Clinical Psychotherapy for
Health Professionals

Clinical Psychotherapy for Health Professionals

(formerly **An Outline of Psychotherapy for Trainee Psychiatrists, Medical Students and Practitioners**)

Edited by

HAROLD MAXWELL, MD, FRCPsych

Honorary Senior Lecturer, Department of Psychiatry, Imperial College of Science, Technology and Medicine, London, Charing Cross Hospital

Emeritus Consultant Psychotherapist
West Middlesex University Hospital

Member British Psychoanalytical Society

W

WHURR PUBLISHERS

LONDON AND PHILADELPHIA

First published 2000 by
Whurr Publishers Ltd
19b Compton Terrace, London N1 2UN, England
325 Chestnut Street, Philadelphia PA 19106, USA.

British Library Cataloguing-in-Publication Data
A catalogue record for this book is available from the
British Library.

ISBN 1 86156 139 3

Printed and bound in the UK by Athenaeum Press Ltd,
Gateshead, Tyne & Wear

Contents

Foreword

STEVEN HIRSCH

This book is suitable for anyone who wants to have a broad introduction to the psychotherapies. Medical students today generally enjoy their periods as students in psychiatry, though they do not expect to do so. Most doctors going through medical school only a half generation ago had less exposure to the speciality. For both generations, the word *psychotherapy* remains one they have heard of and, nowadays, they may have experienced the subject transiently as a member of a seminar group, but this is rarely satisfactory. As teachers of psychiatry, we continue to be asked by students and trainee psychiatrists for something about psychotherapy which is didactic and direct – something which can be written down, thought about and studied. But chapters in textbooks are too short to convey the breadth, depth and relevance of the approach, and books written for the committed tend to be too narrow or too ambitious. For an answer to the questions 'What is psychotherapy?' 'How does it work?' 'What does it consist of?' this book gets it about right. It is not too long or too detailed to lose the reader's interest. It covers the field broadly from psychoanalytically based therapy to family systems theory and conditioning-based behavioural therapy. The main psychoanalytical concepts are well summarized and clearly defined. The possibility for the physician in general practice or any speciality to make use of a psychotherapeutic sixth sense which will help in the management of his patients is explored in a chapter on liaison psychiatry, and in another on general practice. This is a very down-to-earth and practical book which should be useful for anyone who wants to know something of how psychotherapy works and what it has to offer. It will be relevant to those outside the medical profession and in related fields, such as social work.

It is not, of course, a matter of chance that An Outline of Psychotherapy for Trainee Psychiatrist, Medical Students an Practitioners appeared in the 1980s. While general psychiatry was maturing and developing clinical and scientific credibility, it had little time for this area of endeavour which is not necessarily medical, and in which scientific hypotheses that test research hypotheses are still scant. The lack of such reason is the fault of its devotees who, for too long, have clung to early concepts that have heuristic value, but need translation into verifiable operational concepts which can be recognized as right or wrong. A further problem has been the unwilling-ness of psychotherapists and analysts to test the effectiveness of their treat-ment by criteria which lie outside their field of theoretical discourse, such as return to work, resumption of sexual activity, lessening of anxiety and depression scores, lower relapse rates or, in the case of liaison psychiatry, improvement in patients' physical functioning. Yet, recent studies have begun to show that psychotherapy is a powerful technique by these criteria. Another reason for the dearth of research is that practitioners are, rightfully to some extent, convinced by their own experience – because they almost all undergo therapy as a requisite to training. The training is long, arduous and expensive and the commitment of most therapists once trained is to their patients and to the exercise of their hard-won skills; they experience research as antithetical to all this. Fortunately, there is now a small but growing number of psychotherapy research workers who are beginning to demonstrate the efficacy of psychotherapy and earn its respect as a bona fide treatment within medicine.

This book is timely because we have been witnessing an exploding interest in psychotherapy on the part of the public and a growing appreci-ation by the medical profession at all levels of what it has to offer. This may reflect an increasing standard of living for those in society who expect more for themselves and are less willing to tolerate inner turmoil and diffi-culties in their relationship with others.

Although our own Department of Psychiatry at Imperial College is biologically oriented in research, and community-oriented from a service point of view, we require all our psychiatrists in training to obtain experi-ence in psychotherapy, because we believe the skills are essential if the psychiatrist wants to address him- or herself fully to a patient's treatment. This concern is also reflected in recent changes in the membership examinations of the Royal College of Psychiatry. Similarly, our trainee psychiatrists may expect to treat a patient psychotherapeutically and there is now a liaison psychiatry and psychotherapy service in our medical school, which is appreciated by physicians, surgeons and obstetricians alike.

The growing demand by the public for 'humanistic medicine' and the increasing interest in fringe medicine of all sorts is further evidence of this new ethic. If doctors can guard against the erosion of that sensitivity and human interest inherent in them before they even entered an anatomy room, and go on to develop the skills which will enable them to use these qualities as they carry out their medical work, the demand for fringe medicine will be kept at bay. This primer is a very good starting point for such a task.

This volume is dedicated with love to the memory of my parents
Simon and Agnes Maxwell

Preface

The title of this volume reflects the recent remarkable proliferation of trained personnel invoking the "talking cures". For this reason the title has been changed.

Counsellors and psychotherapists as well as members of the medical profession will, it is hoped, look to this volume as a reference guide to the main forms of psychotherapy in use today. The book's contents aim to clarify to all professionals concerned – not only to their clients(!) – the salient features of the diverse treatments in contemporary practice.

Most of the chapters have been revised, and the account of Liaison Psychiatry re-written.

Included for the first time are descriptions of Cognitive-Analytic Therapy, Forensic Psychotherapy, and the Psychotherapy of the Psychoses, the last being a new dimension in the total management of these states, which was previously more the province of the Social and Biological psychiatrists. The authors of this chapter have written a condensed version of their standard work on the subject.

I am again very grateful to colleagues for their helpful comments and suggestions, and especially to Professor Steven Hirsch for his new foreword.

My thanks are also due to Lila Lent and Gabrielle Murphy for their secretarial and editorial help respectively.

Harold Maxwell
London, April 2000

Preface to the First edition
An Outline of Psychotherapy for Trainee Psychiatrists, Medical Students and Practitioners

> If then our judgement be so depraved, our reason overruled, (our) will precipitated, that we cannot seek our own good, or moderate ourselves, as to melancholia commonly it is, the best way for ease is to impart our misery to some friend, not to smother it up in our own breast; for grief concealed strangles the soul, but when as we shall impart it to some discreet trusty loving friend, it is instantly removed, for a friend's counsel is a charm; like mandrake wine it allayeth all our cares.
>
> 'The Anatomie of Melancholie',
> 1621, by Robert Burton

I make no apology for putting together in one volume an assemblage of my own main professional interests: psychoanalysis, psychotherapy and liaison medicine.

Psychotherapy is about people and their feelings. There is no line separating patients, doctors and medical students. At the same time, while not everyone becomes, say, a bronchitic or a diabetic, or has a baby, everyone will at various times experience grief, sadness, elation, envy, fear, paranoia, sleep disturbances, rage and muddled thoughts concerning the problems of living and relating; all these constitute the very stuff of psychiatry and also of this book. Incidentally, it would not have found a market within the world of the medical establishment when I qualified in 1950. Today's mores are, however, thankfully different, being exemplified by the remark of a young male trainee general practitioner who said in a recent seminar. 'Of course in certain circumstances I would feel it natural to hold the hand of, or even put my arm around, a patient, male or female, if in doing so I felt that it would comfort them ...'. The other members of the seminar agreed.

The book was designed with all clinicians in mind, but medical students and other beginners may find it particularly helpful to refer initially to Chapters 1 and 3 as a basis.

It is a pleasure to acknowledge my thanks to the contributors to this book, also to the publishers, and to Aberdeen University Press for allowing Dr Alexander's chapter to appear, the latter being an extended version of that published in *Models for Psychotherapy* by J.D.H. Haldane, D.A. Alexander and L.G.W. Walker. My wife Marianne kindly read the proofs and made many helpful suggestions.

HM
London, December 1985

Contributors

Gwen Adshead, MB BS, MRCPsych, MA (Med Law & Ethics), Consultant and Honorary Senior Lecturer in Forensic Psychotherapy, Broadmoor Hospital, Berkshire. Consultant Psychiatrist, Trauma Stress Clinic, Middlesex Hospital, London

David Alexander, MA (Hons), C Psychol, PhD, FBPS, Professor of Mental Health, Medical School, Aberdeen University, and Director, Centre for Trauma Research, Royal Cornhill Hospital, Aberdeen

Dick Blackwell, BSc, CertEd, MInst GA, Group Analyst, Family Therapist, London

David M. Clark, DPhil, Professor of Psychology, Institute of Psychiatry, London

Alan I. Cooklin, MB ChB, FRCPsych, DPM, Consultant in Family Psychiatry, the Paediatric Liaison Team, University College London (UCL) Hospitals and The Family Project (Major Mental Illness), Camden and Islington Community Health NHS Trust, London. Honorary Senior Lecturer, University College London (UCL)

Andrew Elder, FRCGP, General Practitioner, London, Consultant in General Practice and Primary Care, Tavistock Centre, London

Steven R. Hirsch, BA, MD, FRCP, MPhil, FRCPsych, Professor and Head of Department of Psychiatry, Division of Neuroscience and Psychological Medicine, Imperial College of Science, Technology and Medicine, London

Alan L. King, MRCPsych, Consultant in Cognitive and Behavioural Psychotherapy, Leicestershire & Rutland Healthcare NHS Trust

Geoffrey G. Lloyd, MA, MD, FRCP, FRCPsych, Consultant Psychiatrist, Royal Free Hospital, London. Medical Director, Grovelands Priory Hospital, London

Chris Mace, MD, MRCPsych, Consultant Psychotherapist, South Warwickshire Combined Care NHS Trust. Senior Lecturer in Psychotherapy, University of Warwick

Frank Margison, FRCPsych, Consultant Psychotherapist, Manchester Royal Infirmary

Harold Maxwell, MD, FRCPsych, Honorary Senior Lecturer, Department of Psychiatry, Division of Neuroscience and Psychological Medicine, Imperial College of Science, Technology and Medicine, London, Charing Cross Hospital. Emeritus Psychotherapist, West Middlesex University Hospital. Member of the British Psychoanalytical Society

Anthony Ryle, DM, FRCPsych, Honorary Consultant Psychotherapist and Senior Research Fellow, Division of Psychiatry, Guy's, Kings and St Thomas's Schools of Medicine, London

Marc Serfaty, BSc (Hons), MB ChB, MRCPsych, MPhil, Consultant Psychiatrist, Grovelands Priory Hospital, London. Senior Lecturer in Psychiatry, Royal Free and University College Medical School, University College, London

Barbara Squire, BSc, Medical journalist, London

Chapter 1
Psychodynamic Psychotherapy: An Introduction

HAROLD MAXWELL

The content of this volume pertains to psychotherapy by health professionals, including students. It is necessary however, to note that, unlike medicine, psychotherapy *per se* is a completely unregistered profession and consequently there is no body such as the General Medical Council responsible for monitoring the code of conduct of psychotherapists. Certain members of several core professions, e.g. psychiatry, psychology, nursing and social work, all practise psychotherapy and when doing so are answerable to their own professional bodies. There are, however, other psychotherapists who have trained in various ways, and may not necessarily have a background in one of the traditional caring professions. Some of these people will belong to professional organizations such as the British Psychoanalytical Society, the Society for Analytical Psychology and the British Association of Psychotherapists, although anyone can in fact call him- or herself a 'psychotherapist' or even a 'psychoanalyst'.

Nevertheless, a significant number of people seeking help through psychotherapy will turn to members of the medical profession, which still enjoys a remarkable degree of trust on the part of the general public. Medical personnel who are psychotherapists will usually have been trained as general psychiatrists and, in addition, will have followed courses leading to membership of one of the three bodies referred to above. As far as other medical personnel are concerned, to some extent it will be the degree of *involvement* with the patient, both in intensity and duration, which will affect the 'depth' of the physician's influence. Those with minimum involvement would naturally include, say, clinical pathologists and radiologists, whereas at the other end of the spectrum would be the family doctor with his or her 'permanent' relationship and the general psychiatrist. In between would be every specialist category pertaining to clinical work.

1

Nowadays, there seems to be a greater emphasis placed on what has come to be called the doctor–patient relationship in general medicine and surgery, dermatology, obstetrics and, especially, gynaecology. The *family practitioner's* use of psychotherapy is covered elsewhere (see Chapter 6), whilst the *general psychiatrist* will involve him- or herself in supportive and insight-directed psychotherapy, to an extent that varies with his or her own inclinations, in this way supplementing physical and social measures in the total management of patients.

In the sphere of both general and psychiatric practice the teaching of Michael Balint, which is also discussed elsewhere, will be remembered with its emphasis on the doctor–patient relationship. Naturally, this factor had been known long before Balint described it, but was never so well delineated in practical terms. However, a remarkable paper by Houston (1938) just before the Second World War, emphasized the placebo effect of the doctor him- or herself as a therapeutic agent. The point was made that throughout history the number of pharmacological preparations with a 'genuine' and predictable action was extremely small and the 'greatness' of physicians, effectively up to the nineteenth or even twentieth century, depended upon the *personality* of that physician and its placebo effect (i.e. the faith evoked in the efficacy of the doctor's personality). Hypnosis and other modern fringe procedures may be based on the same mechanism.

Principles of Individual Therapy

What is psychotherapy?

Psychotherapy is a professional way of dealing with unhappiness, both innate and reactive, which may constitute a psychiatric diagnosis, by the interaction of the patient with one or more people. It can be individual, group, marital or family. The most usual method of interaction is through talk and the psychotherapy which ensues may, as already noted, be supportive or insightful, the latter hopefully leading to development of the personality. Psychotherapy in the context of this book is concerned with clinical practice: it may or may not be used in combination with physical methods of treatment such as drugs or ECT.

Where?

The setting is extremely important. Its degree of opulence does not matter, its *constancy* does. Usually a small or medium-sized room, quietly furnished with the absence of distractions of, say, the telephone, with both the patient and therapist being physically comfortable, is adequate.

Who?

The psychotherapist is a professional – for our purposes, a physician. He or she will have had at least some appropriate training, may belong to one of the so-called 'schools' of psychotherapy and will probably have had some personal therapy or analysis.

Features of Psychotherapy

Generally, psychotherapy will be either *supportive*, i.e. 'encouraging the positive', or will hopefully enable the patient to gain *insight* into how and why factors from the past have determined his or her present predicament and how to a large extent he or she is compelled to repeat past patterns of inexpedient behaviour.

With the start of treatment, the patient will, by implication and at the very least, receive the message that he or she is 'worthy of help' and thereby experience enhancement to his or her self-esteem. The installation and maintenance of *hope* will also be a feature, which will be compounded by the constancy of the setting and of the therapist him- or herself. The latter cannot delegate this role to a locum or deputy: *psychotherapy is above all based on a human relationship*.

The initial interview

This is partly a fact-finding process but will differ from a medical model interview because, in addition to facts such as name, address, occupation etc., the patient's demeanour, dress and general attitudes will be noted. The overall mood which the patient evokes in the therapist is also important, especially in coming to an 'empathetic' diagnosis. The more adept and experienced the practitioner, the more accurate will be his or her antennae in receiving emotional messages from the patient.

The psychotherapy sessions

What takes place? Apart from implicit messages of support that are conveyed to the patient, *facilitation* is provided by the therapist by means of his or her interest, recognition and sense of receptiveness. *Confrontation* is also used as a means of making the patient aware of a reaction that has been provoked within the therapist. *Reassurance*, suggestion and direction are also employed, as is *questioning*, although the last should be used sparingly. *Interpretations* are means of conveying to the patient an understanding on the part of the therapist, by which something implied or hidden from the patient's consciousness may be brought to his or her attention. Interpretations sometimes involve the therapist, when they are called *transference* interpretations, and are especially pertinent to orthodox psychoanalysis. *Advice* and *guidance* are also given, as well as reinforcement and behaviour modification. The last is conveyed to the patient by tacit approval, or otherwise, of the patient's activities, statements or decisions. *Silence* may be a problem to psychotherapists in training. It is of several kinds and the overriding mood will hopefully be picked up: hostile, neutral or restful. A therapeutic step forward during a silence would be for the therapist to say to the patient something like, 'I feel a bit lost and don't really know what to say' or 'I'm confused and rather muddled and I wonder whether you feel the same'. This will be a truism and will enable the patient to feel recognized and understood even if it is only in a 'negative' way, so that the basis may be laid for future, naturally more positive, experiences.

Supportive psychotherapy

This is the minimum level of psychotherapy. Evidence of good will, consistency and sincere interest is conveyed with an implicit promise that the patient, with all his or her fears, weaknesses, anxieties and above all his or her aggression, will be received and contained by the therapist. As its name suggests, this psychotherapy is especially called for to support the patient during acute or long-standing periods of crisis. Clear-cut events such as bereavement or divorce may, for a given period of time, call for regular meetings with the patient so that the situation can be worked through and he or she may gradually come to terms with the situation. Those with a low threshold for life's exigencies may need, in the extreme, a life-long availability on the part of the therapist, who ideally will combine this role with that of family doctor. The very fact that the latter 'is there' may often be sufficient to prevent many patients breaking down. (Good GPs have, in fact, had transferred to them aspects of a good parent, who will not condemn or judge, but will *stay* and be available.) Non-medical counsellors are now being trained in considerable numbers to deal with the common-or-garden problems of living with which many patients are unable to cope and which in the past were usually dealt with by the priest, lawyer or lord of the manor.

Insight psychotherapy

This is a process whereby the patient is encouraged to understand that habitual *defences* and methods of reacting to external situations may be inappropriate and unpropitious, and may be seen as provocative by other people. Hopefully, their origin in early life will be understood by both patient and therapist and conscious attempts at modification and change will be made. The use of dreams, slips of the tongue and ruminative free association of speech will be part of the process. Here the aim is more ambitious than in supportive psychotherapy. The patient will be helped to understand that certain patterns of responses to the environment are self-defeating, leading to further negative situations. This type of therapy is a way of showing a patient how he or she can, through reflection and given sufficient motivation, react with different patterns of behaviour. It is an experience based on psychoanalysis, and a certain amount of personal therapy for the doctor may be necessary in order to enable him/her to distinguish between their own hang-ups and those of the patient.

It used to be thought by the early psychoanalysts that the aim of treatment was to 'make the unconscious, conscious'. Nowadays, we would hope that the degree of suffering by the individual may be reduced as a result of *integration*, i.e. the coming together and acceptance of various contradictory feelings and attitudes: that the 'pain' of these *ambivalences* will gradually lessen and become tolerable, so that maturing and positive processes will supervene, thus reducing the need for painful and costly defences to be employed resulting in suffering for the person, the family or even society as a whole (see Chapters 2 and 3).

Clinical Conditions where Psychotherapy may be Considered

1. Supportive psychotherapy may be indicated when any of life's crises affecting the person or his or her family are being negotiated, e.g. divorce, redundancy, retirement, bereavement.
2. Psychiatric conditions, especially recurring states of baseless anxiety or depression; addictions; some of the schizophrenic illnesses.
3. 'Existential conditions' – probably the most common situations which the specialist, in particular, is nowadays called upon to treat. The symptomatology is vague, confused, alters from day to day and accounts for an ill-defined ennui whereby both isolation (loneliness) and its opposite – the too-invasive and too-close proximity of another person – are felt to be intolerable, so that an oscillation of depressive loneliness and suffocating relatedness is experienced, accounting for *difficulties in relationships*, sometimes with recourse to drugs and alcohol. Sexual problems of all types are included in this section.
4. Some medical states of an episodic or chronic nature (e.g. migraine, asthma, musculoskeletal diseases and gastrointestinal symptoms).

These *conversion phenomena* or *psychosomatic conditions* are usually very resistant to change by psychotherapy – frequently, they are best left to sympathetic management by the general physician or family doctor.

Factors to be considered in evaluation of the suitability for psychotherapy

Motivation

This will depend on the degree of real (mental) suffering or distress, usually anxiety and/or depression, and the determination to find a better *modus vivendi*.

Age

Age is not as important as might be imagined. Both the very young and the elderly can be helped.

'Ego strength'

This means the general cohesiveness and state of maturity of the personality, as shown by attainments in general, the sources of happiness, if any, and, above all, the ability or otherwise to *sustain* relationships both in personal life and in work situations.

Intelligence

A minimum is certainly necessary, but again this factor should not be over-emphasized. More important is the capacity or otherwise for insight and reflection, i.e. the presence of 'psychological-mindedness' (see below), and above all the *motivation* for change.

The ability to tolerate anxiety and frustration

This is important, because psychotherapy is often a slow process, not enjoying the instant relief that medication can often provide for symptoms. A history of 'acting out', i.e. the involvement of the patient in unpropitious or destructive activities, is a sign that psychotherapy may be especially difficult.

'Secondary gain'

This means, for instance, that by the maintenance of symptoms the patient may exercise considerable control over his or her environment, sometimes in a blackmailing way.

Reality factors

These include the availability of specialists, the willingness of the patient to invest time and sometimes money in his or her treatment and, ideally, a family situation which is objective towards psychotherapy.

Types of defences (see below)

If it seems that excessive denial, dissociation, confusion or projection are employed, it will suggest that psychotherapy will be difficult, as would evidence of acting out (poor impulse control) or psychosomatic disease.

Discerning 'psychological-mindedness' in the clinical interview

Coltart (1988) suggests some useful pointers, including evidence of 'imagination', the willingness to accept at least some responsibility for the events of one's own life, a record of minimal past successes or gratifications, and especially an 'overall impression' on the part of the observer, drawing on his or her own experience and empathetic constitution.

Psychoanalysis and Psychodynamic Psychotherapy

This is a particular method of psychotherapy devised by Freud, dealing specifically with the phenomenon of transference. This special relationship which develops between a patient and the analyst is analysed and traced back to the patient's earliest relationships. Whilst most other forms of psychotherapy are based on suggestion and encouragement, psychoanalysis is concerned with largely unconsciously derived and transferred feelings and attitudes with which patients invest the analyst. This transference is to some extent fostered by the analyst, who remains relatively 'anonymous'.

Glossary of Some Psychoanalytical Terms

Defences

These are universal phenomena and must be respected. The 'defence' is against overwhelming *internal* anxiety, as opposed to 'real', or outside, physical dangers. It is important to grasp that there is an internal world as well as an external world and that the former does in fact determine many of our basic moods, responses, feelings, attitudes and, in a psychiatric sense, the types of *distortions* which may make human relationships difficult or even impossible. These distortions, especially towards other people, are based on attitudes to important figures from the past, often evoking difficulties which may never have been resolved, and perpetuating feelings which, even at the original time, may well have been inappropriate to the event taking place (*see* 'Transference'). It must be realized that it is only when these mechanisms become exaggerated or habitual, that they can be called pathological and, paradoxically, it is when they break down that psychiatric symptoms begin. Were it not for defence mechanisms which automatically come into play when we meet with any unpleasant reality, life would soon become a severe burden, if not impossible. Such defences include the following.

- Denial
  This is a method whereby unpleasant events may conveniently be 'blotted out'. Examples would include the pain of recent bereavement, an unpleasant sight consequent upon an accident or other trauma, the usage of the 'sour grapes' phenomenon (i.e. something which has not, in reality, been available, has its value denied). 'Splitting' is often associated with denial. It excludes life's grey areas: everything and everyone is black and white, good or bad, etc.
- Displacement
  If hostile feelings or emotions cannot be expressed to authority or other powerful figures, they may be *displaced* on to others less threatening or further away; for instance, it is safe to hate an enemy on the other side of the world. Another example would be kicking the cat to release frustration towards someone whom you could not attack safely.
- Phobic avoidance
  Sometimes very primitive and deep-seated situations which evoke intolerable terror become focused on to specific objects or situations in the external world through a process of subtle and unconscious symbolic transformation. Thus, animals or other creatures, e.g. snakes and spiders, or situations such as open spaces or closed rooms, come to *stand for* these very primitive, sincerely 'forgotten' and very basic situations. The important point is how much of an inconvenience it is to avoid the substituted, external symbol of terror, e.g. it is not much of a problem for a snake-phobic living in a suburb of a big city, but a real fear of flying is, perhaps, a constraint for a businessman. (See Chapter 10)
- Projection
  This is ascribing to others negative feelings and attitudes in ourselves. It is the basis of paranoid states for, if we 'believe' that others are feeling or behaving badly, we are then justified in hating, hurting or attacking them in return.
- Rationalization
  This is a means whereby the true reason for a course of action is hidden by *apparent* explanations.
- Reaction formation
  This denotes going to the opposite extreme towards experiences which may be morally unacceptable, e.g. extreme cleanliness to counteract innate wishes and instincts to be dirty, untruthful, inexact or spontaneous.

- Regression
  This denotes a return to a more child-like state, so that temporarily at least it is possible to re-experience being a child with no responsibilities. The phenomenon occurs naturally in sleep and it is an acceptable event at times of illness when it is a sort of 'secondary gain'.
- Repression and suppression
  A way of putting off, or burying, painful or even exciting feelings or thoughts. As with all defence mechanisms, if it is too successful it is like 'throwing out the baby with the bathwater' and some people are never able to react appropriately or spontaneously to, say, a traumatic or sexual situation. Such people are somehow 'different'.
- States of confusion
  Indecision and other ruminative states of puzzled vagueness may be a way of distancing oneself from unpleasant reality. Conflict and ambivalence, which can be painful, may be avoided in this way.
- Sublimation
  This is a so-called 'higher' solution, whereby anxieties become channelled into positive acts or ways of life (e.g. creativity, gardening and restoring objects).

It is worth repeating that defence mechanisms are present in everyone and it is when they break down that symptoms may ensue.

Oedipus complex

Freud did not invent this, but 'adapted' and extrapolated the scenario from the Greek myth wherein the hero unknowingly slays the parent of the same sex and espouses that of the opposite sex. As in Sophocles' drama, the phenomenon is unconscious. Present-day analysts, whilst still alert to the concept, are equally vigilant to evidence of disturbances at an earlier, or pre-oedipal, time, i.e. when the baby's preoccupation is with the mother (a two-person relationship) rather than later, when the third person (father) has entered the drama (see Chapter 2).

Transference

This is an ubiquitous and everyday phenomenon that occurs between people. Attitudes, feelings and ideas towards significant people from the past become transferred to acquaintances and even friends in the present, often without justification. It is, however, the most important *tool* in psychoanalysis and psychoanalytical psychotherapy, as the patient may invest the therapist with what may well be totally inappropriate characteristics and attitudes, which can be changed or at least modified during the therapy and, by extrapolation, a more realistic appraisal of people in the patient's world may become established. In particular, strangers and acquaintances become less endowed with initial hostility and threat, so that more propitious feelings between the patient and his or her significant persons can become established.

Countertransference

This is the equivalent in the therapist. This will include the therapist's blind-spots of which cognisance and knowledge must be present. Its existence makes a personal therapy on the part of the therapist highly desirable, some would say essential. Countertransference feelings can also mirror attitudes, both conscious and unconscious, originating in the patient, but experienced and recognized in the therapist. With proper timing they may be conveyed to the patient as an aid to the two people's joint understanding.

The unconscious

This refers to both the part of the mind about which the subject is unaware and thought processes that are not within consciousness. Its existence is suggested by three phenomena:

1.   Dreams.
2.   Post-hypnotic suggestion.
3.   Slips of the tongue.

Unconscious processes are linked to what Freud called *primary processes*. These are primitive and unstructured methods of mental functioning: they reduce 'unpleasure' or pain and promote *pleasure*. Images become fused and can readily replace and symbolize each other, as in dreams. *Secondary process* thinking, on the other hand, is logical, orderly and bound up with reality, reducing 'unpleasure' or pain, by adaptation (see Chapter 2).

Projective identification

This is a term from the Kleinian school (see Chapter 3) which is being found to have increasing application (Jureidini, 1990). It is at first a defence mechanism whereby feelings are projected on to the object (therapist) who is at the same time identified with. The latter will also have the impression that a communication of the subject's feelings has become part of his or her own mental experience. For example, a doctor may repeatedly feel hopeless, irritable or even angry whenever a given patient is seen and it may be useful tactfully to 'share' these negative affects with the patient, saying something like, 'it is sometimes difficult to feel optimistic and encouraged and at the moment I have no such feelings. I suspect it is how *you* often feel ...'. Far from being discouraging, the patient may well experience a lessening of his or her isolation and such an exchange may form the basis of more propitious future exchanges.

References

COLTART, N.E.C. (1988). The assessment of psychological-mindedness in the diagnostic interview. *British Journal of Psychiatry* **153**, 819–820.

HOUSTON, W.R. (1938). The doctor himself as a therapeutic agent. *Annals of Internal Medicine* **11**, 1416–1425.

JUREIDINI, F. (1990). Projective identification in general psychiatry. *British Journal of Psychiatry* **157**, 656–660.

Chapter 2
Psychodynamic Therapy: History and Basic Precepts

DAVID A ALEXANDER

The practice of psychotherapy is rewarding, both intellectually and emotionally, but it can also be taxing and difficult and its injudicious application can be harmful. Therefore, it demands a high degree of personal integrity on the part of its practitioners. Unfortunately, psychotherapists share a collective responsibility for failing in the past to pay sufficient attention to the harmful effects of their treatment methods and to the ethical issues related thereto. It is therefore encouraging to find that major attempts have now been made to address such matters (e.g. Mays and Franks, 1985; Lakin, 1988; Strupp, 1994).

Over the last 60 years, schools of psychotherapy have multiplied in such a way that trainees are faced with a bewildering array of approaches. In the absence of convincing empirical data to justify the claims of one school against those of another, it is difficult to decide which theories and techniques to adopt. Powerful determinants of their choice include personal prejudice and serendipity (Nemiroff and Colarusso, 1985; Alexander and Eagles, 1990).

Nonetheless, whatever the factors underlying the choice of model, therapists should be in a position to answer five basic questions which will expose important assumptions underlying their particular choice of therapy. These questions are:

- What factors influence human behaviour?
- What are the basic aims of this therapy?
- What are the characteristic features of the therapeutic relationship?
- What are the techniques and skills associated with this therapy?
- What problems or patients can best be helped by this therapy?

In this chapter, each of these questions will be addressed in relation to the psychodynamic model. Before doing so, however, some of the important historical features of this model are considered.

Most forms of psychotherapy owe something to Sigmund Freud (1856–1939) and to the treatment called 'psychoanalysis' which he developed and which has served as the prototype for later psychodynamic therapies. This does not mean that Freud 'invented' psychotherapy or that all his ideas were entirely novel. Many of his concepts and ideas have long pedigrees. For instance, the notion of a 'talking cure' (as psychoanalysis has been called) is closely related to the Catholic 'confessional' and to the use of the theatre in ancient Greece as a public means of 'purging the passions'. However, such has been the indelible and widespread influence of psychoanalytical ideas that they have fertilized developments not only in medical psychology and psychiatry but also in the social sciences and in the arts.

Inevitably, certain features of this widespread movement attracted a good deal of opposition and criticism. Analytical propositions were attacked on the grounds that they were formulated too loosely to be amenable to verification or refutation by traditional scientific procedures. Theorists and clinicians espousing other models (the 'behaviourists' in particular) have consistently argued that those who practise a psychodynamic form of therapy seem to have been unacceptably reluctant to evaluate the process and outcome of their therapeutic work and to adhere to the conventional canons of scientific enquiry.

Criticisms such as these should not be dismissed readily or be upheld slavishly. However, it cannot be disputed that there is still insufficient research into the process, concepts and therapeutic value of psychodynamic therapy. There is also a need to remove some of the mystery and veneration which surrounds this form of therapy.

Whatever the 'scientific' status of psychoanalysis, however, its significance in the history of Western thought is in no doubt, and this fact has much to do with the personal contribution of Freud himself. Despite his numerous contributions to clinical work, Freud was a reluctant therapist and physician. His main aim was to produce a general theory of human behaviour, and he regarded himself first as a scientist and only second as a clinician.

His intellectual integrity, not to say courage, cannot be questioned, as he had to modify and relinquish some of his most fundamental propositions, such as that about the role of sexual trauma in the development of certain mental disorders. His willingness to adhere to 'the facts' also led him to maintain certain views despite the resultant public and professional criticism and even odium. For example, Freud originally believed that sexual fantasies and attachments begin in early childhood and that early childhood sexual experiences continue to exert an effect in later life. If we think of the moral straitjacket imposed during the Victorian era on the public discussion of sexual matters, it is hardly surprising that these views met with disbelief and disapproval.

Freud's courage in holding to or modifying his theory in the light of empirical and clinical evidence was matched by his physical courage. In the last years of his life he was handicapped by terminal cancer of the jaw, but, in order that he retain all his mental powers, he refused analgesics.

It was, however, his shrewdness and sensitivity as an observer of human behaviour that led to major developments in Freud's theory about human beings. An opportunity to display this ability occurred when he attended the dramatic demonstrations by Dr Charcot in Paris, in which patients, in response to hypnotic suggestions, could manifest symptoms which resembled neurological ones such as aphonia, paralysis and paraesthesia. Impressed as well as puzzled, Freud reflected on some of the patients who had been referred to him in Vienna for the treatment of similar conditions. He wondered if these symptoms had developed in response to the patients' own unconscious ideas – a form of 'autosuggestion'. Freud found that hypnosis was an effective method of directly achieving symptom relief. Despite his initial success, however, he was troubled by the thought that, if he and the patient did not know what underlay the initial development of these symptoms then either the influence of these unconscious factors would begin to reassert itself and the symptoms would reappear or other symptoms would emerge in their place. (The second possibility has been described as 'symptom substitution'.)

Working with the Austrian physician Josef Breuer (with whom he wrote, in 1895, the seminal *Stüdien über Hysterie*) Freud realized that there might be another way of using hypnosis; one which might offer a more durable cure or change (Breuer and Freud, 1964). Instead of using hypnosis as a means of achieving direct symptom relief, Freud used it to explore what had given rise to the symptom. The possibility of the use of hypnosis in this way had been suggested to him by the fact that one of Breuer's patients (immortalized in the literature as 'Anna O') had been able under hypnosis to recall feelings and events previously inaccessible to her and, in doing so, she had been relieved of her symptoms. In brief, therefore, the aim was to treat the underlying cause and not just the symptoms.

At that time, Freud prepared a radical approach by claiming that many symptoms – both physical and mental – had a psychological cause and, moreover, that these symptoms had some personal symbolic meaning for the patient. It is interesting to consider how many common expressions and metaphors there are in our language which reflect the association between emotions and parts of the body. These include, 'he's a pain in the neck', 'she gets on my nerves', 'you're breaking my heart', 'he's a real headache to me' and 'that was a real body blow'.

Later, Freud gave up hypnosis and developed a procedure known as 'free association', whereby patients were encouraged to talk without fear of censure about their past experiences and their most private thoughts, wishes, fears and so forth. In their doing so, Freud believed that the patients and he would be able to unravel the connection between underlying but previously unrecognized factors and the presenting symptoms. Although this procedure of free association was obviously a much more time-consuming one than hypnosis, Freud believed that the results obtained would be lasting. By helping the patient to become aware of events, ideas and feelings which previously had been unconscious, symptom substitution would not occur.

As might be expected, psychoanalysis in particular and psychodynamic theory in general have undergone many revisions and modifications since the days of Freud and his contemporaries (e.g. Holzman, 1995). What remains durable, however, is the role of *conflict* in shaping human behaviour and in symptom development (see Chapter 3).

Obviously, theories about the nature of human beings abound. Some emphasize physical and biological aspects, whereas others focus on interpersonal and social influences, but the theme which tends to link all these theories is that of the potential for and importance of conflict. Indeed, the contribution of conflict to human diseases and dis-ease is a characteristic feature of psychodynamic theory. Some of these other developments, which will emerge as the five basic questions raised earlier, are addressed.

What Factors Influence Human Behaviour?

According to the psychodynamic view of mankind, our behaviour and experience are the result of a number of competing urges, wishes and other influences – some conscious and others unconscious. It is, however, at the unconscious influences that much of psychodynamic therapy is directed. Although there has been much debate about whether the unconscious is a legitimate concept and worthy of study, much psychological research (including that into 'selective attention' and 'subliminal perception') has confirmed the need to acknowledge the influence of unconscious processes. In his earliest writings, Freud regarded the unconscious as a sovereign concept; a concept which included memories, impulses and ideas generally not available to conscious scrutiny, and he distinguished the unconscious from the 'preconscious' and the 'conscious'. The former he viewed as the repository of impulses, sense impressions and memories of which we are not immediately aware, but could be so if required or if the focus of our attention was suitably redirected. (For example, we are not normally aware of our clothes touching our bodies until something directs our attention to these sensations.) The conscious sphere of mental life (a more self-explanatory concept) corresponds to everything of which we are aware at any given time. (Although it is very convenient to talk in terms of the 'unconscious' and the 'conscious' as though they had some spatial existence, this is misleading. It is more accurate to think of all mental activity as occurring along a continuum of consciousness, ranging from complete unawareness to focal attentiveness.)

The distinction between conscious and unconscious mental activities is also associated with different cognitive processes. The conscious level of functioning involves *secondary processes*, which are logical, rational and geared to meet the demands of the real world. In contrast, unconscious activities are associated with *primary processes*, which are not usually adapted to meet the demands of reality, but function to achieve the satisfaction of very basic and urgent needs or drives. We can catch glimpses of these more primitive aspects of ourselves and the processes associated with them when we are dreaming, are emotionally aroused or are under the influence of alcohol or other drugs. Slips of the tongue and slips of the pen, collectively referred to a 'parapraxes' (Freudian slips), may also provide interesting and important clues to the presence of unconscious views, feelings and wishes.

In the 1920s, Freud offered a new model, involving a tripartite division of the psyche into three elements, the *id*, the *ego* and the *super-ego*. Despite its greater complexity, it has the advantage of trying to embrace biological, interpersonal and social aspects of human life.

The first of these elements, the id, on the one hand represents all the inherited biological and constitutional features of the individual, including instincts and basic drives, such as those pertaining to eating, aggression, sex and elimination. These forces, Freud believed, operate according to the hedonistic *Pleasure Principle* in that they avoid being frustrated and seek immediate gratification, regardless of the consequences. On the other hand, the super-ego is very much concerned with the consequences of our actions, since it is built up from internalized representations of the cultural standards and ideals upheld by others who are particularly important to us. For most of us, the first 'culture' to which we are exposed is that of our own family and, consequently, much of our super-ego reflects the impact of parental values and ideals.

The third element, the ego, roughly corresponds to the conscious level of functioning. It develops progressively from birth and its first task is to distinguish between the inner world of subjective experience and external reality. The ego is reality oriented, and therefore it has to find acceptable and appropriate ways of satisfying the demands of the id, although this means that, at least temporarily, the gratification of the id must be delayed.

For example, if we are ravenously hungry, the id drives us to find some immediate way of obtaining food, perhaps by theft or deception, but to do so would be socially unacceptable. Realistically, we can also see that it is likely to lead to further difficulties for us: for instance, we might be caught or we might harm others in the process. Thus, the ego tries to ensure that the satisfaction of such a need is sufficiently delayed to allow us to find some reasonable and socially acceptable means of finding food and satisfying the urge to eat. On other occasions, the ego has to appease the demands of the super-ego. Although the super-ego can be helpful by keeping us out of trouble (rather like a lay person's concept of conscience), it can also act as a source of primitive, irrational and punitive morality and idealism.

In other words, the ego may have to act as an arbiter in the face of the competing demands of the id and the super-ego. Sometimes, the effectiveness of the ego can be compromised by the effects of alcohol, sensory deprivation, insomnia or powerful emotions. Consequently, mental activity, experiences and behaviour occurring during these altered states of awareness appear to be less censored, less rational and more under the influence of the Pleasure Principle. Some dreams may also show the signs of reduced ego involvement, and it is not surprising that Freud described dreams as 'the royal road to the unconscious'.

Freud asserted that there were two mainsprings driving human behaviour. These were the 'life instincts' and the 'death instincts' (conventionally referred to as 'eros' and 'thanatos' respectively). The latter group he regarded as basically destructive in that they seek to reduce us to inorganic matter. The life instincts, however, try to maintain life: in this capacity, one of these instincts – the sexual instinct – plays a particularly significant role. At first, Freud believed that the sexual instinct was served exclusively by a form of energy called the 'libido', but later he concluded that all life instincts drew from this source.

What is more important to note is not the nature of the instincts themselves, but rather their potential for creating competing influences on human behaviour and thereby providing a source of conflict. In Freud's view, we are constantly being pulled and pushed in different directions by powerful antagonistic forces. Thus, behind human experience and behaviour, there lies a constantly shifting dynamic of forces between which we are always trying to achieve some equilibrium. (As applied to psychology, the term 'dynamic', borrowed from nineteenth-century physics and physiology, reflects this particular view.) Freud was aware that, in physics, the resolution of the opposition between two competing forces was sometimes achieved by the emergence of a third force which moves off in a completely different direction from the other two. In terms of human behaviour and experience, the equivalent of the third force would be the development of a symptom. According to this theory, symptom formation is not therefore a random or inexplicable event, but a means of relieving what would otherwise be intolerable conflict.

Some conflicts may be quite transient, whereas others may trouble us throughout our lives, and some may be more characteristic of certain stages of our development. The resolution of some conflicts may be only partial and their impact may be experienced from time to time, particularly when we are under stress. A good example of this, according to psychoanalytical theory, is that of the oedipal conflict. It is believed that children (at least those in Western society) between the ages of 3 and 4 years develop a strong rivalry towards the parent of the same sex, who in turn becomes a source of threat and retaliation. It is argued that these feelings of attraction, and the conflict associated with them, are never thoroughly resolved and that we are likely to experience echoes of this early conflict throughout our lives as we forge new relationships. This may account for the fact that some of our relationships in adult life repeat the dynamics evident in our own family.

What are the Basic Aims of this Therapy?

One of the earliest forms of therapy for mental illness was 'catharsis'. It was initially used when a mental disorder was attributed to demoniacal possession. A cathartic experience can be defined as one in which there is uninhibited and often dramatic expression of pent-up feelings, achieved by the relating and/or 'reliving' of significant past experiences, or sometimes by the acting out of anticipated events or experiences. The alleged value of this is captured in lay expressions – 'letting off steam', 'getting it off your chest' and 'getting it out of your system'.

In the absence of this emotional release, it was believed that the emotional pressure would 'leak out' in some maladaptive way, such as through the development of mental and/or physical ill health. This view certainly has an intuitive appeal but the theory upon which the use of catharsis (or abreaction) is based may owe more to vulcanology than it does to psychology. It may offer only a short-term, symptomatic relief rather than long-term improvement and durable change. One argument raised is that, in the absence of patients understanding why they behave and feel the way they do, there will be only a short-term remission of symptoms followed by the re-emergence of them or the development of new ones.

Insight or self-awareness is not usually a quality with which most of us are over-endowed. People tend to build up their own private view of themselves and of their world, and often this view turns out to be highly deceptive and inconsistent with the view held by others. Sometimes the discrepancy may be quite innocuous or humorous; but, unfortunately, it can also be the basis of a good deal of unhappiness and, worse still, illness. The aim of therapy would be to help a patient to understand the development of his/her view of life and of his symptoms. He/she would have to learn to accept, therefore, some responsibility for his/her feelings, for his/her view of the world and for his/her symptoms.

Unfortunately, even the provision of insight does not guarantee behavioural change because it can be difficult to behave in different ways and to 'give up' symptoms – despite new insights. One reason is that changing our ways and presenting ourselves differently to the world, like any form of change, carries with it a risk that things might turn out to be even worse. For example, some patients fear that if they reveal their feelings or certain facets of their personalities, which they had previously hidden from themselves as well as from others, there is a risk that other people will find them unacceptable and even less desirable. Also, it is undeniable that some symptoms are of benefit to some through 'secondary gain' (e.g. being excused some responsibility or by obtaining sympathy).

Ego Defence Mechanisms

Another important aim of therapy is therefore to help patients adapt to changes in functioning and attitudes which therapy has brought about. The value of this aim is particularly evident when patients are required to give up or modify certain coping strategies called *ego defence mechanisms*. (It would probably be more appropriate to use the word 'processes' rather than the word 'mechanisms'. However, the latter reflects the influence of the physical sciences on the language of psychodynamics.)

The purpose of these defences is to protect us (or our egos) from being disturbed or being overwhelmed by our emotions – anxiety being the most obvious and common example. Anxiety may be created by external factors, such as separation, loss, illness and trauma, but it may also be created by internal ones, such as ideas, wishes, emotions and memories. The protection offered by these mechanisms comes from the fact that they enable us to reject, transform or inhibit our awareness of feelings, ideas, sense impressions and other things which might threaten our self-esteem and composure. Generally, these defences operate at an unconscious level; they should not be regarded as conscious attempts to lie or deceive.

Many defence mechanisms have been described in the clinical and theoretical literature, and a particularly illuminating account of some of them is provided by Anna Freud (1936). For present purposes five commonly observed defences will be described. These will demonstrate how such defences enable us to cope with reality.

Repression

This is the process whereby disturbing ideas, memories or feelings which threaten to become conscious are retained at or relegated to an unconscious level. A good example of *repression* was provided by a patient of mine who, as a child, suffered very serious burns to the throat and neck because of carelessness on the part of her mother. Ten years have passed and the patient is still quite unable to recall anything about the incident or it sequelae, including intravenous feeding and extensive skin grafting. The family have never discussed with the patient what actually happened; instead, it is as though the accident had never happened. Interestingly, her presenting symptom was an inability to swallow food in public places because, as she said 'It sticks in my throat'.

Projection

Another means of dealing with uncomfortable emotions or attitudes is to resist acknowledging them within oneself and to attribute them to others. This is called *projection*. For example, if a person found it difficult to accept his own tendency to be hostile and rejecting, one way to resolve this would be to 'project' (unconsciously) this characteristic on to others, allowing the person thereby to accuse them of being angry and rejecting towards him. An extreme form of this process can be seen in patients who suffer from a disorder called paranoia. Paranoid patients are characteristically hypersensitive to what they consider to be humiliation or rebuffs. They tend to distort their perception of what would have been entirely innocuous or friendly actions and comments by others, and view them as challenging and hostile. Their belief that the world is an aggressive and threatening place thus provides paranoid patients with justification for taking retaliatory action.

Displacement

Scapegoating is a well-known method of ridding oneself of frustration and anger. In psychodynamic terms, this is referred to as *displacement*. For instance, if a doctor were extremely angry with one of his patients, but felt unable to express this feeling directly to the patient, one way to deal with this uncomfortable, pent-up emotion would be to redirect it towards his secretary. Thus, he has rid himself of his anger without threatening his own view of himself; a view which does not include being angry with patients.

Denial

Denial refers to the inability of the individual to acknowledge some reality. Commonly, it is displayed by relatives who have just been informed of the sudden and unexpected death of a loved one: 'Oh, she can't be dead!' is a characteristic response. It may also be seen in people who have a serious or life-threatening illness and yet refuse to recognize the significance of their symptoms, and avoid seeking the appropriate help.

Somatization

Even today it is more acceptable to our *amour propre* to present to a doctor with, say, asthma, migraine, indigestion or hypertension than with recurrent anxiety states, depression or, worse, psychotic breakdown. It is not surprising, therefore, to find that many emotional problems are translated into physical symptoms. It is important for doctors, as a consequence, to try to understand what might lie behind certain physical ailments, particularly when they are resistant to those physical treatments that would normally be effective.

Cautionary notes

Three points should be noted. The first is that we all use such defences – it is not just patients who do – because they can be adaptive by providing a means of coping with events or feelings that would otherwise be too disturbing and disruptive. Medical students are often faced with anxiety-provoking situations which threaten their composure (Alexander and Haldane, 1979). For example, their first experience at the dissecting table can induce denial of feelings. Sometimes defences are used excessively and become more a way of life and they can have a constricting and negative effect on our practice. For example, a doctor's response to anxiety and discomfiture may be to distance him- herself from the patient by being 'cool' and 'objective'. This 'distancing' is frequently seen in the case of terminally ill patients, because staff find it difficult to deal with such patients' emotional reactions (Alexander and Ritchie, 1990).

The second point is that in therapy insensitive assaults on these defences may be damaging to the patient. A former patient of mine (D.A.A.) in the throes of a serious puerperal illness tried to end her own life by setting fire to herself with paint stripper. She survived, but with very obvious and major disfigurement to the head, chest and face. Initially, she made no effort to disguise her disfigurement by the use of a hair piece, cosmetics or carefully chosen clothing. (She was exhibiting denial.) Some of the nursing staff and the other patients in the ward sought to 'confront' her (sometimes rather forcefully) to accept the extent of her disfigurement. This simply provoked further denial, because the unfortunate woman needed time to adapt gradually to what she had done to herself. (An interesting question is, of course, whose anxieties this confrontation was aimed at – the puerperal patient's or those of the staff and the other patients?) A more therapeutic aim would have been to help the patient to use her defence in a flexible and constructive way. Moreover, if the patient can be helped to identify gradually what it is that she needs to be defended from, then other more adaptive and constructive means of dealing with the threat might be found.

The third and final point is that the protection offered by such defences is rarely foolproof. Powerful conflicts and feelings have a tendency to 'leak out' into consciousness, and may present themselves at the most inappropriate time and in the most inappropriate way.

What are the Characteristic Features of the Therapeutic Relationship?

The 'contract'

Despite the variety of theories embraced by the psychodynamic model, there does seem to be a consensus about the crucial role of the relationship between the therapist and the patient. First and foremost, it is a *professional* relationship; thus, there are limits to what may take place between the doctor and the patient: it is a case of disciplined intimacy.

As in other professional relationships, there should be a mutually agreed 'contract' between the two parties. In other words, the therapist *and* the patient should be aware of what it is they seek to do and how to achieve this. Not only does the contract help to ensure that their work together is purposeful, but the process of defining the goals *per se* can be helpful to the patient. Patients often feel so overwhelmed by their symptoms and problems that helping them to define and identify what has to be done, and why, is itself an important and reassuring step in the treatment.

Transference and countertransference

One of Freud's earliest observations was that, in the course of therapy, patients developed strong emotions towards him. Freud regarded these reactions to be unrealistic and related to the patients' experiences in earlier relationships, particularly those with their parents. 'Transference' was the technical term he introduced to describe this tendency of patients to direct to him their feelings and attitudes which would have been more appropriately directed to other significant people in their lives. At first, transference was regarded as a barrier to treatment, but Freud soon realized that understanding the transference reaction was a valuable way of gaining insight into how patients distorted their view of themselves and of others. Thereafter, many therapists saw the understanding and the analysis of the transference as the major focus of psychoanalytical therapy.

Transference feelings may be positive or negative, and often there is a mixture of both. Positive transference can be seen in the way patients describe their therapists, for example, in unrealistically glowing terms, and also in the way they try to translate the professional relationship into a social and personal one. Carefully contrived 'chance' meetings or suggestions to extend the number of appointments, may indicate a patient's positive transference. Negative transference may be shown by expressions of hostility and rejection, by failure to keep appointments, by persistent unpunctuality or requests for a second opinion.

The therapeutic relationship can therefore be seen as a microcosm of patients' world of interpersonal relationships – past, present and future. It provides an opportunity for the close and systematic analysis of how patients behave in relationships, their expectations, needs and defences. In addition, the therapeutic relationship serves as a testing-ground, or an interpersonal 'laboratory', in which patients can explore and experiment with other ways of coping in relationships. Transference probably develops in most relationships, but it is more likely to occur where there is ambiguity and an opportunity for misinterpretation in a relationship. Although the rather passive and enigmatic figure of the psychotherapist is fodder for cartoonists and satirists, this masterly inactivity is not a mere façade but a purposeful tactic. By deliberately limiting the extent to which their own feelings and values intrude in the therapeutic relationship, and by reflecting back to patients those feelings and values they have 'transferred' to the therapeutic relationship, therapists have an excellent means of helping patients to understand how they perceive (or misperceive) themselves and their relationships with others.

Therapists must resist the temptation to satisfy patients' neurotic needs, especially those for love and affection. It is not comfortable being seen by patients as unloving, uncaring and rejecting, when you are dedicated to helping them. Sometimes, the temptation is very strong for us to 'correct' the patients' misinterpretation of what we are trying to do and of what sort of people we are. We may try to 'prove' to patients that we care by creating a highly dependent relationship in which patients feel secure and shielded from all responsibilities. Although it perhaps offers temporary respite for patients, this solves nothing in the long run, because the therapist has colluded in recreating in therapy the type of relationship in which the patients usually become trapped and which usually turns out to be self-defeating and unsatisfying. The therapist has behaved a bit like the parent who never allows the child to grow up.

As is the case with all therapeutic tools, the therapeutic relationship can be put to bad as well as good use. For instance, the relationship does provide therapists with an opportunity for being punitive and hostile to patients under the apparently respectable guise of a therapeutic tactic.

Alternatively, the neurotic dependence and flattery of patients may not be recognized for what they are, and the therapist may unhelpfully and unthinkingly exploit them. A therapist who constantly needs to be flattered and rewarded by patients is likely to become the victim of this need to be gratified. It is more helpful if therapists try to understand what lies behind patients' incessant need to please them.

In the same way that patients bring their past interpersonal experiences into the therapeutic relationship, therapists may also tend to react to their patients in terms of their own experiences in previous relationships: this tendency is known as *countertransference*. As with transference, counter-transference may be positive or negative. Psychotherapists may display negative countertransference by subtle (or sometimes not so subtle!) denigration of their patients, by making impossible or conflicting demands on them, or by 'forgetting' what patients had said the previous week. Positive countertransference may be revealed in various ways, including the offer of additional sessions or extension of sessions well beyond the allocated time. Countertransference can be a barometer of what was going on in therapy; it is not something we need to fear and disclaim. It may be helpful on occasion to share your own feelings with the patient. A therapist saying, 'I'm feeling a bit confused by this and I'm not sure where we should go from here – maybe that's the way you're feeling too' is not an unprofessional admission of incompetence. On the contrary, it conveys an empathic understanding of a patient's feelings and indicates the therapist's willingness to continue to face the patient's problems.

The potential influence of countertransference therefore demands a good deal of basic self-awareness and a willingness to scrutinize our own behaviour and feelings in relationships with patients. Certainly, the significance of countertransference makes the need for supervision of therapy very obvious. It is worth reading Wolstein's (1988) edited series of articles on countertransference, its evolution and relevance.

The therapeutic alliance

More recently, increased attention has been given to another element in the therapeutic relationship; it is called the 'therapeutic alliance'. Freud and the early analysts were aware of the importance of this feature, but they regarded it as another aspect of transference. Perhaps it is easier to consider that there are two 'parts' of the patient. The first 'part' is sick, unhappy and yet resistant to change, whereas the other 'part' is hopeful, co-operative and willing to change. It is with the second 'part' of the patient that therapists have to ally themselves. In this way, patients become active agents in their own treatment, rather than behaving as passive recipients of clinicians' skills and care. This is not the same, however, as describing patients as being 'well motivated' for therapy; many patients are keen to 'get better' but their expectations may be quite unrealistic and based on the assumption that the improvement in their health or circumstances is solely the responsibility of the therapist. As part of the therapeutic alliance, patients must achieve a realistic view of what the therapist can and should offer, and become aware of the extent to which a successful outcome will depend on their own efforts to help themselves. Patients must also be willing to tolerate periods of frustration, disillusionment and emotional discomfort.

The end of the therapeutic relationship is an event of signal importance, particularly if the relationship has been of some months' duration, as is frequently the case. Indeed, it is in recognition of its importance that it is generally argued that termination should be built into the plans for therapy. Under ideal circumstances, we would like the end of therapy to be the natural outcome of achievements of the therapeutic goals. Unfortunately, this is frequently not the reason for the end of therapy. Many factors conspire to produce a premature termination: these include waning motivations of patients, the departure from the region of the patient or the therapist, and significant changes in patients' circumstances. However, whilst accepting that many terminations are not 'ideal', the clinicians should always consider, when formulating with patients the goals of therapy, what criteria would be used to decide when therapy should be terminated.

What are the Techniques and Skills Associated with this Therapy?

One of Freud's patients aptly described psychoanalysis as the 'talking cure' and, from the time Freud stopped using hypnosis, the bedrock of the psychodynamic therapies has been the verbal interchange between patients and therapists. Non-verbal behaviour is certainly important as a dimension of communication, but even this usually has to be dealt with verbally at some stage. Despite the trusting and facilitating atmosphere and relationship, talking in this uninhibited way can be arduous and stressful for patients and they will often show signs of reluctance to continue. A similar reluctance may be shown by patients to grasp what the therapist has suggested or to stick to the therapeutic contract. *Resistance* is the technical term used to describe such efforts of patients to maintain the status quo and to avoid proceeding with therapy. It is not helpful to criticize patients for their resistance. Instead, therapists should try to help the patients to understand what causes the anxiety that lies behind the resistance.

We are not, however, powerless in the face of patients' resistance. We can make use of four techniques: *confrontation*, *clarification*, *interpretation* and *working through*. These are the basic tools of psycho-dynamic therapy to be used to facilitate communication, to enhance understanding, to encourage the expression of feelings and to foster durable change.

Confrontation, as the name suggests, means directing patients' attention to something that they have done, said or experienced, but of which they show little awareness. 'Have you noticed that every time just before your wife goes away on her own your asthma tends to play up?' would be an example of appropriate confrontation.

Another technique for increasing patients' awareness is that of *clarification*, i.e. teasing out of the relevant from the irrelevant features of the material presented by patients. This may be done by rephrasing or reflecting back to patients what they have said, or by skilful questioning around a particular theme or issue.

Interpretation is a rather more complicated technique, and one that has become a source of conflicting opinion. In brief, it refers to that process whereby the therapist *offers* patients a new perspective on, or new meaning to, something they have represented, perhaps in the form of dreams, symptoms, feelings and behaviour. Sometimes, using interpretations the therapist will try to link together what to the patient may seem to be unrelated and discontinuous ideas, feelings and events. This may be achieved, for instance, by helping patients to integrate what goes on in therapy with what has happened in the past or what is happening in the present. 'It seems to me that your frequent silences suggest you are angry with me because you feel as though I am not giving you easy solutions to your problems. Perhaps that is something you have felt before in relationships?'

Learning when, what and how to make interpretations is a skill that is not easily acquired. Poorly timed and insensitive interpretation will probably only jeopardize the therapeutic relationship, leaving patients more disturbed, hurt and confused than they were before the therapy began (Lomas, 1987). On the other hand, some therapists are too reluctant to interpret because they are not sure that their interpretations are 'correct'. This, however, is the wrong way to look at interpretations. The reality is that no therapist has been granted the gift of infallible observation and judgement, and therefore an interpretation has the status only of a hypothesis to be tested. Suggestions such as 'I wonder if you aren't feeling rather angry and fed up just now' are usually more appropriate than are bold assertions such as 'You're feeling angry and fed up'.

Working through is an equally important concept, although it has become a cliché. Correctly used, it applies to the inevitably time-consuming process of exploring and digesting new ideas, experiences and insights. To 'see ourselves as others see us' or to change our view of the world and to test out new ways of behaving are not easy tasks because we need time to consolidate, monitor and adjust to these changes and their consequences, including the reactions of others.

There are two additional points to be noted. The first is that no matter how important the therapy is to the patient, the 'treatment hour' is but one twenty-fourth of patients' day. Neither patients nor therapists can afford to ignore the realities of patients' lives, for the ultimate test of change and development is not how patients fare in therapy, but how they deal with the real world. The second point is that no matter how skilled the therapists are in the use of the techniques and methods just described, they will make no progress unless they listen empathically to their patients. It is a pity that the capacity to listen is often undervalued among clinicians and students.

What Problems or Patients Can be Best Helped by the Therapy?

It will already be obvious that this form of therapy is not suitable for all patients. It is for this reason that the general question 'Does it work?' is a ridiculous one. If anybody asked, 'Do throat lozenges work?', it would not be possible to give an unqualified answer. They may be helpful for certain throat ailments, but they are not too useful if you happen to have a sexually transmitted disease!

Certainly, practitioners of psychodynamic therapy can draw comfort from the increasing body of evidence which testifies to the value of this particular treatment (e.g. Garfield and Bergin, 1986), but there are no grounds for complacency. For a variety of reasons, including theoretical, moral and economic ones, psychodynamic therapy must be subjected to critical and empirical scrutiny, as are other forms of medical treatment. At the same time, however, we must be wary of the possibility that, because verbal therapists often draw the heaviest fire from critics, double standards are not used such that these therapies are more rigorously examined than others.

Although we need to know much more about what particular therapy, carried out by whom, under what conditions, works with patients with what problems, there are some useful guidelines (e.g. Bloch, 1979; Mace, 1995).

First of all, psychotic patients are so out of contact with reality they find it almost impossible to engage in a realistic way with a psychotherapist (although it is worth reading Freeman's (1988) painstaking efforts to relieve the suffering caused by certain symptoms of schizophrenia) (see Chapters 8 and 9). Second, patients of a very limited intelligence and verbal fluency are not going to gain much from a therapy biased towards reasoning, understanding and verbal communication. (It is important, however, not to exaggerate such factors. Even patients of limited intelligence can be suitable for this therapy providing therapists make sufficient effort to work at a level consistent with patients' abilities and experience.) Third, although this is not a problem exclusive to psychodynamic therapy, patients who either have no real motivation to change or have grossly unrealistic expectations of therapy are not good prospects. Fourth, the therapists have a responsibility to ensure that patients' personal, social and family resources would allow them to cope with the demands of therapy. Finally, patients who find it difficult to think in psychological terms, who are not at all introspective and are unable to reflect candidly on themselves, are likely to find this form of therapy unrewarding and unnecessarily stressful.

Even if these guidelines are employed quite strictly, there is no shortage of patients to be helped. Patients with problems in relationships, neurotic disorders, grief reactions or disorders of personality, as well as those with psychosomatic disorders, can be regarded as possible candidates for psychodynamic therapy. With regard to the last group, it is revealing to note that anything between 30 per cent and 40 per cent of patients present to their family doctors with physical symptoms that have no detectable organic cause.

Helping patients in a dyadic relationship is only one way of using psychodynamic principles and techniques. For historical reasons, and for clarity of presentation, individual psychotherapy has been the focus of our attention, but these principles and techniques can also be used in working with couples, families and groups.

Summary and Conclusions

The distinctive feature of psychodynamic therapy is to focus on unconscious mental processes and events thought to underlie patients' symptoms or presenting problems. The therapeutic relationship is regarded as a critical element in therapy because it is in the context of this safe, caring but *professional* relationship that patients can become aware of and explore the significance of this unconscious material.

This form of therapy does not deny the importance of other influences, such as genetics, the environment and culture, and it is not incompatible with other forms of treatment, such as medication or behaviour therapy, provided that there is a sound therapeutic rationale to the concurrent use of other forms of treatment.

Classical psychoanalysis is undoubtedly the prototype of the various varieties of psychodynamic therapy which have emerged. Some of these modifications have developed from the original prototype, whereas others have probably appeared as a reaction against the original mode. Theoretical as well as practical considerations have, for example, fostered a move towards briefer versions of this kind of therapy (e.g. Davanloo, 1994). Sociocultural factors have probably also played a part in the shaping of new therapeutic approaches. For instance, Western society has changed since the early days of psychoanalysis from being highly authoritarian and rigidly hierarchical to being more democratic and egalitarian. Part of this change may be reflected in the therapeutic relationship which has developed from a benign but distant 'father–child' relationship into a more open and flexible one. Another important change is that psychodynamic therapy is not used solely, as it was initially, to treat mental illness and relieve symptoms; instead it is often used to help people with 'problems of living'. The boundary between 'treatment' and 'personal growth' has now become extremely blurred.

To judge from its increasing popularity, it is obvious that psychodynamic therapy is a 'growth industry' but, regrettably, the evaluation of this form of therapy remains a 'cottage industry'. Perhaps the general issue of its effectiveness is no longer in doubt (Garfield and Bergin, 1986), but we still remain in relative ignorance about the effective elements in the process of therapy. In particular, there remain the challenging questions of whether there are effective ingredients specific to psychodynamic therapy or whether there are 'non-specific factors' which Frank et al., (1978) claim to be the potent and ubiquitous influences in any effective form of psychotherapy. Until more data are available, all practitioners will have to act as their own 'researchers', looking candidly at their results and examining the assumptions which underlie their work. Being merely 'caring and compassionate' is not enough (and, in any case, practitioners of psychotherapy have no monopoly on such qualities). On the other hand, therapists must not let the technical aspects of treatment stand in the way of what must be their primary task – the alleviation of suffering. Faced with difficult clinical situations, therapists may be tempted to hide behind techniques, jargon and theories. Facile intellectualizations about patients suffering from an 'unresolved oedipal conflict' may provide insecure therapists with a spurious sense of understanding of their patients' problems, but such statements guarantee no relief of suffering for patients.

References

ALEXANDER, D.A. and EAGLES, J.M. (1990). Which neurotic patients are offered which psychotherapy? *British Journal of Psychotherapy* 6, 401–410.

ALEXANDER, D.A. and HALDANE, J.D. (1979). Medical education: a student perspective. *Medical Education* 13, 336–341.

ALEXANDER, D.A. and RITCHIE, E. (1990). 'Stressors' and difficulties in dealing with the terminal patient. *Journal of Palliative Care* 6, 28–33.

BLOCH, S. (1979). Assessment of patients for psychotherapy. *British Journal of Psychiatry* **135**, 193–208.

BREUER, J. and FREUD, S. (1964). *Studies in Hysteria* translated by J. Strachey. London: The Hogarth Press.

DAVANLOO, H. (1994). *Basic Principles and Techniques in Short-term Dynamic Psychotherapy*. London: Aronson.

FRANK, J.D., HOEHN-SARIK, R., IMBER, B.L. and STONE, A.R. (1978). *Effective Ingredients of Successful Psychotherapy*. New York: Brunner/Mazel.

FREEMAN, T. (1988). *The Psychoanalyst in Psychiatry*. London: Karnac.

FREUD, A. (1936). *The Ego and the Mechanisms of Defence*. London: The Hogarth Press.

GARFIELD, S.L. and BERGIN, A.E. (1986). *Handbook of Psychotherapy and Behavior Change* (Third edition). New York: Wiley.

HOLZMAN, P.S. (1995). *An Outline of Freud's Ideas and their Evolution*. London: Aronson.

LAKIN, M. (1988). *Ethical Issues in Psychotherapy*. Oxford: Oxford University Press.

LOMAS, P. (1987). *The Limits of Interpretation. What's Wrong with Psychoanalysis?* London: Penguin.

MACE, C. (1995). *The Art and Science of Assessment in Psychotherapy*. London: Routledge.

MAYS, D.T. and FRANKS, C.M. (1985). *Negative Outcome in Psychotherapy and What to Do About It*. New York: Springer.

NEMIROFF, R.A. and COLARUSSO, C.A. (1985). *The Race Against Time*. New York: Plenum Press.

STRUPP, H. (1994). *When Things get Worse. The Problem of Negative Effects in Psychotherapy*. London: Aronson.

WOLSTEIN, B. (1988). *Essential Papers on Countertransference*. New York: Columbia University Press.

Further Reading

BROWN, J.A.C. (1961). *Freud and the Post-Freudians*. Harmondsworth: Penguin.

BROWN, D. and PEDDER, J. (1991) *Introduction to Psychotherapy. An outline of Psychodynamic Principles and Practice*. London: Routledge.

ERIKSON, E.H. (1953). *The Interpersonal Theory of Psychiatry* London: Tavistock.

FLANDERS, S. (1993) *The Dream Discourse Today*. London: Routledge.

FREEDHEIM, D.K. (1992). *History of Psychotherapy. A Century of Change*. Washington DC: American Psychological Association.

GLOVER, E. (1955). *The Technique of Psychoanalysis*. New York: International University Press.

GUNTRIP, H. (1977). *Psychoanalytic Theory, Therapy and Self*. London: Hogarth Press.

HOLMES, J. (1993). *John Bowlby and Attachment Theory*. London: Routledge.

KOVEL, J. (1978). *A Complete Guide to Therapy*. Harmondsworth: Pelican.

MALAN, D. (1979). *Individual Psychotherapy and the Science of Psychodynamics*. Guildford: Butterworths.

MASSERMAN, J.H. (1995). *Theory and Therapy in Dynamic Psychiatry*. London: Aronson.

PERLOW, M. (1995). *Understanding Mental Objects*. London: Routledge.

RUTAN, J.S. (1992). *Psychotherapy for the 1990s*. New York: Guilford Press.

SHAMDASAMI, S. and MUNCHOW, M. (1994). *Speculations after Freud*. London: Routledge.

STORR, A. (1979). *The Art of Psychotherapy*. London: Secker & Warburg and William Heinemann Medical.

SUTHERLAND, S. (1976). *Breakdown*. London: Weidenfeld & Nicolson.

Chapter 3
Developments within Psychoanalytic Theory and Practice

HAROLD MAXWELL

Psychoanalysis, based originally on drive or instinct theory, was described in Chapter 2. It proposed that the two drives of sexuality and aggression are inborn, and that frustration of their discharge led to the developing individual experiencing tension and 'unpleasure'. Classical analysts regarded the psychological problems of patients as conflicts occasioned by infantile impulses arising in the id and being countered by the morality of the super-ego (conscience), and the defences of the ego (reality).

The fashioning of a concept of human beings which is reminiscent of the models that were derived from the physical sciences was obviously attractive to Freud, the natural scientist, but this approach was not so appealing to others. Indeed, theory development of this sort became a point of departure for at least two early and significant associates of Freud, namely Carl G. Jung (1875–1961) and Alfred Adler (1870–1937). Both of them became disenchanted with Freud's biological extrapolations and, in particular, with his emphasis on the sexual drive.

Jung produced an offshoot school of his own which came to be called 'Analytical Psychology', the aim of which for patients was *individuation*, i.e. the coming together of various aspects of the subjects' personality, including 'opposite-gender' characteristics. He used the term 'Animus' for the unconscious, masculine side of the woman's female persona and 'Anima' for the equivalent in man. 'Persona' is the front presented to the world as opposed to the 'Shadow' which is kept hidden.

Other terms originated by Jung were: *personal* and *collective uncon-scious*, the latter referring to the myths common to all mankind; *extrover-sion/introversion* which denotes whether an individual's instinctive life is mainly suppressed or overt; and *archetype* which is a symbol and part of the collective unconscious (Jung, 1968).

Adler also founded a school of his own, called 'Individual Psychology', which was more concerned with a social view of human beings, emphasizing factors such as the importance of birth order and sibling rivalry. He wrote also at length about the concept of inferiority, coining the term 'inferiority complex'. The latter can be general or sometimes, according to Adler, concerned with specific body organs either in reality or in fantasy (there is a connection here with hypochondriasis and psychosomatic symptoms). The individual strenuously attempts to compensate in all possible ways and strives to 'become somebody'. These efforts range from healthy adaptive ways to unpropitious neurotic, psychotic or antisocial ways. The concept of 'striving for power' is pertinent here (Adler, 1956).

Modern theories have continued this drift from the emphasis on the dynamic interplay between competing biological drives occurring within the individual. Successors to the early theorists argue that such notions, whilst not to be discounted entirely, are too simple and do not reflect the complexity and subtlety of human behaviour, which when described in terms of 'forces', 'energies' and 'structures' sounds too much like a desperate but inappropriate effort to mimic the style of reasoning and theory development characteristic of the physical sciences.

An equally important fact, which has itself contributed to a revision of theory and practice, has been the nature of the problems and symptoms presented by patients. Nowadays, therapists are confronted with patients whose major concerns are not clearly defined symptoms, such as those with which Freud dealt, but rather a general dissatisfaction with themselves as people and/or with their interpersonal relationships. Bowlby's work on 'attachment behaviour' (Bowlby, 1979; Holmes, 1993), the contributions of Mahler on separation–individuation (Mahler, 1967) and that of the (British) *object relations* theorists, such as Fairbairn (1952), Winnicott (1958) and Balint (1968), are important examples of theoretical developments which reflect contemporary clinical problems. According to these theorists, the motivational drive in humans is to seek relationships with others, and the difficulties or, indeed, the successes, people have in this regard can usually be traced to the influence of very early experiences, particularly those between mother and child. In therapy, this line of reasoning focuses not just on the individual patient's symptoms, or even on the patient as an individual, but rather on the patient in the context of his or her relationship with others (Hamilton, 1988). This object-relations approach is consistent with *systems theory*, which is closely linked with treatment of the family (Minuchin, 1974), and with the neo-Freudian schools of therapy, to which clinicians such as Horney (1939), Erikson, (1950) and Sullivan (1953) contributed.

Melanie Klein

The work of Melanie Klein (Segal, 1964), which had its origins in child analysis, was developed largely in London, where it continues to have a significant influence, and where trainee analysts, especially from Latin America, Spain and Italy, come to study and propagate her work in their own countries. In other parts of Europe and in the USA her teachings are regarded with more reserve, although even here much of what she innovated is selectively valued.

Klein thought that the ego, with its instincts and anxieties, is present at birth, and described *Positions*: the *paranoid-schizoid*, followed by the *depressive* — both referring to anxieties suffered by the individual. These 'positions' recur throughout life, being influenced by external and innate factors (Klein especially emphasized the latter, a source of criticism of her work by many non-Kleinian analysts).

During the 'paranoid-schizoid' episodes, anxiety is predominantly for the self, *splitting* (disassociating) and *excessive projection* being the main defences. When the later 'depressive position' is reached or reactivated, splitting is lessened, and a dim awareness begins — slowly and painfully — that goodness and badness can co-exist within the same person (e.g. the mother and the individual himself).

Other Kleinian precepts include a strict technical adherence to the transference, close attention to projective and introjective mechanisms, and a literal acceptance of the death instinct which, so Kleinians believe, manifests itself as aggression and, particularly, envy. These dismal and pessimistic concepts to some extent further the negativism of Freud and classical analysis wherein primary love between baby and mother is played down in favour of basic aggression, rancour, greed and destructiveness on the part of the former which may — given favourable innate and environ-mental factors or with propitious (presumably Kleinian) analysts — lead to regret, concern and making good.

Klein's teachings have stimulated interest in fields beyond psycho-analysis and psychiatry; educationalists and criminologists, and those concerned with aesthetics have found her work of value (Segal, 1955).

Ego Psychology

Another group of theorists, the ego analysts, who included Hartmann (1958) and Rapaport (1951), have also made a significant contribution to the understanding of human behaviour and experience, by directing attention to the way in which people guide, and are largely responsible for, their own actions. The emphasis by these theorists on human 'self-determination' entailed an important shift in the view of mankind. Human beings are not portrayed as hapless victims of irresistible and turbulent internal (intra-psychic) forces; instead, they are depicted as the major architects in the construction of their own present and future.

Despite these and other more recent developments, strong traces of traditional Freudian concepts reappear, sometimes under a different guise. To some extent this is the case with aspects of Berne's theory of transactional analysis, which for a time enjoyed some popularity, being readily comprehended by both patients and professionals (Berne, 1966). One of the key concepts of this theory is that of the *ego-states*, of which Berne identified three: the 'child', the 'adult' and the 'parent'. The boundaries of the three are not hard and fast but, according to Berne, at different times any one may assume control, giving our behaviour and experience a characteristic 'flavour'. The 'parent' is similar to the more traditional idea of the super-ego, in that it refers to that part of our personality which reflects the ideals and moral values of the family and culture to which we belong. The 'child' makes its presence felt when, for instance, we 'let our hair down' and act on our more basic, egocentric and less socially acceptable impulses. Behaving in this way might also be described as allowing the id to assume control. The remaining ego-state, the 'adult', is that part of ourselves which allows us to deal rationally and maturely with our own internal needs. Again, the correspondence can be seen between this concept and the more traditional Freudian one — the ego.

One particular point, mentioned previously, justifies repetition — the importance of *conflict*. Theories about human nature abound, some of them interpersonal, others social. However, the linking theme of all these theories is that of the potential for, and the importance of, conflict — after all, the contribution of conflict to human diseases and dis-ease is a characteristic feature of psychodynamic theory and its therapeutic counterpart, psychoanalysis.

Modifications of Transference

The unique characteristic of psychoanalysis is the concept of *transference* (the process whereby the analyst is imbued with characteristics of significant persons in the patient's past life) the utilization of which within the analytical situation provides a living experience, both cognitively and experimentally.

In order to foster transference by encouraging free-flowing and regressive fantasies, the analyst traditionally stays out of the patient's physical and emotional sight during the entire course of the treatment, whilst the patient lies on a couch and is invited to 'free associate', generally without interruptions, censure or judgement. But this technical measure of the anonymous analyst, essential though it may be in order to foster projections which can later be assessed more realistically by the patient, has itself been criticized by some writers (Ferenczi, 1932; Suttie, 1935; Lomas, 1987) who have suggested that the use of the transference, as outlined above, may be experienced by patients as coldness and aloofness on the part of the analyst, and could re-enact, in the consulting room, real experiences of rejection in the early environment. Such techniques, these and other authors believe, are the very antithesis of fostering, albeit implicitly, the love and respect for the patient which, it is suggested, is the only basis of success in any psychotherapeutic procedure, including psychoanalysis.

The above authors, among others, whilst retaining the concept of 'transference', maintain that 'scientific' and detached interpretations may serve as a defence on the part of the analyst against sharing patients' painful feelings. In other words, the analyst in this sense employs a stratagem which cannot succeed if the purpose of the therapy is the evolution of change or modification in the patient's state. Unlike other medical specialities, knowledge or information is not enough in this situation. The authors considered here attest their belief that, just like any other helper of a person in deep emotional distress, something more than the foregoing is necessary, and the conviction of Ferenczi that 'no analysis can succeed if we do not succeed in really loving the patient' is strongly supported. Ferenczi at one time advocated a much more open and spontaneous attitude, to the extent that, notwithstanding his position as perhaps the closest of the half a dozen original associates of Freud, was eventually virtually disowned by Freud as a result of his innovative techniques which, startlingly, included 'mutual analysis' with the patient. To the end of his life Ferenczi nevertheless maintained a sense of loyalty and attachment to the psychoanalytical movement and to Freud.

Subsequently, Ferenczi's analyst, friend and colleague, Michael Balint, strove assiduously over many years to explain, modify, clarify and interpret the former's later beliefs into mainstream respectability and acceptance (Balint, 1968).

How Does Psychoanalysis Work?

Originally, as classical psychoanalysis was developing, it was felt to be essential and therapeutic that consciousness should replace that which is unconscious, largely using cognitive measures: ego (reality) should replace id (i.e. basic instincts). *Insight* was the goal, so that a more pragmatic approach to life generally was encouraged. Within the analytical situation, and again according to classical theorists, repressed sexual and aggressive impulses towards early 'objects', i.e. close members of the family (hence the incestuous connotation), were *transferred* to the relationship between the patient and the analyst, and hopefully resolved during the treatment. The focus of the therapy was to examine within the transference the *defences* that emerged, against patients' 'unacceptable' aggressive and sexual drives (Anna Freud, 1936). Interpretations as to the nature of the current transference phenomena were delineated by the analyst who, in Strachey's words, became an 'auxiliary superego' which hopefully attenuated the patient's own punitive superego or conscience (Strachey, 1934).

Kleinian analysts would see the aims of treatment as being the 'integration' of the personality: patients gradually develop a diminished need to *project* endlessly their own bad traits into the environment. These practitioners feel that when any projection takes place, 'good' attributes as well as 'bad' are projected (lost) and impoverishment of the personality inevitably results. Others, already mentioned, believe that for therapy to be successful a modification of the technique employed by the traditional analyst should take place because a detached technical attitude may merely replicate early experiences of rejection, so that a therapeutic impasse may be reached which is damaging and immutable. These authors 'show' themselves to a varying extent, and may openly convey empathy, so that which was not provided, and yet was so much needed, in the earliest formative years of the patient (i.e. the installation of unconditional acceptance and the building of self-esteem), can have a second chance of being developed through analysis. (See also Searles (1965) whose sparkling, human and wise writing is devoted to describing a style of treatment in which the analyst fearlessly merges with patients, even temporarily sharing some of their own psychotic processes, thereby countering the desperate isolation of the latter, and resulting in an unusual depth of understanding and prospect of change and development.)

Kohut and Self-psychology

In recent years, as the type of clinical problems which constitute today's greatest challenge have become more clearly delineated (*see* existential conditions p.5), it is increasingly accepted that in such cases, interpretations, however 'wise and deep', are not enough and indeed may themselves be a source of *intrusive irritation* for the patient. This was actually described in an early psychoanalytic communication (Freud, 1888). In those more complex mental disorders, which amount to distortions of self-esteem, self-cohesion and self-identity, such so-called narcissistic or borderline states have received special attention from the *Self Psychologists*, particularly their founder, the Viennese-born and later Chicago-based psychoanalyst, Heinz Kohut (Kohut, 1971, 1984), who designated virtually the entire range of psychiatric states 'Narcissistic disorders' or 'Disorders of the Self'.

These states have the characteristic defences of splitting, denial, projective identification and omnipotence. Patients will often display a grandiose sense of self-importance, preoccupation with grandiose fantasies, and exhibitionism on the one hand whilst, on the other, sustaining a sense of detachment and indifference to others yet with the expectation of special favours. There is associated rage, shame, poor self-esteem, emptiness, mood fluctuations and depression. Such patients tend to show great sensitivity to criticism, impulsiveness, an ill-defined sense of personal and gender identity, and frequent recourse to drug and alcohol abuse as typical characterological features.

Kohut aimed at providing for what he saw as a developmental lack or arrest in the growing personality which had resulted in these symptoms or characterological defences — especially what he called a specious 'grandiose self', with personality defects and, above all, difficulties in relationships.

The failures, which are inevitable and merely ones of degree, result from the shortcomings of the earliest carers, called by Kohut the 'self objects' which the developing infant requires for coherence and support. These self objects are not persons in their own right, but are felt as a part or extension of the infant's own self. Kohut's belief was that a person's psychological wholeness came about through a narcissistic relationship with primary carers and their later symbolic substitutes (a phenomenon lasting throughout life). The perceived functions of the carers: emotional and physical feeding, holding, touching and soothing, become part of the self, whose boundaries with 'the other' are completely permeable. Kohut also described how self-objects functions may not be actual people or 'objects' at all, but can become abstracted and symbolized into almost any human sphere: patriotism, religion, any aesthetic experience, geographical localities, music, etc. All these may also be considered as forms of 'transitional objects' (Winnicott, 1958; Horton, 1981).

Thus Kohut described how 'narcissism' was normal and not a condition to be described with pejorative overtones. It (narcissism) would hopefully develop along its own channels, not 'maturing' into (adult) object-relations but gradually, with adequate parenting, and later serendipitous events, including the possibility of therapeutic help, become *transformed* into factors such as empathy, humour and self-esteem, creative pursuits and wisdom, in its broadest sense. The requirements of such traits for the self would parallel but be separate from, 'real' relationships.

As there are imperfections in every life, the analyst's target, the basic aim of treatment — especially in dealing with the inevitable borderline features of any analysis or therapy — is to mitigate these imperfections. In this way, life's vicissitudes will be, hopefully, dealt with more propitiously.

Kohut described three elements which he considered necessary for the development of a cohesive character, and further believed that such needs continued throughout life:

- FIRST. The individual's need for affirmation, approval, admiration and, to some extent, an unconditional acceptance and love.

These elements are thought to lay down a sense of self. The parent (therapist) matters only to the extent that they can be experienced by the developing child/patient as a person available to perform these functions and not as a person in their own right. Kohut called this cluster of experiences *mirroring*, and in therapy, *the mirror transference*. The inevitable disappointments in life or therapy lead to a return of relative or absolute fragmentation, in which event the parent/therapist must harness, in another of Kohut's key words: *empathy*, i.e. tuning into or entering the world of the subject and his or her needs.

• SECOND. A safety or strengthening element is needed, and is called *an idealizing transference*.

This endows the parent/therapist with powerful, soothing, knowledgeable and confident qualities, which may be internalized by the patient, leading to a further sense of cohesion and vitality, as well as to inner calm and confidence.

Again, inevitable disillusionments lead to the risk of fragmentation and narcissistic rage and the therapy will be highlighted by reconstructive interpretations which amount to the therapist accepting and living out, for a time, these expectations on the part of the patient. Failures by early carers in *mirroring* and *idealizing* were thought by Kohut to lead either to a general 'weakness' or vulnerability of the personality (ego), or to excessive defensive structures, various symptoms affecting the body or mind or to the development, as a further defence, of a 'grandiose self'.

• THIRD. A sense of kinship or belonging is necessary — again throughout life.

This, also, Kohut, thought could be provided by the therapist by conveying to the patient how basic was this need. This concept makes use of social psychiatry with the fostering of peer and friendship experiences with people of equivalent background.

Thus, in his model, Kohut highlighted above all the concept of *empathy* — which came to mean, in his description, rather more than just feeling for another person, rather suggesting repeated experiences of conscious and unconscious needs on the part of patients being *anticipated* and met by the therapist. In other words, providing or reinforcing the missing or weakly instilled clusters of the above three concepts. He thought that what should be provided is a sort of 'emotional cement' which, over a period of time, could be internalized by those seeking help. The changes rather portentously described by Kohut as 'transmuting internalizations' imply internal changes, mutations hopefully occurring as the individual increasingly develops the capacity to accept the hurts and shortcomings caused by failures in optimal responses by important figures in the early environment. More succinctly, the curative factor could be said to be the development and sustaining of the self-object transference, i.e. a prolonged empathetic response.

By extrapolation, patients benefiting from this approach could more usefully choose modes of interaction with real people and form healthier relationships rather than merely duplicating early ones which again would then be likely to fail. (The enhanced ability of the strengthened self to choose healthier and more appropriate self-objects in the real world will reduce the likelihood of repeating early failures. It could also be said that patients may develop the capacity to manage their own states of tension and incoherence, to regulate their affects in a more propitious way.)

Summary

Some theoretical and practical 'advances' in traditional psychoanalysis have been sketched, but the overall goal is still an enhancement of patients' self-esteem and independence, and an increase in their sense of trust and cohesion.

References

ADLER, A. (1956). *The Individual Psychology of Alfred Adler*. A systematic presentation in selections from his writings. Ansbacker H.L. and Ansbacker R.R., eds. New York: Basic Books.

BALINT, M. (1968). *The Basic Fault*. London: Tavistock Publications.

BERNE, E. (1966). *Games People Play*. London: Deutsch.

BOWLBY, J. (1979). *The Making and Breaking of Affectional Bonds*. London: Tavistock Publications.

ERIKSON, E.H. (1950). *Childhood and Society*. New York: Norton.

FAIRBAIRN, W.R.D. (1952). *Psychoanalytic Studies of the Personality*. London: Routledge & Kegan Paul.

FERENCZI. S. (1932). *Clinical Diary*, edited by Judith Duport and translated by Michael Balint and Nicola Zarday Jackson (1988). Cambridge, MA: Harvard University Press.

FREUD, S. (1888). S.E.2. *Case Histories* p. 62n.

FREUD, A. (1936). *The Ego and Mechanisms of Defence*. London: The Hogarth Press.

HAMILTON, N.G. (1988). *Self and Others: Object Relations Theory in Practice*. New Jersey: [Aronson].

HARTMANN, H. (1958) *Ego Psychology and the Problem of Adaptation*. New York: International Universities Press.

HOLMES, J. (1993). *John Bowlby and Attachment Theory* London: Routledge.

HORNEY, K. (1939). *New Ways in Psychoanalysis*. New York: Norton.

HORTON, P.C. (1981). Solace: The Missing Dimension in Psychiatry. Chicago: University of Chicargo Press.

JUNG, C. (1968). *Analytic Psychology: Its Theory and Practice*. London: Routledge & Kegan Paul.

KOHUT, H. (1971). *The Analysis of Self*. London: The Hogarth Press.

KOHUT, H. (1984). *How does Analysis Cure?* Hillsdale, NJ: Analytic Press.

LOMAS, P. (1987). *The Limits of Interpretation*. London: Penguin Books.

MAHLER, M. (1967). On human symbiosis and the vicissitudes of individuation. *Journal of the American Psychoanalytic Association*. **15**, 740–763.

MINUCHIN, S. (1964). *Families and Family Therapy*. Cambridge, MA: Harvard University Press.

RAPAPORT, D. (1951). *The Organization and Pathology of Thought*. New York: Columbia University Press.

SEARLES, H. (1965). *Collected Papers on Schizophrenia and Related Subjects*. London: The Hogarth Press.

SEGAL, H. (1955). A psychoanalytical Approach to Aesthetics. In: *New Directions in Psychoanalysis*. London: Tavistock Publications.

SEGAL, H. (1964). *An Introduction to the Work of Melanie Klein*. London: Heinemann.

STRACHEY, J. (1934). The nature of the therapeutic action of psychoanalysis. *International Journal of Psychoanalysis* **15**, 127–159.

SULLIVAN, H.S. (1953). *The Interpersonal Theory of Psychiatry*. London: Tavistock Publications.

SUTTIE, I.D. (1935). *The Origins of Love and Hate*. London: Kegan Paul. Reprinted by Pelican Books, 1960.

WINNICOTT, D.W. (1958). *Collected Papers* London: Tavistock Publications.

Further Reading

MEISSNER, W.W. (1991). *What is Effective in Psychoanalytical Therapy*. New Jersey and London: Aronson.

STERN, D.N. et al. (1998). Non-interpretive mechanisms in psychoanalytic psychotherapy. *International Journal of Psychoanalysis* **79**, 903–919.

Chapter 4
Group Psychotherapy

DICK BLACKWELL

Introduction

This chapter comprises six sections:

- Historical background, placing group psychotherapy in the context of the history of ideas, particularly the twin developments in sociology and psychology.
- The structure and process of psychotherapy groups, covering memberships, duration, types of groups and how they function.
- How group psychotherapists are trained.
- How group psychotherapy works — theories about how patients benefit in group psychotherapy.
- Who to refer for group psychotherapy and how to regard the group psychotherapy option in relation to other forms of therapy.
- Wider applications of group psychotherapy theory and practice outside the clinical setting.

Historical Background

The study of human beings and their relationships with their world has a long history, going back at least as far as the Ancient Greek philosophers over 2000 years ago. However, it was only in the nineteenth century that the discipline of sociology began to take shape and to formulate methods of studying whole societies scientifically. Durkheim, in his classic study of suicide, was one of the first to describe how individual behaviour can be understood as a function of social phenomena. Suicide, which had previously been understood as a most individual act, could now be seen as significantly influenced by social factors, i.e. by a person's relationship to others. Marx, too, argued that a person's whole being was essentially a function of his or her social relationships. Although the precise ways in which social relationships influence individuals continue to be matters of further exploration and debate, the fundamental premiss that human social relationships are a crucial dimension of human well-being now seems firmly established.

The first third of the twentieth century saw the development, within sociology, of a concern not only with whole societies and classes that had been the focus of the nineteenth century pioneers, but also with interactions between small numbers of individuals. Sociologists such as Meade and Cooley began to study small social units and the way these influenced the individual's experience of him- or herself. It was at this time that groups began to be used therapeutically.

Joseph Pratt began a group for tuberculosis patients in Boston in 1905, Edward Lazell in Washington treated schizophrenic subjects in 1919, Trigant Burrow treated neurotic individuals in 1920, Alfred Adler used groups generally in 1921, Julius Metzel worked with alcoholics, Cody Marsh used lecture and group discussion in New York in 1930, JL Moreno began psychodrama in the 1930s and Sam Slavson worked with disturbed children and subsequently established the idea of the small group whose structure and process provide the basis of much modern group psychotherapy. It is not clear how directly these pioneers were influenced by the sociological studies, but it is clear that both sociologists and group therapists were participating in the same trend towards an increased understanding of individuals in the context of their relationship with others.

This first third of the century also saw the development of psychoanalysis by Sigmund Freud and his colleagues. Freud was initially a clinician concerned with the treatment of individual patients but he rapidly became a major thinker about the nature and development of the human psyche in relation to its environment. Although he sought to apply his theories to the behaviour of small and large groups, and to whole societies, the individual remained the principle focus of Freud's investigations through his psychoanalytical work. His theories of society were therefore based on his theories of the individual, whereas the sociologists proceeded in the opposite direction, to theories of the individual based on the study of groups and societies. However, it should not be forgotten that the core of psychoanalytic theory is the idea that certain instinctual ideas and wishes have to be repressed in order to allow for the possibility of collective co-existence that is society.

The last 50 years have seen an increasing integration of these two orientations, particularly in the theory and practice of work with small groups of between six and 12 people. This work shows four distinct strands of development: that of Kurt Lewin (1952) with training groups (T groups); the work of Wilfred Bion (1961) analysing the group as a single psychic unit; the investigations of Wolf and Schwartz (1965) doing psychoanalysis of individuals within the group setting; and particularly SH Foulkes (1948) who utilized the communication between group members as a therapeutic transaction.

Lewin emigrated from Germany during the rise of Nazism in the 1930s and settled in the USA. He conducted research on the effect of group membership on individuals and developed the theory of the social field in which each individual existed. This was derived from the concept of a force field in physics. His work was applied in organizations and used widely in management training programmes.

Bion was an English psychoanalyst working as an army psychiatrist when he began his work on groups. Based at the Northfield Military Hospital outside Birmingham, he addressed problems of group morale and was a key instigator of what became one of the first 'therapeutic communities'. Bion studied the group as a single unit and tried to develop group-specific concepts. But ultimately he further explained these group concepts in terms of the psychoanalytical theories of Freud and Klein (the latter had significantly advanced psychoanalytical theory by applying it to the study and treatment of children). Bion thus produced a psychoanalytical theory of groups which has had considerable influence on the development of group psychotherapy in the UK. It has also been used, as has Lewin's theory, in the understanding of organizations and in management training and consultancy.

Wolf and Schwartz were American psychoanalysts who developed a form of group therapy focused on the individual. The group setting enabled them to observe the way each individual behaved in relation to the others. They could then comment on this individual behaviour and offer insights to each one in the traditional psychoanalytical way. They did not apply any particular theories of group behaviour. They regarded the group as a setting in which individual proclivities were revealed and exposed for analysis, rather than seeing group process in itself as an agent of change.

Foulkes was, like Lewin, an émigré from Nazi Germany, coming to England during the 1930s. In Germany he had been closely associated with the Frankfurt Institute for Social Research and his thinking was significantly influenced by the sociological work undertaken there. Like Bion, he worked at the Northfield Military Hospital and played a major part in the development of the 'therapeutic community' there. He was also a psychoanalyst who applied psychoanalytical concepts to the understanding of groups. But he saw the process of interaction *between* members of the group as the primary therapeutic process. The role of the group therapist was to facilitate, or in his word 'conduct', this process. His term 'conductor' to describe the group therapist's role was analogous to the conductor of an orchestra, in which the members of the orchestra make the music, in combination with each other, with the conductor enabling this process and interpreting the musical themes. He regarded the individual as an inherently social being and regarded symptoms as disorders of social interaction, inarticulate ways of communicating with others. His theories, along with those of Bion, have constituted the major strands of group psychotherapy in the UK. However, over the last 20 years the approaches based purely on Bion's model have dwindled. Efforts to study and interpret the development of the group by commenting only on its behaviour as a single entity in the way that he describes doing, tend to have an alienating effect on members who feel their individuality is not recognized but submerged in their membership of the group. Foulkes's approach, which he called *Group Analysis*, has meanwhile incorporated much of Bion's thinking on groups within an overall approach that pays more attention to the contribution and development of individual group members.

In addition to these four strands, five other developments are worthy of note. The first is the development of psychodrama by Moreno in the USA. This was concerned with creating dramatic scenarios, such as role plays and simulations, which enabled individuals to experience and express emotions that had often been suppressed or of which they were not normally aware. Psychodrama is now a growing therapeutic mode in the UK and is sometimes combined with other approaches as well as being used in its own right. It was Moreno who introduced the term 'group therapy' in 1925. The two most influential approaches in the International Association of Group Therapy now seem to be group-analytic psychotherapy and psychodrama.

Second, there has been the work of Gregory Bateson (1972) and his associates studying communication between people. Combining theories of psychoanalysis, anthropology, epistemology and biology, their work has provided the theoretical underpinnings for the rapid growth of family therapy over the last 35 years. They, as Foulkes, saw symptoms as aspects or functions of interactional processes between people, specifically people in the intimate relationships of family life. Whereas Foulkes applied this orientation to work with 'stranger groups' — i.e. groups of people who were not otherwise known to each other — family therapists developed techniques for working directly with those social networks in which symptoms were occurring.

Third, there has been the growth of the encounter group movement, often associated with the West Coast of the USA, but widely known and employed throughout the Western world. Carl Rogers (1970) and Fritz Perls (1971) were both pioneers in this field. Lewin's T groups contributed to some of the developments in this area, which also includes the psychologist Abraham Maslow (1968) and the school of gestalt psychology among its influences. Encounter groups are concerned with promoting the honest and open expression of feelings between people, that is seen as an inherently healthy and growth-enhancing process. Such groups have tended to receive a 'bad press' in more conventional psychotherapeutic quarters, but more detailed study reveals significant similarities between some types of encounter group and more conventional psychotherapy groups (Lieberman et al., 1973). Success was more attributable to leadership style than to actual model. A supportive, non-directive, non-confrontational leadership style was associated with lower drop-out rates and wider overall benefits than more directive and confrontational styles.

Fourth, there is the therapeutic community movement. Tom Main 1946, first at Northfield Military Hospital and subsequently at the Cassel Hospital in Surrey, and Maxwell Jones at the Henderson Hospital, also in Surrey, have been the major pioneers of this approach within the National Health Service (NHS). Other important contributions outside the NHS have come from Elly Jansen (1980) at the Richmond Fellowship, RD Laing at Kingsley Hall in East London, Joe Berke and Morton Schatzman at the Arbours Association in North London and Melvin Rose at Peper Harrow in Surrey. Therapeutic communities mobilize the curative powers of the group on a 24-hours-a-day basis. Patients (usually called *members*, *residents* or even *guests*) live together in the hospital, a hotel or other type of dwelling, forming their own community. Each member plays an active part in the running of the community's affairs. The staff also participate and help to enable the ingredients of communal life — such as co-operating, competing, supporting or challenging — to become therapeutic processes. Over the last decade therapeutic communities have struggled to survive many changes, particularly within health and social services. Peper Harrow (a therapeutic community for adolescents) actually closed, leaving an enormous gap in psychotherapeutic work with them. However, there has recently been an upturn in the development and recognition of therapeutic communities as they have demonstrated their effectiveness in the new age of healthcare.

Finally, one of the more recent developments, pioneered by Pat de Maré (1985) is the study of larger groups. De Maré believed that groups of over 100 or even over 200 individuals, meeting together on a regular basis without an agenda, had a capacity to generate a powerful dialogue among their members. Eventually it would be possible for every member to have a voice and for participants to begin to understand each other, not only at a personal level but also at social, cultural and political levels. Thus, the skills and responsibilities of citizenship could be learned. Such large groups, he believed, could not only civilize the individual but also have a humanizing effect on society. For those of us who have participated in such groups, albeit for limited periods of workshops, conferences and training courses, there is little doubt that the possibilities envisaged by de Maré do exist. However, it has never been possible to sustain such a large group meeting on a weekly basis for longer than 10 weeks. De Maré's effort to organize such meetings led to a group whose membership ranged from 15 to 40 members. This he has called a *median group* (as distinct from a large group) which he sought to develop and understand as a stepping stone from the small group to the large one.

The foregoing overview will have given some idea of the breadth of the field of group psychotherapy. As a group analyst, much of what the author has to say will inevitably reflect that orientation and may not necessarily hold true for other styles of group therapy. However, much of it will be generally applicable to what the author would call *conventional group psychotherapy*, i.e. group psychotherapy as practised generally within the NHS and in other settings, by practitioners with psychoanalytical or psychodynamic orientations and an awareness of the importance of social process.

Structure and Process of Psychotherapy Groups

Frequency and duration

Groups usually meet once weekly, although twice weekly or fortnightly meetings are possible variations. They usually meet for one and a half hours and great importance is attached to prompt starts and finishes, although a therapist may occasionally allow a few extra minutes if he or she deems it necessary to achieve an appropriate ending to the session.

Membership

The group will usually have between five and nine members, selected by the therapist to achieve a suitable mixture for the purposes of the group. In some groups all the patients will have been brought together because they have the same problem, for example alcoholism, drug addiction, sexual dysfunction, school refusal, etc. Alternatively, they may have an assortment of different problems. Similarly, with regard to age and gender, a group may be all of one sex or mixed; it may contain a very narrow age band, e.g. sufferers from mid-life crises, or have a wide spread from 20 to 65. It is preferable, however, to aim for balance in that no one feels him- or herself to be 'out on a limb'. If the group contains both sexes, it is best to have as near as possible an equal number of each sex. If there is not to be just one problem represented, then there should be a good assortment. Five alcoholics, a depressive and someone with sexual difficulties would be unlikely to provide a useful mix. Also, it is not a good idea to have one member much older or much younger than the rest, neither is it desirable to have a member who is isolated according to culture, ethnicity, social class or sexual orientation, or any other socially significant characteristic, though it is sometimes unavoidable. It is particularly problematic where the isolated group member is a member of a minority against which there exists substantial prejudice and discrimination and who consequently has a significantly different experience of the real world from those not similarly discriminated against. In short, the group should be either fully homogeneous along any particular dimension, or fully heterogeneous, and where this is not possible the conductor will have to pay particular attention to the problems created by the lack of balance.

Opinions vary regarding the relative merits of hetero- versus homogeneous groupings. It is argued, on the one hand, that patients get early comfort and support from others with whom they have much in common. This, along with the reassurance that they are not alone in their predicament, can speed the early phases of the group's development and may also lead to more enduring understanding and intimacy, which will promote the therapeutic process. On the other hand, such a group may lack the variety, difference in perspective and, therefore, new information that is available in heterogeneous groups. Homogeneous groups may share common blind spots and will have only the therapist to challenge them.

Co-therapy

There is usually just one therapist to each group except where there are specific reasons for having two people working as co-therapists. Couples' groups, where marital or cohabiting partners come together with other couples, is an example in which co-therapy is widely used. Co-therapy may also be helpful for inexperienced therapists, either learning by partnering a more experienced colleague, or working with another inexperienced colleague for mutual support and confidence. Co-therapy can also provide valuable learning for experienced therapists who may be put 'on their mettle' by the presence of a potentially critical colleague. At the same time, they may find the presence of a colleague provides them with the security to be more adventurous as therapists. It is also likely that groups which have no special reason for requiring it can nevertheless benefit considerably from the input of two therapists instead of one. On the other hand, co-therapists need to be able to play together like tennis partners and, if they cannot harmonize their input and resolve their own inevitable difficulties, they will considerably handicap the group.

Closed and open groups

Closed groups run for a fixed period of time with the same members. They may meet for as few as six or twelve sessions, or they may continue for a year or more. New members do not join during the course of the group, even if one or more of the original members drops out.

Open groups do take in new members as others leave and usually have no fixed time period. They may continue for many years, during which time they will completely renew their membership. Patients remain in these groups for varied periods; from 18 months to two years is usually regarded as a minimum period for full benefit to be derived from the group. However, some patients may stay for over five years, not necessarily in order to resolve their initial difficulty but often because they continue to derive other benefits from being in the group.

Group process

When they meet, the group members sit in a circle with the therapist or therapists.* They will usually stay in their seats for the whole meeting since the process is essentially one of verbal and visual communication. The therapist will not generally ask them to change places, move about or touch each other, nor will he or she expect them to do so spontaneously. Inevitably, however, there will be times when one member will extend a comforting hand to another in distress and the therapist is unlikely to regard this as against the rules. There are a few conventional group psychotherapists who will, from time to time, incorporate psychodrama techniques into group therapy and would then have their patients moving about accordingly.

There is no formal agenda for group discussion and the therapist will not initially offer any direction. He or she will leave the group members to talk about anything they want to bring up and to get to know each other in whatever way they choose. The therapist will allow this process to develop, watching and listening, and will then contribute in his or her own way to enable individuals to learn from their own experience of the process in which they are participating. The sort of interventions the therapist makes will depend on the personal style and the theoretical orientation of that particular therapist.

Among the possible contributions of the therapist are the following: questioning of either the whole group or individuals to elicit information or to encourage further thought and exploration of a particular issue, (e.g. 'How old were you when your father died?', 'How did you feel about what M has just said?'); disagreeing with a particular statement made or a position taken by a group member (e.g. 'I disagree with your view that sex should not be discussed in the group'); drawing attention to aspects of group or individual behaviour which have not been noticed by the participants (e.g. 'I notice that

---

* The rest of this explanation will assume only one therapist.

every time A and B get angry with each other, J clutches the arms of his chair very slightly' and 'Every time P brings up his jealousy, someone else quickly changes the subject'); interpretation of unconscious themes (e.g. 'You have talked a lot about competition in your jobs, I think you are also referring to the competition here in the group'). Sometimes the group will lapse into silence. At such times, the therapist will usually wait with the group until the conversation is resumed. He/she will only break the silence if he feels he has something particular to say at that point. He/she will not see it as his responsibility to keep the conversation going.

Training of Group Psychotherapists

It is generally agreed that group therapists need to have their own experience of receiving therapy. They must know themselves and how they respond to others, and how others respond to them. Some schools of thought would regard individual therapy as an adequate preparation for a trainee therapist, whilst others would insist on experience as a patient in a group. The Institute of Group Analysis requires its trainees to spend at least four years as patients in a twice-weekly analytical group.

In addition to having therapy themselves, trainees will study one or more of the theories of group process and of problem or symptom formation and resolution. They will usually spend two years conducting one or more groups under supervision. This supervision may involve meeting individually with a supervisor to report on and discuss the group but, more usually, it will involve meeting with other trainees in a group led by the supervisor. The supervisory process will then reflect certain important dimensions of the therapeutic process. Institute of Group Analysis students also meet regularly in a large group with all the other students at different stages of the course, and with the staff (see description of a 'large group' above).

How Does Group Psychotherapy Work?

There are a number of theories about how group psychotherapy works. These cover different views about how symptoms and problems arise and how they are resolved.

In the traditional psychoanalytical view, symptoms are manifestations of internal conflicts in the unconscious part of the individual's mind. These conflicts date back to infancy when ideas, wishes, desires and accompanying fears were 'repressed' from consciousness. This repression results from social prohibitions such as the incest taboo or from fantasies such as the male child's fear of being castrated for having incestuous desires. In psychoanalytical psychotherapy the patient re-enacts the infant–parent relationship in the patient–therapist relationship. The patient is said to 'regress' to the infantile state and to transfer on to the therapist the feelings that the infant had for his or her parents. In this way the repressed ideas, wishes, desires and fears begin to manifest themselves. The therapist draws the patient's attention to them so that they can become conscious, be expressed verbally and 'worked through'.

In a psychotherapy group, these unconscious features of the infant–parent relationship become transferred on to other group members as well as to the therapist, and even the group itself may be experienced as if it were a parent, usually the mother. Group members may also represent siblings for each other.

Other theories lay more emphasis on present conflicts and difficulties, and de Maré (1985) has introduced the term *transposition* to describe the way in which a patient treats other group members not as figures from the past (infancy) but as figures from the present — spouses, lovers, friends, colleagues, enemies, rivals, etc. In this view, whole constellations of relationships can be transposed and re-enacted within the group. In this way, patients can become more aware of how they deal with problems in relationships with others and can experiment in the group setting with different ways of relating.

This view sees problems and symptoms arising in an individual's relationships with others. The headache which repels unwelcome sexual advances is an example that has entered contemporary folklore. In a group setting, sufferers from these headaches may learn to say 'no' more directly when not willing to comply with another's wishes. Or in those cases where 'no' does not just mean no, but is also an expression of feelings of anger, sadness, resentment or fear, a patient may also learn to recognize these feelings and express them more directly.

Irving Yalom (1970) has developed the following list of 'curative factors' which operate in groups: installation of hope, universality (the discovery of being like everyone else), imparting of information, altruism, corrective recapitulation of the primary group, development of socializing techniques, imitative behaviour, interpersonal learning, group cohesiveness and catharsis. He regards these as all interlinked in the dynamic process of the group.

Skynner (1983) has attempted to connect historical factors of infantile relationships in the family of origin with contemporary relationship difficulties. He suggests that the individual grows up in a family in which certain aspects of emotional life are avoided. These may be anger, jealously, rivalry, intimacy, sadness, sexuality, etc. The individual's repertoire of behaviour and communication is consequently limited by growing up in this context. Furthermore, he evolves a philosophy of life, chooses friends and enemies, jobs and pastimes, lovers and spouses in accordance with this limited repertoire. In turn, as a parent, he will influence the development of his children in a similar way. If at any point the individual encounters a situation for which his existing repertoire has no satisfactory response, he will encounter an apparently insoluble problem or develop a symptom that brings him to therapy. Because of the diversity and variety of interaction in a therapy group, patients are likely to encounter the very situation that was avoided in their family and which they have successfully avoided prior to the occurrence of the problem or symptom presented for therapy. In the group, patients have to deal with the situation and experience the avoided emotion. It is only after they have done this that they are able to have insight and look back on their previous pattern of avoidance. This theory is particularly interesting in that it describes a scenario of change which need not necessarily be confined to the therapy situation. Such challenges to a person's habitual ways of relating, which were learned in the family of origin, can occur in other areas of life where they cannot be avoided. Thus, psychotherapy is not the only arena in which change and growth takes place. This is in contrast to more traditional psychoanalytical theories which suggest that such change and growth can be achieved only through regression and interpretation of infantile conflicts in the psychotherapeutic setting.

Foulkes (1948) regarded symptoms as forms of communication. They were the result of disorders in the social network of the individual patient who became the locus for the expression of the disorder. Foulkes regarded the group process as essentially one of communication, in which symptoms can be seen to be 'inarticulate' ways of communicating. Through the therapy group process, individuals can learn to communicate more satisfactorily. They will then be able to improve the patterns of communication within their social network, which were the source of the original symptom. Foulkes developed the concept of the group matrix to describe the complex 'transpersonal' network of communication which emerges in a group. As was noted in the historical background, his view has marked similarities to that of Bateson (1972) and the family therapy tradition. Bateson also regarded symptoms as arising from communication patterns in social networks, particularly families, so that changed communication would be the therapeutic goal. He focused on 'levels' of communication and learning, and applied the theory of logical types developed by the philosophers Russell and Whitehead. This resulted in the famous 'double-bind' theory of schizophrenia. But perhaps because this focus was so specifically on families, his theories are widely applied in family therapy but not as yet in group therapy.

Who to Refer for Group Psychotherapy

Again, there is diversity of opinion on this subject. Some therapists have very clear ideas on which diagnostic categories can be helped by group therapy and which cannot. However, Rutan and Stone (1984) point out that 'most exclusionary recommendations in the literature can be countered by other published recommendations that such patients are treatable in groups'. There is also disagreement as to whether traditional psychiatric or even psychoanalytical diagnostic categories are actually useful in deciding on patients' suitability for a group. It is my view that these categories are not very useful, because the success of therapy depends much more on how a particular patient 'gets on' with a particular therapist. Such matching is quite idiosyncratic.

The classification of patients in whatever diagnostic terms can provide only crude guidelines. What is really valuable is for medical practitioners to make personal contact with the psychotherapists to whom they might refer patients for psychotherapy. Obviously, there are limitations to this but, as a general guideline, the better a referrer knows the therapist, the more able he or she will be to make appropriate referrals. A discussion between practitioner and therapist about the *possibility* of referring a particular patient for therapy is in the author's view invaluable to all concerned, and such preliminary pre-referral discussions will also offer doctor and therapist an opportunity to make contact.

Medical students with whom the author has discussed this seem to feel it is incumbent on them as doctors to decide whether a patient should be referred for therapy. As doctors already have to carry a great deal of responsibility, there seems no good reason for expecting them to carry this additional and unnecessary burden, which should more appropriately be shared with their psychotherapist colleagues.

The therapist assessing a patient for a group is concerned not only with how he or she gets on with the patient, but also with how the patient will relate to other members of the group. Apart from being concerned with having a balanced group in terms of age, sex and other dimensions described in the section on group composition, the therapist will also have an intuitive sense of how certain patients might relate to each other. However, despite this need for each group therapist to consider each referral on its own merits, it is possible to make some tentative generalizations to aid referrers, both in terms of who might benefit and who might not.

Clearly, the major criterion must be the view that a particular symptom is amenable to psychological treatment. Many illnesses previously regarded as purely physical are now thought to have a significant psychological component. Medical practitioners themselves will differ in the

extent to which they regard such ailments as tuberculosis, cancer, asthma, premenstrual tension, allergies, etc. as suitable for psychological as well as physical treatment. It is also important that patients themselves are prepared to seek psychological help. A patient convinced, despite his doctor's opinion, that there is no psychological component in his complaint is likely to enter a therapy group with the intention of failing to improve in order to demonstrate the irrelevance of group therapy to his particular problem. Such an attitude suggests a poor prognosis.

This willingness of the patient to try to use group therapy positively applies equally, if more obviously, with psychological symptoms. Whilst the value of group therapy may be obvious to the doctor and psychotherapist, it may not necessarily be obvious to the patient. It is important to distinguish between the patient who is anxious and uncertain about trying something new, but will respond to encouragement and explanation, and the patient who is just not willing to make the investment of time and energy necessary to benefit from group therapy. The former may have a good chance of benefiting from it; the latter is virtually assured of failure.

As well as the type of unmotivated patient described above, there are some other contraindications. One of these is a lack of impulse control, such that the safety of other group members is at risk. Another is an immediate crisis requiring immediate help, with no time to enter a group and establish relationships that can lead to change. Having a speech impediment or other difficulties with language sufficient to inhibit ordinary conversation are also contraindications. In short, if a patient is able and willing to join a group and to participate in its process as outlined above, he or she has the possibility of benefiting from it. Anything that prevents this process from taking place can be deemed a contraindication.

During the current time of economic stringency, groups have gained in popularity because paying one therapist to conduct a group of six or more patients in which the patients help each other is clearly more cost efficient than the therapist having to see each one individually. However, *family therapy* referred to above and described elsewhere in this volume (see Chapter 5) by Alan Cooklin, can turn out to be even more economical because it may take only a few meetings with a whole family to help members overcome a particular communication block, after which they can often continue to sort things out on their own without recourse to a therapist. I, like many others, have grave misgivings about cost playing an inordinate part in decisions about what sort of therapy to offer patients. Care always needs to be taken that patients are not offered inappropriate therapy simply because it is cheap. However, it needs also to be borne in mind that patients can sometimes be offered treatment that is not the most helpful simply because it is conventional, which may in the past have been a barrier to some patients being offered family or group psychotherapy, or any sort of psychotherapy.

Cost is always likely to be a consideration of some sort, both in the NHS and, indeed, in insurance-financed treatment — not to mention the private treatment of patients with limited resources. Furthermore, patients themselves may not wish to spend more time in therapy nor to delve more deeply into their problems than they need to. There is therefore a case for a hierarchy of preferred treatments. First choice is family or marital therapy, which may lead either to a rapid resolution of the difficulties or to the discovery that one or more family members need to do some therapy outside the family. If family therapy is deemed impossible or inappropriate, the next choice is group psychotherapy. If this is not feasible or meets with only limited success then there is the choice of individual psychotherapy for those who need the particular degree of individual attention, focus and perhaps intensity, which it provides.

Wider Applications of Group Psychotherapy

As indicated in the description of the historical development of group psychotherapy, its theories and techniques have not been confined to the field of psychiatry. Group therapy approaches are now commonly used, albeit in modified forms, in education, industry and with staff groups in both health and social services. Usually, the aim of such applications is to facilitate more open and effective communication between groups of people working together. It also provides an opportunity for discussion and sharing of the stresses and strains affecting both individuals and groups in their work setting. In education, Abercrombie has pioneered the use of group approaches to teaching university students (Abercrombie and Terry, 1978). She adopted a group psychotherapeutic approach to create a non-authoritarian climate in seminars which enabled students to learn actively through discussion with each other, rather than passively by being given information and knowledge by the tutor.

Skynner worked with the staff of a comprehensive school. They met as a group to discuss the difficulties they had with the pupils. This resulted in a substantial decrease in the number of referrals from the school to the local child guidance clinic.

Groups are also used for training staff. The emphasis here is not on the functioning of a work group but on the individual development of the members. These groups may be used on management training courses where the participants do not share the same work setting. It is thought that the understanding of themselves and others that participants gain from the group experience will enable them to function more effectively

in their jobs. One excellent description of the way groups can be used to facilitate and develop the work of doctors in general practice is provided by Andrew Elder in Chapter 7 of this volume.

References

ABERCROMBIE, M.L.J. and TERRY, P.M. (1978). *Talking to Learn: Improving Teaching and Learning in Small Groups*. Society for Research in Higher Education, University of Surrey, Guildford.

BATESON, G. (1972). *Steps to an Ecology of Mind*. New York: Ballantine.

BION, W.R. (1961). *Experience in Groups*. London: Tavistock Publications.

DE BOARD, R. (1978). *The Psychoanalysis of Organisations*. London: Tavistock Publications.

DE MARÉ, P.B. (1985). Large group perspectives. *Group Analysis* 18, 2.

FOULKES, S.H. (1948). *Introduction to Group Analytic Psychotherapy*. London: Heinemann.

JANSEN, E. (1980). *The Therapeutic Community*. London: Croom Helm.

JONES, M. (1953). *The Therapeutic Community*. New York: Basic Books.

LEWIN, K. (1952). Defining the field at a given time. In: D. Cartwright (Ed.), *Field Theory in Social Sciences*. New York: Basic Books.

LIEBERMAN, M.A., YALOM, L.D. and MILES, M.B. (1973). *Encounter Groups: First Facts*. New York: Basic Books.

MAIN, T.F. (1946). The hospital as a therapeutic institution. *Bulletin of the Menninger Clinic* 10, 66.

MASLOW, A. (1968). *Towards a Psychology of Being*. New York: D. Van Nostrand.

PERLS, F.S. (1971). *Gestalt Therapy Verbatim*. New York: Bantam.

ROGERS, C. (1970). *Carl Rogers on Encounter Groups*. New York: Harper & Row.

RUTAN, J.S. and STONE, W.N. (1984). *Psychodynamic Group Psychotherapy*. Lexington: Collamore Press.

SKYNNER, A.C.R. (1983). Group analysis and family therapy. *International Journal of Group Psychotherapy* 34.

WOLF, A. and SCHWARTZ, E.K. (1965). *Psychoanalysis in Groups*. New York: Grune & Stratton.

YALOM, L.D. (1970). *The Theory and Practice of Group Psychotherapy*. New York: Basic Books.

Chapter 5
Therapy, the Family and Others

ALAN COOKLIN

Individual psychotherapies, whether based on a model of learning theory or on psychodynamic understanding, have one thing in common: they view the patient from the standpoint that he or she is an integrated discrete organism. Family and other 'systems' therapies differ in that they view the patient as one component in a system or 'organism' (e.g. the family) which may manifest its malfunction through the behaviour of that component — the patient. The purpose of this chapter is to elaborate that difference, the thinking behind it, some of the evidence which supports that thinking and implications for intervention. The goal here is that practitioners should be stimulated to think of alternative ways to use their professional skills, in order to promote healthy changes in families and other human systems. This is not a chapter on 'How to be a family therapist' nor 'What family therapists do'. Its aim is to offer practitioners a broader view of the context of human psychological distress and thus to broaden the range of therapeutic options in practitioners' repertoires. To this end, the material is organized into 15 sections:

- What is family therapy, both as a treatment and as a framework of conceptualization — *Systems therapy*?
- The family interactional model of psychiatry in relation to other models.
- Theories of organization and interaction in families.
- Family patterns and the 'family dance'.
- Short-term patterns and patterns over time.
- Balance and stability versus change in the family.
- The question of intervention: Does it work? It is worth it? What are the dangers?
- Some aspects of family therapy — how it operates.
- Another clinical example.
- Different methods of therapy with the family.

- Family therapy: comparison of principles with individual psychotherapy and group psychotherapy.
- Impacts of race, ethnicity and social disadvantages.
- Applications to different kinds of family structure and to 'non-family' human systems.
- What can practitioners do?
- Further reading and opportunities for learning and training.

What is Family Therapy?

The term *Family Therapy* is potentially confusing because it refers, on the one hand, to a 'treatment' — an activity whereby a therapist sits down for one or more sessions with various members of a family to help them change something — and, on the other, to a framework for conceptualization, a way of understanding and thinking about human behaviour which may then be used in a variety of ways and contexts. This thinking can then be applied to the family or to other proximities in which human beings live and may develop intimate relationships.

Two important components of the thinking are as follows.

First, people are not islands, and their behaviour can only be understood in the context in which it occurs. By the use of **this** thinking, the notion of a person having an 'internal' world has a different meaning and consequences from when the individual is considered in isolation. The internal world is no longer a 'closed shop', viewed only through the portal of dreams and other channels of the unconscious, but is accessible through the day-to-day interactions with others. These interactions are dependent on the context in which they occur. Consider the behaviour of a young mother towards her infant. If the 'individual' perspective is taken to absurd extremes, the mother's behaviour could be seen principally in terms of her unconscious fantasies about the child, or her learned responses. Alternatively, it could be recognized that the mother's behaviour will be affected by many factors. In some Asian cultures the mother would expect her child to be in almost constant physical contact with her for the first year or so of life, whereas in many Western environments she might expect to have longish period of separation from her child very soon after birth. The mother's responsiveness, and its degree of flexibility or rigidity, the degree of playfulness, anxiety, attentiveness or 'over-attentiveness' will, of course, also be affected by the child's response to her. However, if the mother perceives herself as, for example, looking after her child in a relatively hostile environment, she may be highly protective of every aspect of its life. This pattern is likely to be intensified in situations of racial conflict or prejudice. In the first few weeks or months of life, this protectiveness may offer the child the freedom to develop. However, the context changes with time. The same behaviour on the mother's part when the child reaches two, three, four or five years of age may no longer be protective but may have the effect of becoming *restrictive*. On the other hand, if the child is developing in a context in which there are real dangers — such as from racial attack — then this behaviour may continue to be appropriately protective for a much longer period. The mother's and, therefore, the child's behaviour will also be heavily influenced by their relationships with others in their environment. For example, if the mother feels well supported by her husband, she will be less likely to perceive the environment as hostile and therefore be less liable to protect the child inappropriately. However, if her parents are seen as in competition with her husband, or if his family is seen as in competition with her, the mother may be encouraged to isolate herself further with her child for mutual protection. These factors may have an *accentuated impact* on an only child whilst, if there are many siblings, the effect may be diluted. The above illustrates that 'Family Therapy', or rather therapies based on systems thinking, has to take account of the wider social and cultural factors which organize people's relationships, and therefore their behaviour. As a result, 'systems' practitioners are increasingly paying attention to the socio-cultural and even political realities of people's lives, both in their thinking and their forms of intervention.

Second, people in close physical and emotional proximity readily set up stable patterns of interaction. These patterns are made up from a whole series of sequences; repetitive short events involving two or more people. This notion will be elaborated later in this chapter. If the family presents a problem, either as an individual's symptom or behaviour, or as a set of 'problem' relationships, it *may* be assumed that this problem is a manifestation of the total organization of the family and its socio-cultural context. It is not *presumed* that the family 'causes' the problem, but rather that the problem, as it develops, is part of the life and context of the family and can soon become part of what is familiar and comforting. A practitioner offering 'family therapy' will, therefore, be concerned with the total family organization and how this is related to the problem, rather than to any one individual. To do this he or she may use various methods, may be working through individuals, but keeping his or her sights on the whole family organism. The therapist may work with sections of the family, with the nuclear family or with the nuclear and extended family of three generations or more, or even include other members of the community (especially where the family is an ethnic minority in a host culture). The therapy may last for one, two or many sessions of one or more hours. The most common is for the therapist to work for a fairly small number of sessions, averaging about ten.

Family Interactional Model of Psychiatry in Relation to Other Models

Although psychiatry is a branch of medicine, to operate rationally it has to link all levels of human experience: physical, cognitive, perceptual, emotional and, in certain circumstances, philosophical and theological. It is therefore not surprising that, in the struggle to achieve some coherence, there has been much controversy about the correct focus for the subject. Proponents of different views inevitably communicate a different kind of relationship with the patients who seek or are brought for their help (Cooklin, 1973). The *family interactional* model implies a relationship to the client or patient which includes others, which originally might have been expressed as: 'You present me with distress or disturbance. I see this disturbance as representing a problem in the organization of which you are a part, the family. Therefore, I will not respond directly to you: rather, I shall attempt to examine and change the organization of the family in the belief that this will also be of most benefit to you.'

However, although this model sees the therapist as concerned with the patient as *part of a group*, rather than just the relationship between patient and practitioner, this view of the relationship is increasingly being applied to work with individuals as well as with families. However the family interactional model also differs in the way in which it approaches causality: the family interactional model does not imply that the family is noxious and has 'made the patient ill'. Rather, it is concerned with the way in which a number of factors, particularly the family organization and the interactional pattern in the family, have allowed part of the patient's behaviour to become *congruent* to the family's way of living, whereas another aspect of the same behaviour clearly remains *incongruent*. Consider a young anorectic girl in a family where the members have been used to being close and physically intimate with each other, in which conflicts have usually been kept at a low ebb and in which unity of the family has been highly valued. The girl's behaviour is discordant to the family in that she arouses much anxiety and, in such a family, feeding may have been highly valued. On the other hand, it may be congruent to the family in that her sexual development is delayed, she will take less interest in and be less attractive to boys, thus avoiding conflicts common in many families. She will stay at home closely involved with her family, and her behaviour will keep other members of the family closely involved with her. One approach to the problem would be to consider the implications of the family adapting to a growing adolescent girl, to consider how the conflicts which might otherwise arise could be handled differently by both herself as well as the rest of the family. Such an approach could be seen as addressing principally the organization of family relationships, rather than being restricted to the girl's own motivation. However, the family or other relationships could be addressed from the perspective of the girl or other members of the family, and either or both of these could be achieved by working with the whole family together, with her, or others on their own, or by any combination of the above.

Theories of Organization and Interaction in Families

Two related sets of ideas originally provided frameworks for considering the family as a system rather than just a set of individuals. These were *general systems theory* and *cybernetics* (Ashby, 1956; Bertalanffy, 1968).

General systems theory

General systems theory is not a theory of causality, but a theory of organization. It is a way of categorizing systems throughout nature, both living and inanimate. It considers the family as a living system and considers its capacity to adapt in terms of the following.

The boundary around the family and around the subsystems in the family

This relates to the degree to which family members maintain a close unity within the family, or engage actively with the outside world. This, in turn, controls the input and output of information to and from the family. Information includes people. Thus a family with a very impermeable boundary will be likely to adapt poorly to the arrival of new members; babies, grandparents coming to live with them, boy- or girlfriends, and will be intolerant of members moving out (for example, during adolescence or early adulthood).

Differentiation of the subsystems within the family and the degree to which the boundary around these is clear

For example, the marital relationship is a separate subsystem from, say, the parental subsystem. In a family in which members say, 'we always do everything together', the differentiation of the parents having a separate relationship may be poorly recognized. This, in turn, may militate against the development of any other set of separate relationships.

Suprasystems and subsystems

In addition to the extent to which the family is differentiated into subsytems, it will also form part of other suprasystems to varying degrees.

For example, the family will also be part of an extended family network and this, in turn may be part of a dominant or of a minority culture. Furthermore, different members may be part of other suprasystems within the community — work, school, social groups, etc.

Cybernetics

Cybernetics is a set of principles adapted from electronic control systems, the thermostat in a central heating system being the simplest example. Cybernetic principles are used to consider ways in which the family develops habits that tend to neutralize or stabilize any change. In the example of the anorectic girl presented earlier, the father became depressed after his daughter was admitted to hospital and began to improve. Strains in the marriage appeared and the mother developed a number of hypochondriacal symptoms. The youngest sibling began to steal. The girl eventually became so worried about them all that she discharged herself from hospital and soon after resumed her fasting behaviour. The others then improved. Thus, the behaviour of the members of the family could be seen as responding to a change (the young girl leaving home) whilst the effect of their behaviour was ultimately to maintain stability, albeit an inappropriate stability and at a high cost. It was from observations such as these that the term 'family homeostasis' was coined (Jackson, 1957). However, the above assumes that an outside observer — such as a therapist — can make a reasonably objective description of such a system. Increasingly, family therapists have recognized that the observer's perspective and prejudices not only affect what therapists see, but also their presence will both have a significant effect on what is observed as well as being significantly affected by it. Theoreticians such as Von Foerster (1981) have attempted to reformulate cybernetics as 'Second Order Cybernetics' to take account of this process, but some would see these attempts to reformulate an old theory as unnecessarily tortuous.

Family Patterns and the 'Family Dance'

Imagine an event where you are sitting at dinner with some members of your family, say your parents if they are alive, or perhaps your children. Maybe there are others: grandparents, siblings, aunts, uncles or cousins. Imagine that a small and common or familiar conflict develops. Perhaps it starts with the question of who is to visit whom at the weekend, or some comment on your dress or diet. If you can imagine such a scene, you may be able to predict more or less accurately who would say what, roughly in what order, and the sort of tone with which each would speak. You may be able to go further. You may be able to predict to what degree of tension or passion the conflict will develop and two or three ways in which it will 'end'. What you will have remembered is an interactional sequence and one which is likely to be repeated with a similar shape and similar attitudes taken by the various members, despite the fact that the subject of conflict might differ markedly. I put the 'end' in inverted commas because, of course, it is not really the end. It is only the punctuation of a sequence which, with other sequences, makes up the interactional pattern of the family. This sequence could 'end' with a senior member of the household perhaps looking stern, raising his or her voice, perhaps shouting, banging on the table, perhaps threatening violence or perhaps carrying out violence. The amount of feeling and the level of conflict tolerated in different families will be idiosyncratic to that family. However, the ending of a sequence with one member taking a strong and challenging position is one pattern which will occur in many families in a predominately patriarchal culture. However in many cultures both the roles and expectations of women, as well as their physical and economic relative weakness, may be the more significant factor in their adoption of a form of 'toleration' of violence, which may appear to be complementary to the behaviour of an aggressive male. In cultures with a different orientation to gender and power this may be different.

There are many alternative punctuations to such a sequence. It could end with somebody becoming upset, bursting into tears, leaving the room or the house, or with another member placating and 'calming things down'. It could end with a diversion: someone making a joke, an external intrusion such as the telephone or perhaps a child becoming excited or misbehaving. Diversion by a child is a common ending to such a sequence of conflict in many families. In some families, however, the child's over-reaction to increasing tension is in somatic form. If the child has a predisposition to asthma, for example, the child is likely to have an asthma attack at times of high tension, particularly if this concerns the parents. Such an attack will often then divert attention from the conflict in the family, as members of the family co-operate to assist the afflicted member (Minuchin et al., 1978). At this point, the problem of considering causality can be seen. It could be said that the tension in the family precipitates the asthmatic attacks; alternatively, it could be said that the asthmatic attacks control tension in the family.

Short-term Patterns and Patterns over Time

If you were able to imagine a family sequence, you could ask, 'Who made it happen?' The answer has to be, 'Everyone present'. Systemic notions about *complementarity* — the fit between apparent opposites in relationships — would indeed be based on an assumption that all members of a family or other intimate social system share responsibility for all the rational events occurring in that system. This perspective has, however, been the subject of many critiques, originating principally from writings of feminist family therapists (Goldner, 1985; Perlberg and Miller, 1990; Burck and Speed, 1994; Burck and Daniel, 1995) who have pointed out that in most cultures there is commonly a significant imbalance of power between adults and children and between men and women. If the above sequence was experienced as unpleasant, most members of the family would commonly admit that they had individually resolved 'never to let it happen like that again', despite which, as soon as they are together, they may all experience themselves as helpless to prevent a repetition of a similar event.

The kind of sequence the reader has been invited to imagine might be repeated many times over the course of a few hours or days. In the family of 'Susan' (the anorectic young person referred to above) a common sequence would be that she would return from school and suggest to her mother that she was going out. The mother would complain that she did not help in the house but would not directly insist that Susan stay in. As tension developed between the mother and Susan, her younger brother Ben would demonstrate his 'difference' from Susan by offering to help his mother and telling her many things about his school day, Susan would become increasingly angry and provocative in response to Ben's relationship with his mother, so that when her husband returned from work the mother would make demands on him to control Susan. Conflict would then escalate between Susan and her mother, which would be followed by the parents arguing with each other. The children would then fight, and the parents would then interrupt their own argument to control the two children. In various similar forms this complex sequence would be repeated frequently. Susan's failure to eat could then be seen as replacing the fights between the children as a means of interfering with the arguments between the parents, albeit replacing them with other arguments which they often saw as having been 'caused' by her.

More complex patterns may be repeated less frequently. For example, in some families it can be observed that the mother and 'Susan' remain on good terms, whilst the father is 'left out', for approximately 2 – 3 months; perhaps this reverses, with 'Susan' being close to her father for a few weeks, after which she is again closer to her mother. Commonly, the people in a family know that each change is not really a 'change', but only a punctuation. There may be other sequences which are repeated even less frequently. It can often be noted that a particular set of behaviours occurs in one generation, misses a generation, but can then be found between parents and child in the following generation. However, in systemic thinking these patterns do not occur because somebody 'makes' them happen. Rather, they are a function of the organization of relationships which has developed in the family. Although unconscious motives *could* be postulated to explain the behaviour of each member who contributes to the maintenance of such a pattern, another perspective is that these patterns are part of the processes which maintain a certain form of stability in the life of the family. In times of stress the maintenance of stability may be perceived by family members as a means to protect the family and those in it, and may represent an attempt at *mutual protectiveness*.

Balance and Stability versus Change in the Family

A degree of stability is, of course, necessary for a dependent being to achieve physical and emotional development. At the same time, a certain degree of flexibility is necessary for the family to adapt, for example, to the children requiring more independence, privacy or autonomy. Thus, throughout all families, there is a constant tension between these contradictory pulls towards change and stability. Many problems can be understood in terms of the failure to resolve this conflict in the family or, put another way, ways of responding to problems that may have been appropriate and effective in an earlier time have become incongruent to the present focus of development in the children. In the family of the anorectic girl, the various behaviours of the family members could be seen as accommodating to the change in such a way as to temporarily maintain the previous status quo. Several research projects, e.g. Mossigie et al. (1979), have demonstrated that in families where one member has had an episode of schizophrenia there is a greater tendency for that young person to modify his or her opinions and perceptions in order to reflect the 'orthodox family' opinion. The studies by the Philadelphia Child Guidance Clinic of what was described as 'psychosomatic families' gives support to the contention that an illness in a child can play an important role in the regulation of conflict within the family. The most dramatic study by the clinic involved the measurement of the free fatty acid (FFA) levels in severely labile diabetic children and their parents during a standardized task interview (Minuchin et al., 1978). This level has been shown to rise in ketoacidosis but is also a useful measure of emotional stress. The 'labile group' of diabetic children required hospitalization for correction of acidosis as often as once per week. The symptomatic child was initially left outside the room but was allowed to observe a family argument which the parents had been asked to resolve from behind a one-way mirror. During this period, the FFA levels in at least one of the parents would rise markedly whilst the FFA level in the child would continue to rise slowly. The child was then brought into the room and invited to join in the discussion. At this point the FFA level in the parents dropped markedly, whereas it continued to rise sharply in the child. The level remained high in the child long after the end of the interview. In practice, it seemed as though the intervention of the child, and even the beginning of symptoms in the youngster, was associated actually with a lowering of the level of stress in the parents.

The Question of Intervention

Despite a plethora of research, there are few controlled trials that successfully demonstrate the therapeutic efficacy of family therapy in comparison with other treatments. An early review was included in the *Handbook of Family Therapy* by Gurman and Kniskern (1981). In the 'labile diabetics' referred to earlier, the re-hospitalization rate was negligible following 3 – 12 months' family therapy. Leff et al. (1982), demonstrated that a factor defined (somewhat inappropriately in my opinion) as 'Expressed Emotion' or 'EE', may be critical in determining relapse rates of patients with schizophrenia. Patients who return to live with a relative who has been assessed as high in 'EE' may have as much as a 98% chance of relapse, which may be lowered by about 20% if they take their medication regularly. This contrasts with a relapse rate of only 12 – 15% for patients who return to live with a relative who has been assessed as low 'EE'. Later studies (Anderson et al., 1980; Hogarty et al., 1986; Leff et al., 1982, 1987, 1990, 1994; Strachan, 1986; Randolph, 1994; Xiong et al., 1994) demonstrated that family therapy could markedly improve the relapse rates in these families in comparison with control subjects. Asen et al. (1991) have demonstrated that 'EE' is also a useful generic measure of family change, and a recent study has suggested that family therapy is superior to drug treatment for depression (Leff, 1998). Family therapy may last only a small number of sessions (between two and ten), and has been said to minimize the dangers of the patient developing an unhelpful dependence on the therapist, or of those close to him or her perceiving that the solution is 'out of their hands'.

Some practitioners fear that bringing the whole family together may lead to the erupting of terrible family dramas. They may further fear that any mistake may lead to the 'break up' of the family, for which the therapist will be responsible. In the experience of most family therapists the meeting of the family makes this 'danger' *less* rather than *more* likely, partly because the impact of the therapist is diminished by the presence of more family members, and partly because of the ability to 'survive' which many families have developed through 'stabilizing' or 'neutralizing' change.

Some Aspects of Family Therapy

The goals of family therapists will vary widely, but they are almost universally concerned to encourage in different ways, the development of an experience of some new *information* in the family. This notion of information

(Bateson, 1973) refers to a different way of perceiving the events of which family members complain, rather than some new didactic data or knowledge. Some writers would describe this process as the development of different discourses or stories. This may occur through the family members being helped to understand the origins of the problem, through trying to understand or sharing unconscious fantasies, but it is more likely to take place through a series of interactions occurring in the session, which initiate a process of change in the meaning of what had recently happened in a different way.

One approach to generating a different experience would be for therapists to encourage the creation of a family event which may be familiar in may ways, but therapists would then aim to help the family resolve it or to end the sequence or 'dance' in a different way. By having a different experience, the family members may then experience differences in perception of events that had previously been felt as unpleasant exchanges. For example, in one family in which there was a 16-year-old deaf daughter and a 12-year-old boy who was not attending school and had been defined by the family as 'retarded', the mother complained that the whole load of worry about the family fell on her shoulders. Both she and her husband seemed to agree that the husband was 'distant, detached and disinterested'. The therapist suspected that this was a collusive relationship, i.e. he believed that the mother and the children (and the father as well) were all behaving in a way that kept the mother over-burdened and kept the father distant. The therapist believed that this view of the family was inefficient, and was playing an important part in keeping the young boy behaving much less competently than he was able. In order to change this view of the roles of the mother and father, the therapist needed first to challenge the idea of the father as distant and, secondly, to compère an event in which he and the mother begin to play their customary parts. As a way of challenging the idea of the father being distant, the therapist asked the father how his wife coped when she realized that her first child was deaf. The father answered that 'it took its toll'. The therapist pressed the father to recall from whom the mother gained her support: had it been from the children, had it been from her mother or had it been from him? He answered, 'I don't know'. The previous descriptions of him might have led the therapist to assume that this was because he was disinterested. The therapist defined the situation differently:

> Therapist: 'It sounds like she does not tell you much about what she is thinking.'
> Father: 'Probably not.'
> Therapist: 'So you seem to get left out quite a lot.'
> Father: 'No.'
> Mother: 'No, he likes to be left out.'

The therapist now begins to challenge this definition.
Therapist to father: 'Just a minute. Is this really true?'
Father: 'I do, yes.'
Therapist: 'Ah, but who sold you the idea?'

This interpretation eventually leads the father to acknowledge that he actually finds it very difficult to play an active part in the family as his wife has already decided everything. Which of these definitions of the father is 'true' is not strictly relevant, but *the latter provides a definition of the relationship which is more likely to promote at least some experimentation with a new pattern*. The therapist has opened up an alternative way of viewing things. This couple were unaccustomed to continuing their disagreements to a point of resolution. Commonly, disagreements would end by the mother taking a decision, or by the children providing a diversion. In the presence of the therapist, both partners turned to him with their point of view, assuming that he would resolve the disagreement. It is at this point that the therapist has the opportunity to provoke an event which ends in an unfamiliar way for the family. That is that the couple begin to face and resolve their differences.

Therapist: 'No! Sort it out together!'
(To the wife) 'With him! He's your husband, not me!'
The mother finally turns to the father and complains.
Mother: 'I took Ben to the doctor's. I tried to get it all straightened out. You just spoke about it, but I did it.'
Father: 'Right'.'
Therapist to father: 'Go on.'
Father: 'No, no, no.'

The therapist challenges the position the father is taking by defining him as compliant rather than disinterested. The therapist asks the father, 'So is this what happens at home? She makes a speech and you say "right"?' Eventually, the father confronts the mother with the fact that he feels unable to stand up to her as she is always much more verbal so he eventually 'gives up and ignores her'. Subsequently, the couple begin to experiment with an alternative way of responding to each other, particularly in relation to their roles as parents. In doing this, the therapist has temporarily increased the level of conflict beyond the level which usually occurs in the family. The goal is not so much to help them to understand the conscious or unconscious 'reason' for their difficulties, but rather to experience a different view of their relationship so that they can begin to respond to the children and each other differently. In general, family therapists would not see interpretation as a useful way of introducing this information.

However, consider the following sequence:

Pamela (11) is brought to the therapist by her mother and stepfather with the complaint that she is crying constantly. Her mother also states that at times she (the mother) has 'felt like strangling her', and that there was a time when she threatened to have her taken into care. Also present are her two younger brothers who seem to observe mother and daughter in a rather 'distant' manner. As the interview progressed it was revealed that Pamela was approaching the age (12 years old) of two previous children who had been left by their mother with their different fathers. In both cases, the mother had left, or the family had broken up when the eldest reached the age of 12. The family was seen for five sessions, in the third of which Pamela is fingering a little box, looking away and generally refusing to speak. The excerpt illustrates the interaction of the therapist, Pamela and her family around the box:

Therapist: 'You keep showing that to me. It must be very important. What is it?'
Pamela: 'It is a box.'
Therapist: 'Can I have a look? I feel I am supposed to see it. Am I allowed to look inside or don't you want to show it to me?'
Mother: 'I don't think there is anything in it, is there?'
Therapist: 'You decide, Pamela, is it private?'
Mother: 'It is all the silly things she brought out with her.'
Therapist: 'The family think it is all rubbish; is that right?'
Stepfather: 'It is not rubbish, just her own things.'
Therapist: 'Yes, private things?'
Stepfather: 'They are not really private, they are what girls of her age collect.'

Pamela pulls out a broken bracelet and other broken trinkets from the box.

Therapist: 'I think it is very important that you carry all the different bits and pieces that are broken and keep them with you and look after them and that is rather like what my colleague (who was observing from behind a one-way mirror) thought Pamela is doing for the family; that she was doing some crying, that we didn't really understand what the crying was about yet, but carrying some of the broken things, things that have broken in the past for the family and that that is why it was unbearable for the family because she was carrying in her all these hurts and broken things which really you (addressing the mother) must have felt as well.'

In this example, a piece of behaviour is defined as *representing* an expression of a family dilemma. It is not of immediate concern to the therapist whether this idea is conscious or unconscious, or even if it is 'true' or 'untrue', but rather that the idea may have a useful function if it links Pamela's behaviour to that of the rest of the family.

Another Clinical Example

The following case illustrates:

- The tension between stability and change.
- The intensity and perceptiveness of the sequences and patterns in the family: 'the family dance'.
- The impact of change in the wider system (retirement and the stabilizing effect of the day hospital treatment).
- The case therefore illustrates also the intervention of the family therapist in the wider system of family and professional.

Wendy

Wendy was an only child, aged 20 when referred. Her mother, Anne, had not known her own mother and had been brought up by an aunt and her grandmother. She was nervous when she had Wendy, and this was aggravated when the paediatrician suggested that Wendy may be partially sighted. This later turned out to be untrue, but it was one factor which pushed Wendy and her mother closer together in the first few years. Another factor was that the father Simon, aged 60, was often away. He had recently retired from an active life as an officer in the army. He had had long periods away from home on missions to which his family either could not, or had chosen not to, follow him. Wendy and her mother continued to live in Scotland. Simon's retirement almost coincided with the time when Wendy would be leaving school and perhaps leaving home.

Eighteen months before referral to the family therapy clinic Wendy had been attending a day hospital run for the armed forces near her home in Scotland. She had been 'unable' to work because of 'obsessional rituals'. These involved washing and, most specifically, clothes-washing rituals. She claimed that these were caused by 'contaminations', which she experienced in crowded places, particularly in two nearby towns where there happened to be many young soldiers, but also if accidentally touched by either of her parents. At home she was perceived by her parents, and behaved, as irritatingly incompetent. She would insist that her parents help her with any activity, writing a letter, filling the washing machine, etc. In the day hospital she attended groups with other patients, had the almost full attention of one senior nurse, spent two hours a week with her psychiatrist and was particularly attached to her psychologist. The latter had attempted several behavioural training programmes with frustrating results.

In the first session the therapist noted that as they came into the room the parents motioned Wendy where to sit, then they suggested which clothes she should remove for comfort and watched her anxiously if she was asked any questions, clearly ready with the 'correct' reply. Wendy seemed unable to say anything on her own behalf, and to expect her parents to speak for her. Alternatively, she seemed to assume that the therapist could rely on the reports received from the other psychiatrists, nurses, psychologists, etc. The therapist chose to ignore the parents and repeatedly asked Wendy why she had come? Finally, and with great difficulty, she was able to say, 'It's because of the crossed wires'. Although a small statement, it was at least one from Wendy herself. As the discussion continued the therapist gained the impression that the way that the family was organized seemed in some way to fit with Wendy remaining incompetent. The presumed need to do things for her brought the parents together in their relatively new role as shared parents (the father recently having retired). As a result, Wendy's behaviour seemed to fit more with that of a young child. As the therapist began to challenge the parent's interruptions, Wendy could be seen to reactivate them in subtle ways; by glances, stammering, being lost for words or appearing confused. Gradually, Wendy began to take on more responsibility at home, but despite this continued to attend the day hospital. The therapist realized that the latter was providing Wendy with a life which was richer than anything she could conceive of outside. Having no siblings and no friends, she had little impetus for change. The therapist asked her whether her parents would welcome the effect on her which more independence might bring (such as speaking up for herself more clearly or taking a more independent line). To the great surprise and shock of her parents she answered, 'No, I don't think they are ready, I think they would prefer me to remain a baby'. The therapist suggested that perhaps the day hospital was a good solution for everyone. It allowed the parents to continue to feel they were doing the 'right thing' by their daughter and it allowed Wendy to have a life, apparently as an adult, whereas in reality she was treated as a child. The therapist suggested that maybe this is what they should settle for and prescribed caution about any abrupt change. The goal of this was to face Wendy and her parents with a different framework — for thinking about her symptoms — as representing a 'costly' (in terms of lost life opportunities) solution to a real dilemma which they all shared. He left the family without offering another appointment. Two weeks later the therapist received a letter from Wendy, the first that she had written herself, saying that she had discharged herself from the day hospital and would like another consultation for the family.

In this case it was not until the therapist realized that two aspects of the wider system were playing an important part in Wendy's problems — the father's retirement from an institution on which he was highly dependant (the army), and Wendy's involvement in an institution on which she was highly dependent (the day hospital) — that she could begin to change. The staff of the day hospital were unintentionally mimicking her parents by responding with anxiety whenever she made a bid for more independence. The repetitive sequences of behaviour by the family could not be changed without reference to the wider context. Thus, by suggesting that the family settle for the status quo, with Wendy remaining as a patient in the day hospital, the therapist had forced both Wendy and her parents to face their conflict about change and to make a real choice. From this point on, therapy moved more quickly but, after discharge from day hospital, Wendy complained more acutely of her 'contaminations'. The therapist suggested that the family should not attempt to 'cure' these, but rather they should think of them as a problem of loneliness, i.e. that 'nobody could understand just exactly what Wendy felt like when having these feelings'. He therefore asked Wendy if she would agree to her parents making these feelings worse so that she could describe them with more passion and the parents could understand them more fully. He therefore asked the parents to push Wendy into crowded places and touch her whenever possible, for one week. The parents were amazed when Wendy agreed to this, as they had always avoided confrontation with her and had accommodated her every request. The mother then acknowledged that she had a phobia about cats and the father and Wendy agreed to bring cats into the house to do the same thing for her. Finally, the father acknowledged that he had a phobia of heights and the mother and Wendy agreed to take the father for a walk along the nearby cliffs. This session ended with great jocularity and on their return, not surprisingly, they had been unable to elicit the expected symptoms in any of these situations. Thus, the symptoms had ceased to have a stabilizing influence in the family and had become part of a more playful behaviour which allowed more freedom and experimentation. Later aspects of the therapy were concerned with helping Wendy to think about how to get a job without her parents doing it for her, helping the mother to take charge of the father, so that he became less anxious and therefore less intrusive on Wendy and, finally, helping Wendy to leave home and find her own lodgings. Only then was she able to make friends and develop her own life. In this case, the initial interventions were of a type described as direct intervention in the process of the session. However, the intervention which prescribed that Wendy should remain in the day hospital as a fitting solution to her and her parents' requirements of each other was designed to offer the family a caricature of an aspect of their shared perceptions of each other and one which had not been previously acknowledged. This rather exaggerated portrayal created a crisis which allowed Wendy to leave the hospital and allowed Wendy and her parents to be courageous in facing questions of change.

Different Methods of Therapy with the Family

The kind of direct approach described in the second example does rely on the family members making an alliance for family change with the therapist. This, in turn, requires that the pressures for stability are not so great that the opportunities for a change cannot be welcomed. When the family is thoroughly entrenched in a particular pattern, the members may be at a loss to experiment with alternatives or may see any alternative as a great threat.

In these situations, it is common for therapists to adopt a more 'strategic' approach, which often uses tasks that are not obviously directed towards change or may even be apparently prescribing what is already happening (Haley, 1977). The most coherent body of such work has been developed by the Centre for Family Studies in Milan. There is not, however, space in this chapter for further elaboration of this approach. Other approaches particularly explore the inter-generational patterns running through the family and may involve grandparents and extended family members in exploring these. The goal of this is to help the family members to feel less 'programmed' and more able to take autonomous decisions.

What is common in all the approaches, however, is that in general therapists are less concerned with pathology and with dysfunction, and more concerned with blocking dysfunction and encouraging the discovery of latent or new repertoires of behaviour in the family.

Psychotherapy and Individual Therapy

Table 5.1 illustrates some distinctions between aspects of family therapy, individual therapy, and 'stranger' group therapies. Although there are often many overlaps, in practice there are important distinctions between the thinking underpinning them. Family therapists would often assume that a significantly different experience, perhaps as a result of a different 'event' from that expected, can lead to altered perceptions of a problem. Naturally, the kind of small changes in behaviour illustrated so far in this chapter would not in themselves lead to any such lasting change. Such changes would need to recur frequently in situations of emotional intensity for such an effect to be achieved.

Impacts of Race, Ethnicity and Social Disadvantage

Some would argue that race and ethnicity should play no special part in the principle of therapeutic intervention. They would argue that people are people the world over, and stress that *they* are not prejudiced. Most employers, doctors, teachers, police or members of the judiciary would similarly protest their lack of racial discrimination. At the same time, it is known that Black people are much less likely to be appointed to senior jobs; that they are much more likely to be hospitalized as psychotic; that they do much less well in the educational system despite comparable

Table 5.1 Comparison between family group therapy, 'stranger' group therapy and individual therapy

Individual therapy	'Stranger' group therapy	Natural (family) group therapy
The patient/therapist relationship exists only as a context for therapy	The group exists only as a context for therapy	The family has a life of its own, with a history and an anticipated future
Therapy occurs in the context of the intensity of relationship between therapist and patient	Therapy occurs in the context of the intensity of relationships between the therapist and group members, and between group members	Therapy occurs in context of a change in relationship pattern in the context of the current intense family relationships
Thus — the therapist is central	Thus — at different times the therapist or some part of the group may be central	Thus — the therapist is principally an agent of change rather than a central actor
The therapist *allows* the intensity of affect from the patient to him or her to develop (although the setting may provoke it)	The therapist facilitates the 'integration' or 'gelling' of the group in the service of therapy	The therapist is more likely to be concerned to develop the differentiation of the group
Therapist and patient maintain a non-social relationship (to varying degrees depending on the model)	The members are discouraged from meeting between sessions	The members remain in an intense relationship between sessions
The therapist does not try to develop structure in the therapeutic relationship, and interpretations may be used to highlight inappropriate structural patterns sought by the patient. In child psychotherapy the therapist *may* be forced to be a parental adult	There is no permanent structural organization of the group. That which evolves is transient and often seen by the therapist as a re-creation of past or 'inner' families of the members. The members are usually of similar age, as may be the therapist. The therapist aims to be *meta* to the group	The family has an inherent and necessary hierarchical organization, relating to the different ages, developmental positions and responsibilities of the members. As the therapist is an adult, this will affect how he or she is used by the family. The therapist aims to *think* from a meta-position, but may *act* in a partisan manner
Change occurs through understanding the meaning of an old pattern in a new context. This change has then to be generalized to other contexts. The pattern in the original context *may or may not* change	Change occurs through understanding the meaning of an old pattern in a new context. This change has then to be generalized to other contexts. The pattern in the original context *may or may not* change	Change occurs through changing the pattern in an 'old' context, so that the context itself is changed

levels of intelligence, and they are much less likely to be granted bail while on remand than are whites for the same crimes. The staff of the Marlborough Family Service noticed that Black people and people from other ethnic minorities made proportionately much less use of the service whilst often having as many or more problems for which it was thought the service could potentially be useful. In such situations some subtle process must be operating which acts to discriminate unfairly against ethnic minority groups, but the professional staff who participate in that same process may be partly or wholly unaware of if. This process has sometimes been called *institutionalized racism*. The staff team of the Marlborough Family Service decided to employ Black consultants to provide anti-racist training for the whole group in an attempt to ensure that the service served equally all ethnic groups in the community. In the follow-up to that training, the building, literature, language, and in fact all our practices, were examined in terms of what would make them more friendly to ethnic minorities. One of the practices adopted was to talk to families about feelings about having a white therapist, when they must have experienced discriminatory relationships with other white professionals who may have been in positions of relative power in relation to them. We would further point out that they could not as yet be sure that we would not behave similarly.

I had been working with a young couple in which the husband, Rajiv, was of Indian Hindu background. His father had brought the family to Great Britain after the Tanzanian government introduced discriminatory legislation against the employment of Asians in academic jobs. He was married to a French woman and they had one child, aged three years. They were both well educated. Although when I first saw the family the husband was unemployed, they could not have been described as obviously socially disadvantaged. Three months later Rajiv had been asked to run an engineering firm. A year later it was expanding fast. The problem the wife, Odette, complained of was that after he had had an affair, Rajiv had become obsessed with work and never listened to her. He complained that she was depressed and depressing, as well as sexually restrictive. When she was pregnant with her second child these problems were exacerbated; she considered an abortion but instead they consulted me again. When I saw them he told me that Odette was always complaining that his mind was never with her and that she would speak and he would not hear her. I imagined the voices of my team asking, 'Why are you not discussing the racial issue with this man?' In my head my voice answered that with this middle-class successful man it would be insulting; after all he is so 'British'. The voices continued to argue with me. Rajiv was telling me about the problems of relocating his factory, and there was something in his description which led me to wonder why he was moving from one part of the country to another. My team won and I rather clumsily asked whether there was some racial prejudice issue in this move, and that he had never even acknowledged his racial difference, so perhaps he thought I would be prejudiced against him in favour of

Odette. He was extremely surprised and relieved by this statement, said he had never talked to anybody about his race, including Odette. When the family had emigrated to England his father had moved from an academic job to a lowly manual one, and he blamed this for his father later becoming depressed and alcoholic. He had bitterly despised his father's reaction, and vowed never to allow himself to be in a situation in which he was vulnerable and could be humiliated. This explained the move, as he felt the community in which his factory was placed to be prejudiced against him because of his colour, but had not been able to say this to Odette. He then linked this to the way he kept aloof from Odette. The result of this initially uncomfortable conversation was that we broke a taboo — one that had been operating on me as well as on him. Having broken it, however, Rajiv was left in some sense vulnerable in relation to me — perhaps before he was ready. One practice the team had recently developed was to try to find some area of life that may be shared by therapist and family or patient, that can cut across differences in terms of culture and power. Actually, I was not thinking of this but Rajiv kept talking of the way he absolutely could not hear Odette when he was so obsessed by work. I told him that the only real time I had that experience was when I was working on my wind generators. He said 'What!' I told him of the three wind-driven electric generators I had developed. I would often go there to work with them or play with them, which involved working up a ten-metre pole. At these times I was exactly like him, and could hear nobody, but I added that it was more limited and pleasurable. The next time he came with Odette he brought a design for a new wind generator with a cordless motor that he was considering developing.

Thus, through the process of my eventual challenge of what had become a shared taboo subject, and through one might say accidentally discovering an area of mutual interest, both he and I were freed of some unhelpful constraints. The result was that he was then able to use the consultation to examine some incongruent aspects of his adaptation to the host culture. This, in turn, led to a more mutually respectful debate by the couple about the management of their family life.

This vignette illustrates how therapist's and family members' feelings about race can lead to realistic mistrust of the therapist, with consequent interference with his or her usefulness to the family. Rajiv, however, had much in common with the therapist in terms of social class and interests. An even greater sensitivity and a greater effort to connect is called for when the family is also socially disadvantaged through, for example, poverty.

Ayo
Ayo was aged 34, and the mother of two boys, Alex, aged 13, and Jason, aged 11. The boys were by two different fathers, and had both been made Wards of Court in infancy on the basis of injuries received from Jason's father. The two boys had been placed in long-term foster care with different foster parents. Ayo, however, had never accepted this, and had fought hard to get her children back. She had kept in as much contact with them as the Social Services would allow, and several years ago had used the Marlborough Family Service Intensive

Treatment Programme as a way of being united with Alex, as a result of which he was eventually returned to her care. The situation with Jason had been a bit more difficult. Jason was fostered to a family in the country, in a community and culture that was totally different to that of his original family, and quite different from that in which he would live in London. Ayo, however, was determined to get him back and complied with every possible ruling made by the Social Services Department. She now had a stable boyfriend called Fred, who had made a good relationship with Alex. In a family meeting in which all members of the family (including the grandfather and Fred) were present it became clear that there was some kind of, but unspecified, problem about Jason returning. Jason was a lively intelligent and outspoken young man. I began to realize that Fred was not sure if he had Ayo's permission to say what was on his mind. I raised the question as to whether there was not some racial issue about the way in which Jason had been brought up, but that Fred would assume that I would be on the 'side' of the foster parents. Eventually, after considerable uneasiness, Fred explained that he was worried that Jason would get into trouble with the police in the area where they lived, as he was too 'trustful'. If he was going to survive 'in our area' he would have to learn to mistrust the police and all 'white' authorities and to avoid contact with them. It transpired that each member of the family had tried to say this to Jason in different ways, but had been so worried about saying it aloud that they had not acknowledged it to each other. I pointed out that they had no certainty about my trustworthiness either, and we would have to discuss how they were going to deal with that. After many reassurances to me that I was 'OK', Ayo eventually admitted that she felt she must hide from me any potential problems about Jason returning or she would lose her fight to get him back. She then acknowledged that she had believed that the two children had been made Wards of Court without any other options being considered, and that she believed this was because of her being black. Once all of this had been acknowledged, and the therapist had recognized the bad relationship between the police and the Black community in their neighbourhood, the family was able to plan much more realistically for Jason's return home.

We can and should expect people in such circumstance to be appropriately suspicious and mistrustful. It is then important for therapists not to interpret this as pathology, but to find a way of acknowledging the disadvantage faced by the family while encouraging them to see the aspects of this disadvantage which they can fight realistically. Therapists also need to show respect for the successful ways they have managed despite these extra burdens.

Applications to Different Kinds of Family Structure and 'Non-family' Human Systems

An obvious question is: For what diagnostic categories is family therapy applicable? The goal of family therapy is not to remove a 'cause' but rather to interfere with patterns which maintain a problem and to promote the development of more healthy patterns. This can be applied in any context where such an agreement can be worked out, and yet it has been found to be a particularly potent form of therapy in the behavioural and psychosomatic disorders of children, in neurotic and relationship problems in adults and in substance abuse. In addition, it has been used with the families of schizophrenics, particularly those in the process of rehabilitation, and in families where there is a seriously ill or dying member, or the consequences of a recent bereavement.

The model of family on which the illustrations have been based, for convenience rather than for truth, has been that of the traditional white, Western European nuclear family. Many people, however, do not live in the tidy group of two parents and 2.4 children and in many cultures this is not the traditional structure. Three family structures are of particular importance:

- Single-parent families, whether as a result of divorce, bereavement or the lack of a partner.
- Extended family organizations as, for example, when a young couple or a single parent live with parents, perhaps siblings, other family members, and other co-opted family members.
- Remarried families, sometimes called 'blended families' or 'reconstituted families'.

For each of these three structures, there are particular issues of which therapists need to be aware and incorporate into their views concerning intervention. In the single-parent family, the parent needs more support, and non-family social contacts take on greater significance. However, the parent's authority may have to be more autocratic, or he or she may need to delegate authority to elder siblings. It is easy to see what can go wrong when an elder sibling takes authority unilaterally. Alternatively, if a parent responds to the loneliness of being single by befriending the children, he or she may then be unable to help them make necessary developmental transitions.

In the extended family organization, there is a particular danger of confusion between the roles of parents and grandparents. For example, will grandparents' support be seen as underpinning or undermining parents' authority, and how can parents help grandparents to find a useful role which is not in competition with them? In addition, children and grandparents may be allied against the parents. In a positive way, this may allow children freedom of access to someone with whom they are less emotionally involved, but in a negative way it may be perceived by parents as 'stealing their child'. However, in some Indian, Chinese and other cultures, it may be expected that the grandparents would retain primacy of influence.

In the remarried family, all these issues are still poignant, but in addition:

- The problem of the children resolving the conflict of loyalty between the step-parents and absent parents continues to be an issue and it depends particularly on the degree to which, for example, the divorced couple are still fighting or have accepted the new liaison.
- There is also the problem of the children having changed their 'position' in the family. Thus, an elder child in the original family may have older half-brothers or half-sisters and find him- or herself becoming the younger child, or vice versa. Each structure has its own strengths and weaknesses in terms of the goal of promoting the development of the children. The job for family therapists is, firstly, to understand the organization and structure in which the individuals live and, secondly, to plan their interventions on the basis of what is most functional for that family at that time. For example, in the single-parent family, it may be appropriate to encourage the mother to rely more on an elder sibling for certain functions such as helping with the younger children. In another family, this may have happened to a degree where the elder sibling is in competition with the parent. In the latter case, parents may need to be helped to re-establish authority so that an appropriate generational boundary develops between adult and elder child.

Thus, the task for therapists is to think about the organization and functioning of the system and to use themselves to create a new balance in the dilemma between stability and change. This thinking can then be applied to a child living in a children's home, to a school classroom situation or, with certain modifications, to a social delivery agency or even an industrial organization.

What Can Practitioners Do?

The training of nearly all practitioners, whether in medicine, psychology or social work, has underlined the individual integrity of the patient. This chapter has been about seeing patients as part of a wider system, the family and 'others', and seeing their problems as, in part, a manifestation of those relationships.

The author would like to feel that this chapter has introduced therapists to the process of thinking in terms of *relationships*, rather than *causes*, and to consider the whole system rather than just its parts. It is hoped it has also illustrated how therapists can use this thinking to engage actively in the processes of the family. Of course, they are then also part of the system which is struggling between stability and change. To a degree, all therapists and practitioners are part of the system which they treat. This was well illustrated in the case of Wendy and her therapist in the day hospital, as well as in the case of Rajiv in which the therapist had to make an ethnic bridge with the patient. It is hoped that practitioners will be stimulated to think how to increase the *competence* in the family rather than the *incompetence*. Lastly, the chapter has demonstrated that practitioners may need to develop and maintain a quite different perspective from that held by the family members, and to think how to engender a different set of perceptions in those who are concerned to achieve a change. It has also described in some detail some of the forces in a family which tend towards the maintenance of stability. It is therefore not surprising that when practitioners offer what they think are rational solutions, they are frequently not welcomed as warmly as might be hoped. In fact, to get through this, practitioners may often need to think of solutions which are quite 'irrational' in everyday terms. One such solution was used in the case of Wendy.

However, this chapter has not provided a recipe of how to 'do family therapy'. Learning from the written word has severe limitations in acquiring any active skill. In the final section some useful reading is listed, as well as more useful suggestions as to how practitioners can acquire skill in understanding and intervening in families.

Further Reading and Opportunities for Learning and Training

A clear exposition of what has been described as 'Structural Family Therapy' is contained in three books by Salvador Minuchin: *Families and Family Therapy* (Minuchin, 1974); *Psychosomatic Families* (Minuchin et al., 1978); and *Family Therapy Techniques* (Minuchin and Fishman, 1981).

For a clearer exposition of a slightly different, but related, approach, *Problem Solving Therapy* (Haley, 1977).

A good exposition of the Milan systemic approach can be found in Jones's book, *Family Systemic Therapy: Developments in the Milan Systemic Therapies* (Jones, 1993). *Family Therapy in Changing Times* (Gorell Barnes, 1998) perhaps offers the best overview of the state of the field as it relates to the structures of family living that are prevalent in Britain and Western Europe today.

However, the best way for practitioners to develop some skills is to join up with one or more colleagues who have decided to explore their thinking and work with families. They can use discussion, observe each other's work, perhaps play tape recordings, or arrange sessions together and consult each other. Forming of such a group can allow the development of the inventiveness and imagination of the members — essential ingredients for working with families. Details of how to carry out this kind of consultation/supervision are also the subject of many of the courses currently available. There are now many training courses available in the UK, most having university accreditation at either MSc or Advanced Diploma level. There are also at least two doctoral programmes. Information on conferences, a journal and courses is available from: Chris Frederick, Membership Secretary, Association for Family Therapy, 12 Mabledon Close, Heald Green, Cheadle, Cheshire SK8 3DB; (Tel/Fax: 0161 493 9012; e-mail chrisfrederick@compuserve.com).

References

ANDERSON, C.M., HOGARTY, G.E. and REISS, D.J. (1980). Family treatment of adult schizophrenia patients: a psycho-educational approach. *Schizophrenia Bulletin* 6, 490–505.

ASEN, K., BERKOWITZ, R., COOKLIN A.L. et al. (1991). Family therapy outcome research: a trial for families, therapists and researchers. *Family Process* 30, 3–20.

ASHBY, W.R. (1956). *Introduction to Cybernetics*. New York: John Wiley.

BATESON, G. (1973). *Steps Towards an Ecology of Mind*. St Albans: Paladin.

BERTALANFFY, L. VON (1968). *General System Theory*. New York: Brazillier.

BURCK, C. and SPEED, B. eds. (1994). *Gender, Power and Relationships*. London: Routledge.

BURCK, C. and DANIEL, G. (1995). *Gender and Family Therapy*. London: Karnac.

COOKLIN, A.L. (1973). Consideration of the 'contract' between staff and patient and its relationship to current hospital practice. *British Journal of Medical Psychology* 45, 279–285.

GURMAN, A.S. and KNISKERN, D.P. (1981). *Handbook Family Therapy*. New York: Brunner/Mazel.

GOLDNER, V. (1985). Feminism and family therapy. *Family Process* 24, 31–47.

GORELL BARNES, G. (1998). *Family Therapy in Changing Times*. London: Macmillan.

HALEY, J. (1977). *Problem Solving Therapy*. California: Jossey-Bass.

HOGARTY, C.E., ANDERSON, C.M. and REISS, D.J. (1986). Family psycho-education, social skills training and maintenance chemotherapy in the aftercare treatment of Schizophrenia. I: One-year effects of a controlled study of relapse and expressed emotion. *Archives of General Psychiatry* 43, 633–642.

JACKSON, D.D. (1957). The question of family homeostasis. *Psychiatry Quarterly Supplement* 31, 79–80.

JONES, E. (1993). *Family Systemic Therapy: Developments in the Milan Systemic Therapies*. Chichester: Wiley.

LEFF, J., KUIPERS, L., BERKOWITZ, R. et al. (1982). A controlled trial of social intervention in the families of schizophrenia patients. *British Journal of Psychiatry* 141, 121–134.

LEFF, J., WIG, N.N., GHOSH, A., BEDI, H., MENON, D.K. and KUIPERS, L. et al. (1987). Expressed emotion and schizophrenia in North India. III: Influence of relatives' expressed emotion on the course of schizophrenia in Chandigarh. *British Journal of Psychiatry* 151, 166–173.

LEFF, J.P., BERKOWITZ, R., SHAVIT, N., STRACHAN, A., GLASS, I. and VAUGHN, C. (1990). A trial of family therapy versus a relatives' group for schizophrenia. Two-year follow-up. *British Journal of Psychiatry* 150, 571–577.

LEFF, J., THORNICROFT, G., COXHEAD, N. and CRAWFORD, C. (1994). The TAPS Projects. 22: A five-year follow-up of long-stay psychiatric patients discharged to the community. *British Journal of Psychiatry Supplement* 13–7.

LEFF, J. (1998). Clinical and economic value of a randomized controlled trial of couple therapy versus antidepressants. Presentation at the Family Research and Family Therapy Conference. London: Institute of Psychiatry.

MINUCHIN, S. (1974). *Families and Family Therapy*. London: Tavistock Publications.

MINUCHIN, S., ROSMAN, B. and BAKER, L. (1978). *Psychosomatic Families.*. Cambridge, MA: Harvard University Press.

MINUCHIN, S. and FISHMAN, C. (1981). *Family Therapy Techniques*. Cambridge, MA: Harvard University Press.

MOSSIGIE, S., PETTERSON, R.B. and BLAKER, R.M. (1979). Egocentrism and inefficiency in the communication of families containing a schizophrenic member. *Family Process* 18, 405–425.

PERLBERG, R.J. and MILLER, A.C. (1990). *Gender and Power in Families*. London: Routledge.

RANDOLPH, E.T., ETA, S., GLYNN, S.M. et al. (1994) Behavioural family management: outcome of a clinical-based intervention. *British Journal of Psychiatry* 164, 601–600.

STRACHAN, A.M. (1986). Family intervention for the rehabilitation of schizophrenia: toward protection and coping. *Schizophrenia Bulletin* 12, 678–698.

VON FOERSTER, H. (1981). *Observing Systems*. Seaside, CA: Lukesystems.

XIONG, W., PHILLIPS, M.R., HU, X., WANG, R., DAI, Q., KLEINMAN, J. and KLEINMAN, A. (1994). Family-based intervention for schizophrenic patients in China: a randomized controlled trial. *British Journal of Psychiatry* 165, 239–247.

Chapter 6
The Role of Psychological Treatments in Liaison Psychiatry

GEOFFREY G LLOYD

Introduction

The relevance of psychological factors in medical and surgical practice is now widely accepted and research continues to clarify their influence. Many studies have shown there to be a high prevalence of psychiatric illness among patients attending general hospitals, whether they be in-patients or out-patients (Mayou and Hawton, 1986). *Liaison psychiatry* is that area of psychiatric practice which forms an interface with other branches of medicine. Its practice covers the whole range of psychiatric disorders, and treatments used are similar to those employed in other areas of psychiatry. They include both physical and psychological approaches. The term *consultation–liaison psychiatry* is used by some clinicians to denote two different styles of practice. Consultation is regarded as essentially a patient-oriented process, the psychiatrist responding to a specific request from another medical specialist to assess a particular patient and advise on treatment. Liaison, by contrast, has a more ambitious aim in which psychiatry is considered to have a preventive as well as a therapeutic role. This requires the psychiatrist to develop closer links with a particular clinical team, for example an oncology or transplantation service. The liaison role involves mediating between patients and staff to improve communication, reduce conflicts and prevent the deterioration of clinical care (Lipowski, 1974). These two styles are not mutually incompatible. In the UK, most psychiatric services within general hospitals operate a consultation service, largely because of constraints imposed by staff shortages. Nevertheless, several clinicians have been able to establish close links with particular units with whom they work.

An influential report on the psychological care of medical patients (RCP and RCPsych, 1995) emphasized the importance of a readily available

83

liaison psychiatry team and recommended that purchasers should not purchase healthcare in hospitals where a liaison psychiatry service is not available. The suggested level of staffing includes a consultant psychiatrist, one or more trainee psychiatrists, two clinical nurse specialists, a social worker and a clinical psychologist. Unfortunately, few hospitals currently possess a multi-disciplinary team such as this despite increasing demands on liaison psychiatry, particularly from services dealing with chronic and terminal conditions including HIV infection and rehabilitation and palliative care units. The future development of liaison psychiatry will almost certainly depend upon evidence demonstrating the efficacy of various types of psychiatric intervention for general hospital patients with psychiatric problems. The current fashion for evidence-based medicine means that services will not be developed unless they are supported by the results of reputable, controlled therapeutic trials. Liaison psychiatry, in common with other areas of practice, therefore needs to demonstrate that the treatment methods it employs are effective in terms of reducing levels of psychiatric morbidity. There is also a need to demonstrate cost effectiveness in terms of avoiding the use of unnecessary investigations and reducing the length of stay of hospital in-patients. Improvements in the general quality of a patient's life must also feature prominently in any assessment of therapeutic efficacy.

Clinical Problems in Liaison Psychiatry

Three broad areas of practice make up the bulk of the work of a liaison psychiatrist, namely: the psychological consequences of physical illness; somatization; and deliberate self-harm. The nature of the psychological problems in each of these three areas is discussed separately in this chapter, with an evaluation of the effectiveness of various types of psychological treatment. It should be remembered, however, that psychotherapy is an important aspect of all medical treatments and its significance is not confined to psychiatry. Indeed, psychotherapy probably underlies all other treatments in medicine and is much more pervasive in its influence than many physicians and general practitioners realize. It forms the basis of all good doctor–patient relationships, involving, as it does, mutual trust, understanding and a reasonable degree of dependence on behalf of the patient.

Psychological consequences of physical illness

Physical illness predisposes to psychiatric morbidity through a variety of mechanisms, including toxic effects on the brain, as is the case in delirium and organic affective disorders, and also through its emotional impact on the patient (Lloyd, 1997). Many different factors determine the nature and severity of the psychological response to illness, including pre-morbid personality, severity of illness, treatment required and the patient's social circumstances at the time of onset. In the latter context the response of key relatives and friends to the patient's illness is crucial. The type of psychological response is not specific to the type of illness, similar reactions being seen in patients with AIDS, cancer, heart disease and other serious conditions. The most frequent reaction is an adjustment disorder which is characterized by anxiety, depression or, most commonly, a combination of both. The symptoms develop within a short time of the recognition of illness, sometimes within a few days. The duration of these psychological symptoms parallels closely the progress of the underlying physical illness and complete resolution can be expected in nearly all cases when the physical illness has resolved. Patients are preoccupied with the effects of illness on their lifestyle, career prospects and family relationships. There may be a concern about the prospect of persistent pain and long-term invalidism, and in the case of the terminally ill patient they may be associated with preoccupations concerning death and the process of dying and the effects of bereavement on relatives, particularly young children.

Symptoms of anxiety occasionally persist beyond the time when the acute physical symptoms have started to resolve. The anxiety symptoms may be generalized but are more likely to be linked to specific aspects of the illness, including the treatment. Phobic anxiety disorders are well recognized among diabetic patients, who may develop a needle phobia and find it impossible to administer insulin injections. They also occur among those who are undergoing chemotherapy, which can produce unpleasant side-effects, such as anorexia and nausea. A small proportion of patients come to link chemotherapy with these undesired complications and may develop anticipatory anxiety which is associated with nausea and vomiting and which lead to avoidance of further treatment. Patients treated for cancer may become morbidly anxious about the risk of tumour recurrence, and some check their body in an obsessional manner, searching for bumps, enlarged lymph nodes or other signs of tumour recurrence.

Post-traumatic stress disorder (PTSD) is a specific anxiety syndrome which is observed in those who have been involved in a trauma of an exceptionally threatening nature, of a degree not encountered in everyday life and which would be expected to cause almost universal distress. It follows traumatic events such as road traffic accidents, physical or sexual assault, terrorist activity or natural disaster. More recently, PTSD has been described after major complications of medical procedures, including childbirth. Victims may not necessarily have sustained serious physical injuries but they nearly always have perceived themselves to be in mortal danger, even if this perception has lasted for only a few seconds. There is often a delay, ranging from a few days to several months, between the traumatic event and the onset of psychological symptoms. The characteristic symptoms include variable depression, irritability, hyper-arousal, emotional blunting, social withdrawal, sleep disturbance, nightmares and recurrent, intrusive memories of the event (flashbacks). These symptoms invariably lead to avoidance of the location of the trauma and of situations or activities which are reminiscent of the traumatic event.

Depression is a well-recognized complication of physical illness. Conservative estimates suggest that a depressive illness develops in at least 20% of patients during the 12 months following the diagnosis of a serious physical disorder. In establishing a diagnosis of depression the characteristic somatic symptoms (such as anorexia, weight loss and fatigue) cannot be given their usual significance because they may all be related to the underlying physical condition rather than to accompanying psychological symptoms. Greater importance has to be attached to the psychological symptoms of depression, particularly anhedonia and loss of interest in the patient's usual activities.

Depression also appears to be particularly common among patients who perceive a sense of loss in association with their physical condition. They may fear that they are going to be unable to resume previous leisure activities, they may be unable to return to work and may fear financial ruin. Depression can lead to marital, sexual and family tensions and it increases the risk of suicide, which is much higher among physically ill patients than in the rest of the population. It is an important cause of prolonged invalidity after physical illness; it is often undetected and untreated or it may be regarded as an inevitable and understandable consequence of physical illness. This is a misleading trap for the clinician. Depression should be diagnosed if there are sufficient symptoms of the condition and it should not be explained away on the basis of it being an understandable reaction.

In addition to the emotional impact of physical illness, a number of other factors contribute to the onset of depression. The treatment environment in hospital is very important in this context. Nursing patients in isolation, because of immunosuppression or methicillin-resistant *Staphylococcus aureus* (MRSA) infection, often appears to have a profound, adverse effect on mood state. Patients should be kept in such surroundings for as brief a period as possible. Whilst they are in isolation it is important to maintain the maximum possible degree of contact with the outside world. Drugs also contribute to depression in the physically ill. Steroids are probably the most common single group; other drugs which are well known to cause depression include beta-blockers, calcium channel-blockers, beta-interferon and other immunosuppressants.

In some patients, the degree of functional disability appears dispropor-tionate to the underlying physical pathology. Physical symptoms appear to be abnormally persistent; return to work and resumption of other daily activities are delayed and no satisfactory physical explanation can be found on physical examination or laboratory investigations. This pattern of elaboration of physical symptoms can be observed in patients involved in litigation for compensation for illnesses or injuries which are believed to be due to someone else's negligence. In some cases dissociative symptoms can occur in the presence of physical illness. Symptoms such as these are often reinforced by relatives and friends, who become over-protective towards the patient, reversing previous dominance hierarchies and unwittingly rewarding the pattern of invalidism and need for atten-tion.

A rare complication of physical illness is an *acute transient psychosis* which is likely to be seen in patients who have been admitted as emergen-cies to hospital, particularly to an intensive care unit (ICU) or a coronary care unit (CCU), settings that most patients find threatening and unfamiliar. The sudden emotional impact of the illness appears to disrupt the patient's familiar routine and this is the crucial factor in precipitating the psychotic reaction. The characteristic feature of the psychosis is an acute delusional symptom, which usually involves the belief that medical or nursing staff are planning to harm the patient, who may then retaliate in an aggressive manner. An alternative response is to insist on self-discharge. It is essential that this type of psychosis be distinguished from acute delirium by the absence of signs of an organic mental disorder.

Psychological treatment and physical illness

Effective psychological care is an essential part of good clinical manage-ment. The prevalence of psychiatric morbidity in physically ill patients is such that specialized intervention is not feasible for most patients, nor is it desirable because it runs the risk of splitting physical and psychological care. In most cases the nature of psychological treatment consists of supportive psychotherapy which should be undertaken by members of the medical and nursing teams involved with the patient's day-to-day care. The role of consultant physician or surgeon is crucial in this respect. Doctors should allow sufficient time to listen to patients' complaints in an empathetic manner and to provide explanation, reassurance and directive advice, as appropriate. Reassurance should always be based on adequate information and should not be given merely to placate patients. If clinical information is lacking it is better for doctors to acknowledge this and not to disguise ignorance by offering false platitudes. Much psychological distress accompanying physical illness can be alleviated by effective communication between doctor and patient. There is abundant evidence that patients wish to be more fully informed about the nature of their illness and its treatment than they have been in the past. Medical practice is changing to accommodate this and many hospitals are now providing patients with information leaflets giving them specific information about a particular illness and the treatments which are available. Counselling services have been established, particularly in departments dealing with malignant disease, HIV/AIDS, genetic disorder and obstetrics.

The effectiveness of supportive psychotherapy in physically ill patients has been evaluated by Spiegel et al. (1989) who studied a group of women with metastatic breast cancer, comparing those who participated in psychotherapy with a control group who received only routine medical care. In this study, psychotherapy consisted of weekly meetings over a period of 12 months, during which patients were encouraged to express their feelings about their illness and its effects on their lives and to discuss ways of coping with cancer. They were also taught pain control by use of a self-hypnosis method. The psychotherapeutic intervention appeared to have a significant, beneficial effect on the course of the malignant disease as demonstrated by the observation that patients in the treatment group had a significantly longer survival time than those in the control group. The effectiveness of interpretative or analytical psychotherapy has proved more difficult to establish. Rosser et al. (1983) conducted a well-designed study to evaluate psychotherapy in patients with chronic obstructive airways disease (COAD), now called chronic obstructive pulmonary disease (COPD). Patients engaging in interpretative psychotherapy were compared with those who received supportive psychotherapy; with another group given practical advice by a nurse without training in psychotherapy; and a fourth group receiving standard medical care. Psychiatric symptoms were reduced in those who received supportive psychotherapy but not in those who had interpretative psychotherapy. Sustained relief of dyspnoea was better in patients given practical advice by a nurse. More encouraging results were obtained by Moran and Fonagy (1993) who evaluated an in-patient programme of combined psychoanalytic psychotherapy and ward management with routine in-patient care for adolescent patients with unstable diabetes. Patients in the psychoanalytic group received therapy up to five times weekly for a period of ranging between five and 28 weeks. Parental involvement was arranged in most cases. The group receiving psychoanalytic psychotherapy showed significant improvements in diabetic control as measured by glycosylated haemoglobin and the improvement was maintained at follow-up one year later.

The shortage of suitably trained psychoanalytic psychotherapists and the complexity of this type of treatment have shifted attention towards developing briefer methods of psychological treatment, of which cognitive behaviour therapy has become firmly established. This approach has been shown to modify the characteristics of Type A behaviour associated with the development of coronary heart disease, namely competitiveness, time urgency and hostility. Patients who had already experienced a myocardial infarction can be helped to modify these characteristics, thereby reducing the risk of recurrent episodes of ischaemic heart disease (Friedman et al., 1986). Cognitive therapy is now established as an effective treatment for patients with PTSD and it has also been evaluated in patients with cancer. Greer et al. (1992) studied a consecutive series of patients with various types of cancer whose scores on screening had revealed psychological morbidity. They were invited to participate in a randomized trial comparing adjuvant psychological therapy with routine medical care. The adjuvant psychological therapy consisted of a cognitive behaviour treatment programme conducted with individual patients and, where appropriate, their spouses. The therapy focused on the personal meaning of cancer to the individual and on the patient's coping strategies. The treatment was directed at current problems as defined jointly by the patient and the therapist and aimed to enhance self-esteem, overcome feelings of hopelessness and promote a fighting spirit towards the cancer. Patients were also taught to identify negative thoughts underlying their anxiety and depression, and helped to challenge such thoughts. The course of treatment consisted of approximately six sessions, each lasting at least one hour. Patients who participated in the cognitive behaviour therapy programme showed significantly greater improvement than control subjects on several measures of psychological outcome.

Eight weeks after commencing therapy patients reported significantly less anxiety, helplessness, depression and other negative attitudes towards cancer. Significant improvements on several measures were maintained at four months' follow-up. The authors concluded that the treatment results in significant reduction in psychological morbidity related to cancer, with consequent improvement in the psychological dimension of the quality of life.

However, a similar type of treatment, evaluated in patients with testicular cancer, did not find such positive results (Moynihan et al., 1998). In this study, 60% of eligible men declined to participate in the evaluation of psychological treatment and in those who did complete the treatment no clinically important differences were observed between those who received the treatment and those who were in the control group. The psychological treatment consisted of a cognitive and behavioural treatment programme of six sessions, each lasting one hour; the sessions were conducted by a specially trained mental health nurse who was experienced in caring for patients with testicular cancer.

The role of psychological treatments in physically ill patients has yet to be fully defined. It is unlikely that specialized intervention, even if it were available, is necessary for all patients, not even those diagnosed as having serious, life-threatening diseases. Psychological treatment is likely to be effective if it is offered to those who are most at risk and who have been identified as having psychological problems or a diagnosable psychiatric disorder. For these patients, cognitive therapy appears to be the treatment of choice. Further development of focused, brief psychological treatments is clearly required.

Somatic Presentation of Psychiatric Illness

This phenomenon is often referred to as 'somatization', a term that is widely used to describe the presentation of psychiatric illness with physical symptoms which cannot be explained by organic pathology. The patient presents to a doctor with somatic symptoms and does not complain of psychological problems. The symptoms are attributed to physical illness, the patient requests physical investigations and treatment, and resists attempts at a psychological explanation. However, if a thorough history, clinical assessment and appropriate investigations are conducted, physical illness can be excluded as a sufficient cause for the symptoms. Direct questioning reveals psychological symptoms, which indicate the patient to be psychiatrically ill. Somatization is not a psychiatric diagnosis but it can be the pattern of presentation of a wide variety of underlying conditions, including adjustment disorders, anxiety disorders, depression, somatization disorder, neurasthenia and somatoform autonomic dysfunction. In general practice, patients with a psychiatric disorder are more likely to present to their doctor with physical rather than psychological complaints and this may mislead the doctor into diagnosing a physical illness and requesting referral to a physician or surgeon for further investigations. The style in which the consultation is conducted is crucial in influencing the doctor's ability to respond to emotional cues and to probe behind the façade of somatic complaints.

The presenting physical complaint can draw attention to nearly any organ system. The nature of the symptoms may be determined by previous experience of physical illness and doctors in primary and secondary care often miss the underlying psychiatric problems because they are misled by the somatic façade. Pain is a common presenting symptom. It is usually localized in the head, chest or abdomen but it is poorly defined and its distribution does not conform to anatomical pathways. There is often an association with external stress and with variations in the patient's mood. Fatigue is another symptom which has been studied widely in recent years. Chronic fatigue syndrome, or neurasthenia, is characterized by extreme fatigue after physical or mental exertion, poor concentration, reduced exercise tolerance, muscle pain and sleep disturbance. It may follow a well-recognized viral illness such as influenza or hepatitis but in the majority of patients with chronic fatigue there is no convincing evidence of any such infection. Up to 80% of patients with chronic fatigue fulfil operational criteria for a psychiatric illness, most commonly a depressive episode. Other symptoms which bring somatizing patients to medical attention include dizziness, disturbance of higher cortical functions, palpitations, breathlessness, upper abdominal pain and bowel disturbance, predominantly irritable bowel syndrome.

Somatization is seen commonly in patients presenting in primary care. Indeed, there is evidence that this is the most common pattern of presentation, rather than the atypical presentation, that some people consider it to be. Psychiatric illness still carries a stigma, which prevents patients complaining of psychological symptoms. Many people are not aware of their emotional feelings and if they become psychiatrically ill they are more likely to perceive the bodily changes that accompany psychiatric illness. The pattern of somatic complaints is often reinforced by doctors who become preoccupied with the fear of missing organic pathology and who therefore arrange an increasing number of laboratory investigations while remaining unaware of the possibility of an underlying psychiatric explanation.

Psychological Treatment of Somatizing Patients

These patients make up a substantial proportion of out-patients in secondary and tertiary referral centres. The symptoms cause considerable distress and functional disability; somatization is costly in terms of medical time and unnecessary investigations and it is, therefore, important that patients are correctly identified and treated. A number of studies have shown that psychological treatments are effective in reducing the severity of symptoms and altering the pattern of patients' behaviour.

Two well-designed control studies (Svedlund et al., 1983; Guthrie et al., 1993) have shown dynamic psychotherapy to be superior to routine medical treatment in the management of patients with irritable bowel syndrome, a disorder of gut motility which is known to be associated with high levels of psychological symptoms and which is the most common diagnosis made in hospital gastroenterology clinics. In the study conducted by Guthrie et al. (1993), patients with overt depression and anxiety did particularly well after psychotherapy, and improvement in bowel symptoms was considered to be mediated via an improvement in mental state. It was considered that most patients who improved symptomatically did so as a result of learning to understand the link between their symptoms and emotional state and then to share with the therapist their internal feelings of distress and despair. Understanding the transference relationship was also important and led to significant change (Guthrie, 1991).

Cognitive behaviour therapy is also being used in the treatment of somatizing patients. Sharpe et al. (1992) outlined the principles of cognitive therapy in treating patients with functional somatic symptoms. A key element of treatment is to re-evaluate the nature of the presenting complaints and to link them with identifiable stressful events or with persistent, unresolved conflicts in the patient's life, particularly those involving interpersonal difficulties. The patient should be helped to re-attribute symptoms so that they are not perceived as arising from physical causes but are linked with psychological factors. It is then important to aim for behavioural change, altering dysfunctional responses to symptoms such as excessive rest, repeated medical consultations, seeking reassurance and adopting a life of invalidism. Such an approach has been shown to benefit patients with atypical, non-cardiac chest pain (Klimes et al., 1990). The approach has also been applied effectively in the management of patients with chronic fatigue, a particularly difficult form of somatization to manage (Sharpe et al., 1996; Deale et al., 1997).

Attempted Suicide

Attempted suicide, or deliberate self-harm, remains an important cause of admission to general hospitals. Recent increased rates of deliberate self-harm, especially among young people, suggests there are approximately 140 000 hospital referrals annually in England and Wales. Approximately two-thirds of cases are women, this being in marked contrast to the sex distribution of people who kill themselves. Attempted suicide is more common in younger age groups and in the lower socio-economic groups, particularly those living in overcrowded, inner city areas. There is often a history of an acute life crisis which appears to act as a precipitating factor for the attempt. However, chronic personal problems and social deprivation are very common in patients attempting suicide. Many have a history of marital disharmony or divorce, long-term unemployment, substance misuse and previous suicide attempts. In the UK most hospitals aim to provide a psychosocial assessment for all patients admitted following an episode of deliberate self-harm. This assessment does not necessarily have to be conducted by a psychiatrist because evidence has been produced to show that other professional groups, including suitably trained nurses and social workers, assess these patients just as effectively as psychiatrists in training. It is known that approximately 20% of patients repeat the episode within the following 12 months and 1 per cent actually kill themselves during this period. It is, therefore, important to try to identify patients at high risk and to plan appropriate management, thereby reducing their psychiatric morbidity, their associated social problems and the risk of repetition of the suicide attempt.

A substantial proportion of patients discharge themselves before completing the initial assessment and these have a considerably increased rate of repetition (Crawford and Wessely, 1998). Hawton et al. (1998) conducted a systematic review of randomized control trials of psycho-social and physical treatments and found promising results for problem-solving therapy and long-term psychological therapy for women with borderline personality disorder and recurrent self-harm. Positive results are also found for interventions which enabled patients to make emergency contact with services and also for depot flupenthixol for recurrent self-harm. In view of the magnitude of the clinical problem these authors believed there was insufficient evidence to indicate the most effective forms of treatment for patients who deliberately harm themselves, and advocated large-scale trials of interventions shown to be of possible benefit and also the development of further treatment approaches. In the meantime psychiatrists need to identify those who are most vulnerable to repeated attempts. These include patients with a distinct psychiatric disorder, substance misuse, chronic, unresolved social difficulties and personality disorder, especially of borderline type. A variety of physical and psychological therapies may be utilized. For patients with personality disorders, long-term psychotherapy may be the most effective way of achieving psychological change and preventing further self-injurious behaviour.

All general hospitals need to have a clearly defined policy for evaluating these patients and a consultant psychiatrist should be responsible for supervising those mental health professionals who conduct the assessments and co-ordinate further care.

References

CRAWFORD, M.J., WESSELY, S. (1998). Does initial management affect the rate of repetition of deliberate self-harm? Cohort Study. *British Medical Journal* **317**, 985.

DEALE, A., CHALDER, T., MARKS, I., WESSELY, S. (1997). Cognitive behavior therapy for chronic fatigue syndrome: a randomized controlled trial. *American Journal of Psychiatry* **154**, 408–414.

FRIEDMAN, M., THORESEN, C.E., GILL, J.J. et al. (1986). Alteration of Type-A behavior and its effect on cardiac recurrences in post-myocardial infarct patients: summary results of the Recurrent Coronary Prevention Project. *American Heart Journal* **112**, 653–665.

GREER, S., MOOREY, S., BARUCH, J.D.R. et al. (1992). Adjuvant psychological therapy for patients with cancer: a prospective randomized trial. *British Medical Journal* **304**, 675–680.

GUTHRIE, E. (1991). Brief psychotherapy in patients with refractory irritable bowel syndrome. *British Journal of Psychotherapy* 8, 175–188.

GUTHRIE, E., CREED, F., DAWSON, D., TOMENSON, B. (1993). A randomised controlled trial of psychotherapy in patients with refractory irritable bowel syndrome. *British Journal of Psychiatry* 163, 315–321.

HAWTON, K., ARENSMAN, E., TOWNSEND, E. et al. (1998). Deliberate self-harm: systematic review of efficacy of psychosocial and pharmacological treatments in preventing repetition. *British Medical Journal.* 317, 441–447.

KLIMES I., MAYOU R.A., PEARCE M.J. et al. (1990) Psychological treatment for atypical non-cardiac chest pain. *Psychological Medicine* 20, 605–611.

LIPOWSKI, Z.J. (1974). Consultation–liaison psychiatry: an overview. *American Journal of Psychiatry* 131, 623–630.

LLOYD, G.G. (1997). Liaison psychiatry. In: R. Murray, P. Hill and P. McGuffin, eds. *The Essentials of Postgraduate Psychiatry* (third edition). Cambridge: Cambridge University Press; 534–550.

MAYOU, R., HAWTON, K. (1986). Psychiatric disorder in the general hospital. *British Journal of Psychiatry* 149, 172–190.

MORAN, G.S., FONAGY, P. (1993). A psychoanalytic approach to the treatment of brittle diabetes in children and adolescents. In: M. Hodes and S. Moorey, eds, *Psychological Treatment in Disease and Illness*. London: Gaskell; 166–192.

MOYNIHAN, C., BLISS, J.M., DAVIDSON, J. et al. (1998). Evaluation of adjuvant psychological therapy in patients with testicular cancer: randomized controlled trial. *British Medical Journal* 316, 429–435.

ROSSER, R., DENFORD, J., HESLOP, A. et al. (1983). Breathlessness and psychiatric morbidity in chronic bronchitis and emphysema: a study of psychotherapeutic management. *Psychological Medicine* 13, 93–110.

ROYAL COLLEGE OF PHYSICIANS and ROYAL COLLEGE OF PSYCHIATRISTS. (1995). The Psychological Care of Medical Patients: Recognition of Need and Service Provision. London: RCP and RCPsych.

SHARPE, M., PEVELER, R., MAYOU, R. (1992). The psychological treatment of patients with functional somatic symptoms: a practical guide. *Journal of Psychosomatic Research* 36, 515–529.

SHARPE, M., HAWTON, K., SIMKIN, S. et al. (1996). Cognitive therapy for chronic fatigue syndrome: a randomised controlled trial. *British Medial Journal* 312, 22–26.

SPIEGEL D., BLOOM J.R., KRAEMER H.C. , GOTTHEIL E. (1989) Effect of psychosocial treatment on arrival of patients with metastatic cancer. *Lancet* ii, 888–891.

SVEDLUND, J., SJODIN, I., OTTOSSON, J.O., DOTEVALL, G. (1993). Controlled study of psychotherapy in irritable bowel syndrome. *Lancet* ii, 589–592.

Chapter 7
Psychotherapy in General Practice

ANDREW ELDER

'Hearing secret harmonies' (Anthony Powell)

The Setting

Specialized psychotherapy is concerned with the treatment of selected patients in a highly organized setting. The treatment of patients in general practice is very different; the surgery doors open on to the everyday world. In general practice, doctors are not set at such a careful distance, monitoring the various aspects of transference and projection, but are enmeshed — fellow travellers — more involved with their patients and their illnesses. It is High Street medicine. This difference gives rise to many of the difficulties of the setting but also to some of its advantages for psychotherapeutic work. In general practice, doctors are not concerned with the clinical applications of a particular therapeutic philosophy, but with whatever psychotherapeutic use they can make of the opportunities that arise as part of their everyday work. They are *opportunists*. General practitioners carry whatever skill and awareness they posses in whatever they are called on to do — visiting a dying patient at home, dealing with a 'minor' illness in the surgery, responding to an emotional crisis, or a problem concealed in a 'While I'm here, Doctor'. The general practitioners' (GPs) psychotherapy is dressed in ordinary clothing.

Psychoanalytical theory provides an essentially developmental view of human life, placing 'each individual in his own unique cultural and developmental context' (Brown and Pedder, 1979) and lays great emphasis on the quality of the human relationships that enable an individual's development from the earliest moments of life 'to promote growth and facilitate the patient's own potential' (Bateman and Holmes, 1995). Difficulties and conflicts, as well as satisfactions and achievements, are constantly present and may build up in such a way that a crisis or illness develops. For a few patients this may lead to formal psychotherapy, but for the overwhelming majority it is neither sought nor appropriate. Doctors in general practice,

95

however, are often already present at first hand, helping their patients with many of the experiences that are some of the psychological determinants of people's lives: the problems of birth and early childhood, sexual development and marriage, illnesses, death and losses of one sort or another. Morbidity and presentations to the doctor are known to increase when people are negotiating these major transitions of life, or life events. This means that doctors are often involved when psychic history is being made. They can therefore influence this process, a little, both for better and for worse.

Listening

In this chapter, the need for doctors to 'listen' to their patients and 'hear' what they are saying is emphasized. However, this does not mean a passive process of sitting back and listening to someone talk. It refers to the quality and intensity of the *listening to feelings* that lie behind patients' words, and the sensitivity with which things are heard that patients are only *half saying*. This is an *active* process and requires attention to detail: how patients look and behave, their mood, what words are chosen, when they falter and change tack and what is left unsaid; it involves respecting patients' need to express emotion in their own way and hearing what thoughts and feelings are elicited by all this, in the doctor's own mind.

Most communication from which something new may be learned by the person trying to communicate exists in a half-lit world of things that are only 'almost known' to that person. This is true of patients communicating to their doctors and also true of doctors when they attempt any change in *their* understanding of their patients or their involvement with them. Both worlds, the patient's and the doctor's are constantly changing, and influencing each other. It is the relationship between the two, referred to in this chapter as the *doctor–patient relationship*, that is of central importance in general practitioners' psychotherapy.

Incidence

It is a commonplace that the incidence of emotional or psychiatric disorders seen in general practice is high. Figures vary widely; the problems of definition are great and the diagnoses made in general practice consultations depend as much on doctors' own characteristics and attitudes, as on patients' presentation. It is generally accepted that between one-quarter and one-third of a GP's patients have some significant psychiatric disorder (Clare and Blacker, 1986; Department of Health, 1991). In a practice with a special interest in psychological disorders, 43% of all patients seen had symptoms which were regarded as being of emotional origin; 11% suffered from formal psychiatric illnesses and 32% from a variety of stress disorders (Hopkins, 1956). In another survey (Goldberg and Blackwell, 1970), a GP who was again described as having a particular interest in psychiatric disorders, recorded an incidence of only 20% of consecutive attenders as having evidence of psychiatric morbidity. It may be that another doctor, steadfastly physical in his or her approach and determined not to notice his or her patients' emotional problems, could achieve a significantly lower incidence still. Doctors are as variable as their patients.

Despite these differences in doctors' diagnostic thresholds, it seems that the average GP in the UK is likely to have a significant number of his or her consultations, probably at least 30% (Royal College of General Practitioners, 1981) with people who have been propelled towards the surgery by apparent psychological symptomatology of one sort or another, and the figure would be far higher if all patients are included in whom the doctor feels that a significant element of emotional difficulty is being presented.

Some people consult their GPs much more often than others. Approximately 50% of the GP's workload is generated by 10% of their patients, and the members of each doctor's '10% group' will have more psychological characteristics in common with each other than with a group of less frequently consulting patients who may, nevertheless, belong to the same diagnostic category (for instance, migraine, dysmenorrhea or depression). Among the population who do not go often to the doctor are individuals who have similar symptoms to those who do (Miller et al., 1976). It is not the possession of the symptom or the disorder that characterizes the more frequently-attending patients, but the fact that they attend whilst others do not, and the reasons behind this. This realization is vital to the GP's work. A broader approach is needed.

What Kind of Diagnosis?

Although the results of these surveys give something of a statistical background to the GP's work, they do so in over-simplified terms. Diagnoses of this sort belong to a psychiatric classification derived from what has often been called the medical model. The doctor presides, uninvolved with his or her patient, and diagnoses the patient's illness according to certain symptoms and signs. Such a model encourages the doctor to think only about making the 'right' diagnosis and not about the patient, and inclines both the patient and the doctor to define the problem outside themselves, thus discouraging the doctor from thinking about his or her relationship with the patient. It is a model much used in hospital-based thinking, but it transfers very uneasily into general practice, where the emphasis is shifted more to people and away from illnesses;

more to a longer-term perspective and away from a two-dimensional 'snapshot' view at any one moment. It makes little sense to place two totally different consultations with people of different personalities and backgrounds with different problems and expectations into a single category called, say, anxiety state.

> A large woman in her 60s, who always has a timid look about her, comes to see the doctor about her painful neck, which prevents her from sleeping. She is a bit overweight, tends to visit the doctor about once a month and is recently retired from her work as a cleaner. She comes to ask for a repeat script for her arthritis tablets and wonders if her blood pressure is up (which it is, slightly). She cries when the doctor asks about her brother whom he knows she has been worried about and who is now dying of cancer. She is single, rather shy and has always felt large and awkward. She has remained closely attached to her large number of brothers and sisters since their father died when she was 9. They mostly live a long way from her and she is constantly anxious about them. The doctor has got to know her and how she uses him. He is happy to see her and takes her blood pressure, listens to her and prescribes more tablets. The consultation lasts ten minutes and will be repeated many times, in one form or another, as it has been already in the past.

Such a consultation is very typical of a GP's work. Which diagnosis is the doctor to choose? Even sticking to traditional medical diagnoses, it would be difficult to choose between obesity, mild hypertension, cervical spondylosis, anxiety or depression. All play a part.

If we shift the emphasis from the medical diagnosis towards a more personal one, we immediately begin to include some life history, any important recent events, present tensions with other people and something of the patient's relationship to herself: her self-esteem and confidence, and her capacity for change and adaptation. These things may help us learn more about her emotional needs and what she may require from a visit to the doctor. *The single page becomes a biography*.

It does, however, still leave out any account of the doctor's own particular viewpoint. The importance of this omission increases as the patient's subjective world is taken more into account. The diagnosis has to broaden again to include something of the doctor's own reactions and how he or she sees the patient. Today's view may be different tomorrow and the same patient would be seen differently by different doctors.

Knocking on the Doctor's Door

Among the sea of people who come in and out of a doctor's surgery, some people will have a relatively clear idea of why they have come and what they can reasonably hope to gain. Others are propelled by a less well-differentiated urge, a more generalized need for understanding or help, which they initially transmit to the doctor through their symptoms. These may resolve quite quickly or continue until the doctor and patient eventually settle on a distance and a language that is acceptable to both of them. This is then the 'illness'. It is particularly important for the doctor in general practice to tolerate uncertainty and not organize the patient's illness too soon. He or she may otherwise prevent important developments from emerging and contribute to what Illich has called the 'medicalization of life'. The groundswell of need which brings people to doctors is present in everyone. For some, it is more successfully met in their personal relationships than for others. The doctor is a relatively freely available figure. Maybe in previous times such a need sought its expression elsewhere, through the church or within the extended family, but in today's world it *knocks on the doctor's door*. Both the patient and the doctor contain numerous possibilities for the outcome of their consultation together. They each have the potential for many different directions and levels of contact with each other. Nothing is static. Patients alter their patterns to fit their doctors, and seek out doctors who reflect their needs. For many patients it may be more important that there is a channel of communication open to them when they need it, rather than its particular medical content.

Doctors develop different ways of responding to this challenge. Each doctor's own approach may be valid to himself. There is a risk in too great a conformity. If a doctor does decide to undergo appropriate training and learn to make himself more accessible to his patient's emotional needs, he must first become aware of the history and development of the thought that has already gone into trying to understand the nature of the general practice setting for this kind of work.

History

The history of psychotherapy in general practice is essentially the history of the impact of two psychoanalysts, Michael and Enid Balint, and their work with GPs. The story begins with general practice at a low ebb in the early 1950s, very much the junior partner within the medical profession. There was 'widespread dissatisfaction amongst general practitioners' (Collings, 1950) who at that time lacked any specific training for their work. The mismatch between the skills acquired through undergraduate medical training and those needed by GPs in their work was even more acute then than it is now. Apart from their heavily disease-centred training, those doctors had mainly their commonsense and endless outpatient referrals to help them through.

In 1948, at the Tavistock Clinic in London, Enid Balint had begun leading a group of non-medical workers who were working with people having marital difficulties. Michael Balint, a Hungarian psychoanalyst whose father had been a family doctor, became interested in applying this method to study the difficulties GPs were having and to see if new techniques could be developed to help them in their work. In 1954 and 1955, the first reports of this work were published (Balint, 1954, 1955). This initiated far-reaching changes in the ways doctors and patients were subsequently to relate to each other. Much was learnt from this early work and was published in 1957 as *The Doctor, His Patient and the Illness* (Balint, 1957), one of the masterpieces of medical literature.

From the beginning, this work was a marriage between the psychoanalytical background of the Balints and the medical work and attitudes brought to the groups by those first GPs. The Balints contributed the setting, the aims, the open-mindedness of their enquiry and a belief in the value of human beings (doctors as well as patients). They also contributed their understanding of the unconscious and a basic trust that, from the ruminations of the doctors themselves, new patterns would emerge. They were non-moralizing and non-didactic. They did not attempt to instruct the doctors in psychoanalytical theory or give them psychodynamic explanations of their patients' behaviour, or of the doctors' own behaviour for that matter. Through their own listening skills, enhanced by psychological training, they helped doctors to listen better to their patients. Winnicott and others have shown how a mother can respond more sensitively to her child if she has herself received what he called 'good-enough mothering' (Winnicott, 1972). By the same token, doctors are better able to respond to their patients' problems if they have had the experience of being listened to sensitively themselves in their training. They are then able to learn more from the main source and stimulus to education for doctors, *patients themselves*.

The doctors also had much to contribute. They brought their openness and willingness to learn, which is never an easy process, and their preparedness to stick at a difficult task for a considerable length of time. They required what Balint came to call the 'courage of their stupidity' (Balint, 1957). This meant being prepared to use their minds imaginatively (Elder, 1996) and contribute freely to the thinking of the group — not being too cautious and correct. This courage remains the main driving force for any Balint group.

Training

The method of work and its aims have remained essentially the same over the years. A small group of GPs meet each week with a suitably trained leader and present cases that are giving them difficulty. They do so without notes, which enables the doctor to give a more spontaneous presentation, disclosing to the group some of their own subjective reactions to the patient. With the help of the leader(s), the group then examines the doctors' and the patients' interactions, often focusing on the detail of a recent consultation, but in the context of their longer-term relationship together; 'Why did you say that?', 'How did she react?' 'I feel that by prescribing for her at that moment, you were dismissing her', 'I don't think this patient can get through to you', 'I think you were caught in a difficult situation', etc.

> The doctor comes to the group with the real burden of a difficult case. In reporting his case and joining in the discussion, he tests his own ideas against those of his colleagues. In a way, the reporting doctor takes on the role of his own patient, and the group becomes the doctor. They share his anxieties and may pick up what he has missed due to his blind spots. (c. Gill, 1985, personal communication).

The group process does not teach skills or manoeuvres, but aims at a 'limited but considerable change' (Balint, 1957) in the doctor's personality. It helps participants to extend their range and methods of working by enabling them to use their own personal potential more fully. Doctors gain additional understanding of their involvement with the patients, and over the years gain a greater understanding of themselves too.

There are many aspects of a doctor's work. It is the *integration* of these various elements and their appropriate use that is the aim of successful training. If the training results in doctors who carry on their general practice regardless, but perform what might be described as 'psychotherapy on Sundays', it has failed. And if it results in doctors who become so interested in pursuing their patient's psyches that they persecute them with inappropriate curiosity, e.g. 'How's your sex life?', and become dissatisfied and neglectful of the rest of their medical work, then again training has failed. A successful marriage produces a *new individual*, not just a chip off one or other of the old parental blocks.

It is the leader's job to preserve the aims of the group and help it remain focused on its primary task. Groups often prefer to do almost anything other than this. They take refuge by a flight into other preoccupations and the leader has to watch out for these, steering a course between anecdotal chit-chat, journeys of psychological speculation into the patient's past, constant questioning of the presenting doctor or drowning him or her with 'helpful' advice, at the same time avoiding anything that might be too personal or painful for the doctor (Gosling, 1999).

This method is both a technique for training, still remaining the principal one for training GPs in this sort of work, and a technique for research, and *observing* the effect of a GP's work with patients. The main thrust of Balint research work has been towards a deepening of understanding of the therapeutic possibilities (and limitations) of the doctor–patient relationship (Elder and Samuel, 1987; Balint, et al, 1993; Courtenay, 1999, personal communication). Some groups have also met to research particular aspects of their work, such as marital problems (Courtenay, 1968), repeat prescriptions (Balint et al., 1970), abortions (Tunnadine and Green, 1978) and accidents (Campkin, 1999).

Developments

An important change of emphasis and technique occurred in the 1970s. During the early years, the doctors tended to become semi-psychotherapists, devoting long sessions to their patients with psychological problems. This was an inevitable side effect of the training and reflected doctors' need to model themselves on the work of the leaders, a defence against the real difficulty of achieving an independent and appropriate professional identity for themselves.

Doctors' psychotherapeutic work had to become better integrated with their everyday work, making it less of a foreign body. New techniques had to be discovered to fit GPs' timescales. A research group, again with the Balints' leadership, began meeting in 1965 to study this problem. The findings were published in a book called *Six Minutes for the Patient* (Balint and Norell, 1973). The change in thinking that lay behind this work was as significant as the original work itself. The change from a history-taking style of interview, which they called the *detective inspector* approach, are described with the doctor conducting a search of the patient's life for significant events and feelings, to one in which doctors listen intently to the patients' presentation, trying to tune in to how the patient wants to use the doctor and what this means. In this style of work more autonomy is left with patients who set the pace, and doctors have to be content to abandon their central role and follow their patients, being more aware of their relationship and less curious about secrets in the patient's inner world, or finding out what makes the patient tick. This is a more appropriate method for the brief encounters characteristic of general practice and leaves the patient's self-esteem intact. While working in this way, *flash* interviews may occur, in which there is a sudden mutual awakening between doctor and patient with a consequent change in their relationship. 'Often the flash concerns the relationship between doctor and patient, but even if it does not, the relationship is changed by the flash' (Balint and Norell, 1973). Relationships in general practice often seem to progress through these 'flashes' or 'important moments' (Elder and Samuel, 1987). A later research group focused on following up the therapeutic effects of such 'surprising' changes in the doctor–patient relationship (Balint et al., 1993).

Balint had a considerable literary gift and used many metaphors which are still highly resonant. He described doctors as possessing an *apostolic function*, by which he meant:

> ...the way in which every doctor demonstrates a vague but almost unshakably firm idea of how a patient ought to behave when he is ill. Although this idea is anything but explicit and concrete, it is immensely powerful, and influences the way in which the doctor not only talks to the patient and relates to him, but how he prescribes drugs, and the way in which he expects to be treated by the patient. It is almost as if every doctor had a revealed knowledge of what is right and what is wrong for patients to expect to endure, and further, as if he had a sacred duty to convert to his faith all the ignorant and unbelieving amongst his patients. (Balint, 1957)

Doctors' apostolic functions are shaped mainly by their own personalities and their personal attitudes to suffering and illness, but are also influenced by the social culture in which they live. Every culture has powerful apostolic beliefs of its own about health, as well as other things, and these are changing all the time. The apostolic attitudes of 40 years ago may no longer be relevant now. In our world, we may expect people 'to work through their grief appropriately' or 'to take responsibility for their own health, not using alcohol, or drugs but attending exercise classes instead'. It is worth examining what is meant by such phrases and whose concerns they reflect: the patients' or the doctors'?

Balint also often referred to the doctor as the *drug doctor*, saying he was the most frequently used drug in medical practice and calling for further study of his or her uses and side effects. Revealingly, it is the most frequently misquoted of Balint's aphorisms. Doctors usually describe the 'drug doctor' as 'the most powerful drug used in medical practice'! The apostolic function is alive and well.

General practice owes the Balints (and other later analysts who have continued working in this tradition) a great debt of gratitude. It is almost inconceivable to imagine people coming from positions of outside expertise, bringing the same painstaking willingness to study, listen and learn from the doctors as did the Balints, and not adopting a position of 'telling them what they ought to be doing' — an invitation that only very exceptional people can refuse as is revealed by the ubiquitous phrase in the medical literature, '*the GP is ideally placed…*'.

Wider Changes

Since the 1950s, there have been many developments that have influenced general practice: a Royal College of General Practitioners was founded, vocational training became firmly established, departments for teaching general practice and primary care are now present in all medical schools. Since 1990 there have been further radical changes which have led to the NHS internal market and the most recent reorganization of fundholding into Primary Care Groups. Alongside these changes, there has been a considerable growth in the number of 'therapies' and 'techniques' of a broadly psychotherapeutic nature and many of these are now well established within the compass of general practice and primary care. Different counselling techniques, cognitive analytic and behavioural approaches, and an understanding of the systemic foundations of family therapy, as well as different approaches to the therapy of sexual discord, all contribute to the ways in which individual GPs can choose to develop their own style and repertoire of work. The are like *articles of clothing* for GPs to try on, taking something from this one and other things from another one, adding to their range of techniques and skills to be integrated alongside those acquired through medical training. They have to find out how well they 'fit' into the 'GP setting' and how well they fit their particular *personality*. It is important for GPs to study and to distinguish between the ways in which these different approaches aid their primary GP task with patients, or whether they are useful as distinct treatment modalities that can be offered from within the surgery setting. There is of course no inherent contradiction between these two positions, but there is potential for confusion. Much thought is being given to these questions in relation to the teaching of systemic (family therapy) thinking to GPs (Launer and Lindsey, 1997) and to the introduction of psychodynamic counselling (Wiener and Sher, 1998).

Body and Mind

GPs have to try to achieve an integration in their work between those skills and attitudes that come from the more authoritarian tradition of the medical profession with those other quieter listening skills that come from the psychoanalytic and humanist tradition. When to ask questions and when to listen? They have to learn *sufficient flexibility* for the one to be part of the other.

> A young man comes to the doctor, looking rather sleepy, and complains of a heavy chest, wondering whether it could be his 'heart'. The doctor can find nothing obviously wrong. The consultation seems lifeless, but in an aside which the doctor easily might have overlooked, the patient mentions that his father died a year ago. His father had been less than 60 when he died of a heart attack and his father's father had also died young, raising the question of a familial hyperlipidaemia. The patient expresses little grief and does not feel his father's death has affected his life much. He mentions that he now visits his mother more often and seems to resent this.

The doctor has to balance his or her medical responsibilities, such as investigating this patient's possible hyperlipidaemia and giving him necessary
advice about this, whilst also noticing their own reactions and the patient's
appearance and listening for clues to this young man's heavy heart. The
patient seems depressed without knowing it, quite unconsciously bringing
his complaint to the doctor. He does not seem to feel as much grief as the
doctor first expects. But the doctor must allow the patient's own story to
unfold, without superimposing his or her own expectations.

This is a typical brief encounter, where there is a balance between
medicine and listening, both being part of each other, not an 'either/or'.
The patient has had some limited but relevant help at a time when he
presented himself for it. He may leave it there or return some time later. If
he does come back, the first impressions have been laid, on both the
doctor's and the patient's side.

The illness or health of an individual depends on a complex inter-
relationship between the total person and his environment. Within the
individual there is a constant interaction between the body, the mind, with
its powerful emotional world both conscious and unconscious, and
whatever moral and spiritual life the person possesses and through which
he relates his life to other people and the world at large.

Doctors have a relationship with the *whole person* and often with the
whole of a family too. The body and the mind reflect and influence each
other all the time. The distinction is not as clear as is often made out. The
split between the two is a very common feature of illness, where a physical
tension, an ache or a rash remain quite unconnected in the patient's mind
to the conflicts that may be associated with them. Medical thinking is often
also split in this way, with physical illness being considered first, leaving
the mind as a sort of remainder. The patient is put through a *sieve* marked
'physical' in order to catch only those aspects that doctors feel they understand and can do something about. The antagonism sometimes observed
between medical consultants and psychiatrists is an expression of this
divide, with the two seeming to inhabit different worlds; and psychoanalysis, in isolating the mind for particular study, is also prone to accentu-
ating this problem.

GPs are uniquely placed for an understanding and healing of this
relationship. They are working across the 'body/mind' boundary practically all the time. The whole spectrum of illness is brought to them, from
the almost entirely physical to the almost entirely psychological. These
differences are simply reflections of the different densities of disturbance.
At the most concrete end, serious physical illnesses (such as cancers and
arterial disease), always have important psychological consequences; in
the middle range there are large numbers of illnesses in which body and
minds seem to be inextricably bound up with each other (such as asthma,

irritable bowel syndrome, hypertension, migraine and abnormalities of menstruation), and at the lighter end there are the transient physical expressions of tension — odd pains, headaches and autonomic symptoms that occur according to personal patterns of anxiety and depression.

Doctors handle, touch and listen through their stethoscopes while also keeping alert and listening through the human ear as well. They examine the body at the same time as noticing the patient's reactions to this process. Not everything has to be verbalized. If psychological tensions are expressed, which had been close to the surface anyway, their physical counterparts may resolve as well, but such connections are most often quite inaccessible. Doctors must learn to mediate their medicine through whatever language, be it largely physical or largely psychological, that the patient is using at that time.

> Mr C. is a tall young banker in his late twenties, married to a schoolteacher. They are expecting their first baby and Mrs C. comes regularly for her antenatal care. She is rather jolly and seems pleased to be pregnant. The doctor has seen the husband only once or twice and on this occasion Mr C. seems rather more reserved than before and the two do not easily get on to the right track. He has been having intermittent diarrhoea and abdominal discomfort for some weeks. The doctor and patient fence around a bit but do not seem to get anywhere. Maybe this is the beginning of ulcerative colitis? The doctor sends him for some tests that all turn out to be normal. Mr C. is still pretty unforthcoming when he comes again, but is perhaps a little keener for the doctor to get on to the right wavelength this time and drops more of a hint. He describes his symptoms as 'blowing out' and says he is 'almost as big as his wife'. The doctor senses an important area, makes some exploratory remarks, and when he is more sure of his footing says, 'You can look forward to the birth of babies but you can dread them too.' With doctor and patient now better tuned, the patient can express some of his feelings about the forthcoming baby, '... he hates babies, they puke and make a noise, the smaller they are the worse they are, he can't stand his friends' babies because he has seen how they have changed them, *ruining their lives* ...'

The patient seems to resent the intrusion of the pregnancy and is frightened by the changes that it may produce. He fears they may have to move, as there will not be enough space for the baby (or himself?) and nowhere to retreat in peace, as he is someone who dislikes displays of strong feelings. He is angry and fears the baby will change his life, leaving him left out of the relationship between the baby and his wife. It is possible that this strong feeling of the patient's was echoed in the doctor–patient relationship where he may have felt left out by the doctor and his wife, something that very often happens in antenatal care. Perhaps they had left him with an unfair amount of the negative resentful feelings attached to the forthcoming birth? The patient afterwards felt that both sides of his experience, positive and negative (for he was also looking forward to the birth), been accepted by the doctor, making him feel less of an outcast. He had earlier described the baby as a 'monster'. It is also possible (and there was some evidence from later joint antenatal visits) that after this consultation, Mr and Mrs C. were able to communicate with each other about such an important change in their lives in a more open and balanced way.

Still within the psychosomatic sphere, the body may literally almost break under a psychological strain:

> Mr J., an earnest young man of 26, had been sent to his doctor by his employer because he had collapsed with back pain six weeks earlier and had still not fully recovered. The doctor had not seen him before but he gave the history of his back pain clearly. He was an only child who had always done well academically. He had 'passed everything' until recently failing some exams to become a solicitor. He had been working very hard to retake them and his parents had suggested he went away with them for a Bank Holiday weekend. He was pleased he went, but returned home earlier than his parents, in order to continue his studies. After he left, his mother had suddenly died. Normally, he would have phoned them on his safe arrival, but that night he did not. He was devastated. He had always found emotion less easy to share with his father and he adopted a role of 'carrying on', throwing himself into hard work, redoubling his efforts to do well in his retake exams. These he passed. As the pressure began to relax, only a few days later he 'collapsed' with back pain and was taken to a hospital casualty department, where he was sent home with analgesics and told to rest, advice which his firm's doctor had later repeated.

During the consultation described, in which this history emerged, the patient's emotions also emerged at the same time. He was able to break down in tears, particularly when reliving the bitter anguish he felt that his mother had not been able to share in his examination success. What had it all been for?

The patient had himself half-known that his back had cracked as a result of the tension and strain of his suppressed feelings after his mother's funeral. But he needed a doctor who could allow him to make the connection more confidently and who could help him express some of the half-hearted emotions which he had bottled up inside his body in order to carry on with his work.

'The helping him express' is often written about as 'allowing the patient to express'. It is more than that. It is doctors experiencing some aspect of their patient's predicaments and feelings, and giving them back through their words and reactions as a rightful experience for the patient to be having. It is a reinforced or positive echo returning to the patient from the doctor. The patient leaves feeling 'Yes, that *is* what I feel'. His or her *authenticity* as an individual *is strengthened*. This is, of course, helpful only if the experience does have the feeling of *truth for the patient*. Otherwise, it may be that the feeling of conviction belongs more to the doctor's end. This is an ever-present danger.

Living in the Present

Patients often apologize when they take the doctor's time. 'I'm sorry to take up your time again, doctor'; 'I won't keep you a moment, doctor'. Sentences which can carry many different emphases and meanings, and which most often doctors hardly notice. *The way* in which patients ask for the doctor's attention *matters*. Why does this patient always seem unsatisfied or unable to tolerate other patients in the waiting room? Why is this one over-apologetic and another anxiously over-friendly? *How* people present their problems to their doctor may reveal important patterns in other relationships and these may be closely related to their current difficulties. Doctors must allow such patterns to develop, being careful not to do so only to gratify their own need, say, for patients to be appreciative or friendly. They may sense, when they are with a particular patient, that they are perceived as a parent who has to be appeased or a lover who must not come too close, or an old friend or somebody the patient always has to do battle with but never completely defeat.

Doctors have to try to recognize, *there and then*, when one of these characteristic patterns of relating is being enacted with them and whether it is relevant. Their listening must be efficient; hearing is what is important *at that moment*:

A young woman in her thirties, Miss E., seems to the doctor prematurely grey and burdened. She has a likeable seriousness about her but is depressed. She had what she describes as a big emotional breakdown three years ago and has been depressed on and off since. She has a strong sense of duty and seems to live in a predominantly female world. She has a responsible job which she does very conscientiously, but feels that her supervisors do not take her work seriously enough. She is new to this doctor, who can feel how heavily depressed she is, but also how difficult it is for her to do anything with this, other than to endure it worthily. He is content to let her communicate in her own way and has to remain in the dark about many of the details of various relationships she hints at as current difficulties. If he does ask or enquire, he appears to add to her burden and she says, 'Oh, it would take such a long time, it's all so complicated anyway'. She comes seldom. On this occasion, she had not been for some time, but clearly had been very depressed. The doctor felt that he wanted her to realize that he was available for her as her doctor and finished the consultation by saying that she was able to come and see him if she felt depressed and that it was legitimate to make an appointment if she felt dreadful. It was not breaking any rules. At this point she conveyed that he had enough to deal with already and would not want to be burdened or spend more of his time seeing her. This was said genuinely, not evasively. She said it in such a way that she seemed to make *herself* responsible for *his* burden. He pointed this out to her, suggesting that she had enough to carry already, without also having to worry about his decisions in allocating his time and energy. He would look after that himself.

The doctor could feel her conflict. It was not just that she did not want to burden him. If it had been, his remarks would have made no impact. It was that she desperately wanted to burden him, but also could not allow herself to do so, and that in part her depression was related to her habit of carrying other people's responsibilities as well as her own, a pattern perhaps originally established with her parents, but certainly persisting into the present as well.

This was a crystallizing point in the relationship and clearly meant something significant to the patient. It had arisen with the doctor, but it was important in her difficulties all round. The same or a similar point may often have come up; after all, such a problem is not uncommon, but it seemed *particularly true* at that *particular moment* and was intimately related to the problems the patient was suffering in her current life. It has much of its impact for the patient because of the feelings contained in the doctor–patient encounter in which it is verbalized.

Miss E. did return after quite a short interval and this time was able to talk to the doctor more about her distress, initiating a series of appointments with him at a time when she needed help.

It is worth noting that the doctor at this stage knows nothing about the patient's father, her mother or her siblings, and very little of her present relationships. He does not know about her sex life, whether she has a boyfriend, a girlfriend or no friends. If he had asked her, he would have been unable to help her in the way he did. He had to be *prepared to follow the patient*, trying to make sense of whatever patterns emerged.

Time

It is often said that GPs do not have enough time to listen to their patients. This is far from the truth. The GP's timescale is one of the setting's great strengths. They build their knowledge of their patients and their patients' families through repeated short contacts, sometimes over many years. It is their use of the time that matters. Their appointments system is flexible. They can see a patient for five minutes on one occasion, 20 minutes on another. They can see people frequently for a short time and then not need to again for months. Of course, if listening is simply a process of letting people talk, then indeed they do not have enough time. But it is not. It is the accuracy of *attention to the moment* that counts and an ear that 'hears' what is being said in the echoes and resonances behind their patients' words. No long preamble and fact-finding is needed. The doctor and patient can get to the point quickly. Much of what is important will already be known.

> Mr R., a widower in his sixties, seldom comes to the doctor, but does so one evening near Christmas, about two years after his wife's death. She had been a frequent attender whom the doctor knew well, an incessant talker with a great many complaints. Mr R. is dressed in dull clothes, and comes with a 'croaky cold'. No time is needed for his own doctor, who has known his whole situation over the years, to understand his croaky (tearful) cold(ness) and the lack of warmth he has felt in his life since his wife's death. The doctor gives him simple treatment for his cold and a few minutes of time, tears, and some memories of the unexpectedness of her death, the shock ...

That is all that is necessary. A brief consultation not necessarily requiring any follow-up.

For some patients the doctor remains one of the few fixed points. They may not come often, but know that he or she is there, as a reference point, *a secure base*. Most important is the patient's pattern of use over time. Is there a change? Is the patient coming more often or less often? One axis of the doctor's timescale is long term, but the rhythm of use along the way can be very variable. This reflects the distance patients may feel they need at different times, sometimes coming to the doctor for quite intense help and then staying away. This pattern may have important echoes.

> Miss J. is a slim 23-year-old student. She is a northerner and often comes to the surgery with a friend who stays in the waiting room. When she joined the doctor's list, she came for a repeat prescription of her pill, a routine visit in which no problems were mentioned. She returned a month later to tell the doctor she was having a difficult time with sex with her present boyfriend. She felt dry and was put off by the thought of intercourse. She was shy and embarrassed with the doctor, but told him that she had known Robert for two years, that he had been prepared to build up their relationship slowly, which had been important for her as she had felt easily pushed into bed by men previously. She had recently changed digs and so was new to the doctor's area, but felt her 'present home' would suit her better. She had felt tense with her past family and feared someone might walk into her bedroom at any moment if she had her boyfriend there. The doctor and Miss J. managed to establish enough contact, and Miss J. would attend every few weeks, sometimes more often, sometimes less, to talk to the doctor and report on progress in her relationship with Robert. The doctor had suggested seeing them together as a couple and had discussed referring them for specialist psychosexual help. Neither of these suggestions had worked out. During this time she also talked a little about her family background and other relationships. Her mother and she were 'peas in a pod'. Her father, in fact her stepfather, had been very strict but she was his 'favourite'.

The doctor felt he had to be careful not to undermine the patient's relationship with Robert, hoping instead to help Miss J. become more receptive to him.

The doctor was careful to let her dictate the pattern and frequency of her attendance, as she had carefully signalled that this was important to her in her relations with men. She did not like to be pushed. It seemed to be the doctor's task to respect this aspect of her, but not too much. He had also to push her a bit as well, towards examining some of her reactions and possible reasons for them; gently steering a course between 'too much' and 'too little'. On one occasion the doctor finished an interview feeling he had probably overdone it and gone into things more deeply than was comfortable for the patient. However, on the next occasion she returned she looked more feminine and said she had a confession to make. They had successfully made love. On that occasion her friend had not accompanied her to the waiting room

This kind of work seems to progress, then run into new difficulties — backwards and forwards. Miss J. seemed to keep attending when she wanted to and the doctor continued to try to balance his encouragement with allowing her to set the pace.

This work goes on amidst all the other demands that are made on doctors' attention. They have many other difficult tasks to perform and their minds may often be far from being tuned to their patients. Doctors will need to find a balance for themselves between engaging and identifying with their patients, on the one hand, and gaining sufficient distance from them, on the other, for thoughtful professional reflection. They will need both if they are to remain useful to their patients, and become neither too defensive and 'clinical', nor be too close to think clearly and see their patients from an angle different from the one at which they see themselves. GPs can then show respect for their patients' own way of living and treat them as other human beings and not only as the bearers of a diagnosis for doctors to discover.

Summary

I have isolated some aspects of GPs' work in order to draw attention to the possibilities the setting offers for psychotherapeutic work of a certain kind. I hope that some of the characteristics of this work can be seen from the cases I have discussed, all taken from a GP's everyday work: doctors' relatively easy personal accessibility, their involvement with patients at times of need and change, their 'being there' for people (regardless of how little or often consulted) for long periods of time, often for many years; the relationship with the 'whole' patient; the fact that patients hold the key and can therefore dictate the pace, coming at a time of their own making (*Why now?* What is important to *this* patient at *this* time?); listening all round patients as well as to echoes within themselves; being content to do *just enough* and not more, so that patients may leave feeling free to use the doctor at another time, or in a different way, without having to bare their souls more than they want or having their lives interpreted. The patient remains in charge of his own life and, hopefully, is strengthened and not undermined by his contact with the doctor.

References

BALINT, M. (1954). Training general practitioners in psychotherapy. *British Medical Journal* 1, 115.

BALINT, M. (1955). The doctor, his patient and the illness. *The Lancet* i, 683.

BALINT, M. (1957). *The Doctor, His Patient and the Illness*. London: Pitman Medical.

BALINT, M., HUNT, J., JOYCE, D. et al. (1970). *Treatment or Diagnosis: A study of Repeat Prescription in General Practice*. London: Tavistock Publications.

BALINT, E. and NORELL, J.S. eds, (1973). *Six Minutes for the Patient*. London: Tavistock Publications.

BALINT, E., COURTENAY, M., ELDER, A. et al. (1993). *The Doctor, The Patient and the Group: Balint revisited*. London: Routledge.

BATEMAN, A. and HOLMES, J. (1995). *Introduction to Psychoanalysis. Contemporary Theory and Practice*. London: Routledge.

BROWN, D. and PEDDER, J. (1979). *Introduction to Psychotherapy*. London: Tavistock Publications.

CAMPKIN, M. (1999). Proceedings of the International Balint Conference, Oxford 1998. *Journal of the Balint Society* 27.

CLARE, A.W. and BLACKER, C.V.R (1986). Some problems affecting the diagnosis and classification of depressive disorders in primary care. In: M. Shepherd, G. Wilkinson, and P. Williams, eds, *Mental Illness in Primary Care Settings*. London: Tavistock.

COLLINGS, J.S. (1950). General practice in England today: a renaissance. *Lancet* i, 555.

COURTENAY, M.J.F. (1968). *Sexual Discord in Marriage*. London: Tavistock Publications.

DEPARTMENT OF HEALTH (1991). *The Health of the Nation: Consultative Document for Health in England*. London: HMSO.

ELDER, A. (1996). Enid Balint's contribution to general practice. *Psychoanalytic Psychotherapy* 10, 101–108.

ELDER, A. and SAMUEL, O. eds, (1987). *'While I'm here, doctor'*. London: Tavistock Publications.

GOLDBERG, D.P. and BLACKWELL, B. (1970). Psychiatric illness in general practice. *British Medical Journal*. 1, 439.

GOSLING, R. and TURQUET, P. (1965). *The training of general practitioners: the use of the group method*. Karnac Reprint, London 1999.

GOSLING, R. and ELDER, A. (1996) in Michael Balint *Object relations pure and applied*. The New Library of Psychoanalysis 25, Routledge. Part 2: *Applied psychoanalysis*.

GOSLING, R. (1999). *Use of Small Groups in Training General Practitioners*. London: Karnac.

HOPKINS, P. (1956). Referrals in general practice. *British Medical Journal* 2, 873.

LAUNER, J. and LINDSEY, C. (1997). Training for systemic general practice: a new approach from the Tavistock Clinic. *British Journal of General Practice* **47**, 453–456.

MILLER, P. McC., INGHAM, J.B. and DAVIDSON, S. (1976). Life events symptoms and social support. *Journal of Psychosomatic Research* **20**, 515.

ROYAL COLLEGE OF GENERAL PRACTITIONERS. (1981). Prevention of psychiatric disorders in general practice. *Report of General Practice* **20**. London: RCGP.

TUNNADINE, D. and GREEN, R. (1978). *Unwanted Pregnancy — Accident or Illness?* Oxford: Oxford University Press.

WIENER, J. and SHER, M. (1998). *Counselling and Psychotherapy in Primary Health Care: A Psychodynamic Approach*. London: Macmillan.

WINNICOTT, D.W. (1972). *The Maturational Process and the Facilitating Environment*. (The International Psychoanalytical Library, No 64.) London: Hogarth Press.

Chapter 8
Psychotherapy for Psychosis

CHRIS MACE AND FRANK MARGISON

Introduction

What is a psychosis?

Psychosis is a fairly recent concept and has been said to be no more than the doctor's word for 'mad'. It is only in the last 100 years that it has come to be more or less synonymous with schizophrenia and bipolar illness (with a few extras such as delusional states, psychogenic psychoses, or psychoses directly caused by a physical illness). Still, the main features are seen as involving a loss of contact with reality through the development of delusions and hallucinations.

For many years, particularly in the USA, psychotherapy was seen as the only alternative to long-term custodial treatment. Evidence about its effectiveness was weak, and with the new drugs introduced in the 1950s, psychotherapeutic approaches were put on the back burner. Slowly, there has been an increase in our understanding of the psychological mechanisms involved in psychosis and tailor-made treatments have been developed. The first breakthroughs came with family treatments which reduced the conditions in families which made further breakdowns more likely. This idea was quite different from previous ideas that families actually *caused* the psychosis, or at least made psychosis the only escape route.

Later, the successes of behavioural and cognitive therapies were extended to psychoses and there are now effective strategies to reduce symptoms, improve coping strategies and reduce relapse rates (see Chapters 9 and 10). Finally, the early ideas from psychoanalytic psychotherapy have been revised and there are treatments based on understanding the meaning of psychotic symptoms in terms of patients' attempts to deal with conflict.

These three principal approaches were previously seen as distinct, but the most effective treatment strategies draw on all three traditions as well as medication and social interventions to deal with the devastating effects of psychotic illness.

114

Within the range of mental disorders, schizophrenia and bipolar affective disorder are relatively rare. However, the disabilities they impose, the huge resources required to provide adequate care, and some of the limitations of physical treatments for them, ensure that research into effective psychological treatments is a major area of activity.

History of psychotherapy and psychosis

When Freud developed psychoanalysis he had no experience of people with psychotic disorders, having worked in neurology rather than psychiatry. He believed psychotic disorders to be unamenable to treatment. An ego that was too weak to prevent the primitive contents of the id breaking through into consciousness was also thought incapable of forming the kind of relationship with an analyst that he thought was necessary for psychoanalytic cure. Subsequent psychoanalysts, with more personal experience of psychotic patients, have had very different views.

An early example was Carl Jung, Freud's pupil turned rival, who first described the collective unconscious. Jung had worked as a psychiatrist in Switzerland in the Burghölzi clinic of Eugen Bleuler, originator of the term 'schizophrenia'. Jung believed schizophrenia was inherently treatable by a sympathetic analytic approach, and noted extraordinary resemblances between the apparently psychotic outpourings of schizophrenic patients, many of whom were illiterate or had little education, with the myths and symbols of earlier civilizations. The psychotic person, therefore, was not only somebody whose defences had broken down in a catastrophic way and failed them, but someone with a greater access to collective unconscious in which everybody participates. On this account, psychotic experiences have something of a prophetic quality. Progress was thought to depend on completion of a major readjustment leading to permanent psychic change rather than a return to functioning in much the same way as before the illness struck (Jung, 1939).

Although Jung's ideas have inspired many figures in literature and religion as well as his heirs within analytical psychology, his views on the scope of analytic treatment have not had anything like the impact on psychiatric practice as that enjoyed by several American psychoanalysts during the 1940s and 1950s. This was a time when there was a large hospitalized population of psychotic patients, few effective treatments, and widespread interest in psychoanalytic ideas among North American psychiatrists. Harry Stack Sullivan, who has been dubbed the father of American psychiatry, moved beyond orthodox psychoanalysis to an explicitly interpersonal theory. He believed the origins of schizophrenia lay in faulty interpersonal communication, ideas elaborated in his posthumous book, *Schizophrenia as a Human Process* (Sullivan, 1974). He taught a generation of psychiatrists how to attempt to cure it by intensive psychotherapy that offered an opportunity to renegotiate damaging earlier experiences, social as well as familial.

R.D. Laing was a British psychiatrist who, inspired by Sullivan, famously emphasized both the meaningfulness and social origins of psychotic episodes (Laing, 1961). It was a corollary of his understanding that psychiatry was intrinsically harmful in such situations, and that social action was as relevant as family change. These, together with a faith in the potential of psychotic experience to assist personal growth, were tenets of the so-called 'anti-psychiatry' movement with which Laing was identified. Whilst very different in their personalities, theory and practice, Jung, Sullivan and Laing were all deeply affected by their work. Jung described living at the edge of psychosis himself. Sullivan also suffered significant illness, whereas Laing was prey to chronic addictions that contributed to his early death.

Other approaches to psychosis

Contributions to the psychotherapy of psychosis were a significant part of the rise of behavioural and cognitive psychotherapy also described in this volume. The learning theory on which behaviourism is based had evolved from experimental studies with animals. Difficulties in establishing good collaborative relationships with the large number of chronic, institutionalized patients in psychiatric hospitals inspired therapies which aimed at change through manipulation of the environment rather than talking alone. 'Behavioural modification' was thought to be an important strategy in psychotherapy of patients whose apathy was attributed either to negative symptoms of schizophrenia, or to the effect of institutionalization. Behaviour modification is not used widely now, but the principles of examining in detail the environmental factors which help or impede social adjustment remain important aspects of a treatment programme.

Until the 1990s, cognitive therapy was thought of almost exclusively as a treatment for neurotic disorders, including many forms of anxiety and depression. In its early days, however, Aaron Beck had reported success with a patient with delusions (Beck, 1952). Recent research has confirmed that, contrary to previous clinical opinion, it is possible to challenge patients' delusions in a constructive and effective way with cognitive therapy techniques. It is essential that this is done in a supportive way so that it is the unjustified ideas that come in for critical attention, not patients themselves. When successful, bizarre beliefs that have been maintained with great conviction can be re-evaluated by patients and were discarded. Although these symptom-focused techniques are consistent with cognitive theory, they had been anticipated by the 'moral management' practised in the late eighteenth century within asylums adopting liberal methods of restraint and rehabilitation.

Links between the behaviour of families and the occurrence of schizophrenia were elaborated in the 1950s through concepts such as the 'double bind' (Bakeson et al., 1956). Most clinicians no longer accept that these communication patterns cause schizophrenia. However, close observation of family interactions led to novel approaches to treatment that attempted to alter the pattern of family communication. This branch of theory and a related school of family therapy became known as 'systemic'. Systemic thinking understands people to exist through their communications, with each individual being part of several communicative systems at any one time.

Family approaches have subsequently concentrated on modifying common elements of family behaviour (often termed 'expressed emotion') (Brown and Rutter, 1966) associated with higher rates of relapse. The methods combine educational and behavioural techniques. In fact, the 'expressed emotion' is a critical kind and needs to be sustained for over 15 hours of face-to-face contact each week to have these large effects on relapse rate. Strategies to reduce relapse aim either to reduce the amount of contact, or to reduce the proportion of communication which is critical in tone. Families are responding to the distress of seeing a relative behaving in odd ways and a key element is to explain to the family why, as a consequence of illness, the odd behaviour is so persistent.

Combining therapeutic approaches

Although each of these approaches to the psychotherapy of psychosis arose relatively independently, there is growing recognition of the importance of allowing these approaches to complement one another in the work of clinical teams and in the treatment of a given patient. Silvano Arieti was a pioneer of such an 'intergrationist' approach to the psychological management of schizophrenic patients, and his descriptions of how behavioural, psychodynamic and family interventions can be brought together remain relevant reading today (Arieti, 1975).

Current Practice

This will be considered in terms of three diagnostic groups: people with schizophrenia and schizophreniform psychoses; people with bipolar disorder (previously known as manic-depressive psychosis); and people who can sometimes resemble those with psychotic disorders, but whose diagnosis is borderline personality disorder.

Schizophrenia

By definition, schizophrenia embraces a wide range of symptoms and handicaps ranging from hallucinations, delusion and thought disorder to apathy, withdrawal and deficits in social and emotional perception. Because schizophrenia is a relapsing illness that may also be chronic, somebody can also have very different needs according to the stage they have reached in their clinical and social history. By the same token, it is possible to assist with one or more of a patient's difficulties, without this amounting to a 'cure'. Symptoms such as delusions might be improved without any social change; conversely, a patient might rekindle an ability to participate in social networks without evident change in their hallucinations. Nevertheless, many treatments aim to diminish the likelihood of future relapse, as well as simply influencing the course of an ongoing episode.

Improving specific symptoms, acute and chronic, is a direct goal of cognitive-behavioural treatments (Kingdom and Turkington, 1997). We might take as an example a patient who complains that other people are able to read her thoughts and place unwelcome thoughts that she is a whore in her brain. The therapist's first steps will be to try to establish a working alliance and detailed enquiry into these as a source of concern for the patient. The history of these complaints and the contexts in which they have occurred would be pieced together while the therapist also listens for other, less dramatic, examples of how the patient may be misinterpreting and misconstruing events around her. A phase of active negotiation follows in which therapist and patient try to correct the mistaken beliefs by reattribution, analysis of evidence, and by generating plausible alternative explanations. In this instance, the patient may admit that guilt over an illicit liaison, fear of discovery, and a belief she ought to be punished are encouraging her to think other people actually know what she has done and are torturing her for it. The misinterpretation can be normalized during sympathetic discussion of the effects on this patient of the sleep loss she reports, or other people's sensitivity to non-verbal cues she is actually giving off. If this kind of challenge to the specific features of the complaint fail to prompt change, further exploration is likely to be necessary to establish whether it has been persistent because it also expresses a less conscious set of negative self-beliefs or schema. If so, the schema is likely to be longstanding, pervasive and also manifest in other ways. It will need to be addressed directly for therapeutic change to occur. In this example, the woman may have already thought herself to be fundamentally bad and dirty. These beliefs would need to be framed in the context of their origins (e.g. being raped as a child). In so doing, an individual formulation will be derived that the therapist uses to guide further interventions once the working relationship is sufficiently strong for these core beliefs to be exposed and challenged.

Some of the specific symptoms for which treatment is sought reflect loss of previous capacities rather than disturbance of thinking and sensation. Again, cognitive-behavioural treatments following a symptom-led programme, are widely used. The token economy, in which selected behaviours for each patient are consistently reinforced by trained staff issuing rewards in a local currency that patients have to use instead of pocket money to obtain a range of everyday goods at a ward shop, has been cited already as an example of behaviour modification. Although the use of tokens simplifies administration of reinforcers, the same goals can be achieved by consistent social reinforcement (i.e. praise and attention) provided this follows a rigorous schedule. Less intractable social deficits are often helped by social skills training, in which patients are taught how to recognize feelings from facial expressions, and how to present themselves and interact in progressively more demanding social situations by use of modelling and role play.

Still other symptom-focused techniques attempt to minimize the impact and distress of intrusive experiences by enhancing patients' capacity to distract themselves as these occur. Coping skills enhancement (CSE) is a set of cognitive techniques based on a thorough assessment of patients' existing methods of reducing the distress experienced from hallucinations and delusions. Examples may include distraction to lessen the auditory impact, shouting in defiance of negative messages, and substance misuse to numb the distress. Where coping tactics are adaptive and likely to be successful, these are encouraged through *in vivo* practice. When they have disadvantages, they are reshaped in discussion with the patient. For example, listening to the radio may be encouraged as an alternative form of distraction to endless revving of a car engine. Patients may also be helped to rationalize critical negative voices so they are understood to be symptoms rather than real voices — an internal argument in effect taking the place of a shouting match. In addition, to help patients become less dependent on random use of tranquillizers, relaxation might be taught as an anxiety-reducing measure that is under their personal control.

Prevention of relapse, irrespective of the form this takes, has been an explicit goal of family-based interventions. The classical approach arose out of the research on expressed emotion, being specifically designed to reduce levels of criticism, hostility, and overall duration of contact between patient and family. Expressed emotion was attributed to a family's failure to understand a variety of anti-social behaviours that were the consequence of their relative's illness rather than laziness or badness. The key to intervention, therefore, was full and patient explanation of the nature of the relative's condition, and the need to adjust the family's behaviour. Discussion of troublesome incidents in this light could be followed up by provision of non-critical feedback to the family as they interacted with the patient *in situ*. Increasingly, elimination of harmful behaviour has been accompanied by efforts to improve communication on all sides through specific exercises.

More recent approaches have been based on raising family sensitivity to other aspects of their relative's behaviour, especially those that represent the earliest signs of onset of relapse. These prodromal features can differ considerably from case to case. Typical examples include dysphoria, inter-personal sensitivity and low-level psychotic experiences, such as visual and auditory disturbances, that do not amount to fully-formed hallucin-ations. Therapeutic strategies rest on identification of the prodromal features, increasing awareness of the importance of acting within a critical 'time-window', and interventions in the form of counselling, advice and regular medication.

Although the approaches discussed so far clearly offer help for defined problems and procedures by which they can be addressed, they do not necessarily address the suffering that accompanies psychosis. Psychotic breakdown can be both a source of extreme mental pain, and represent a desperate method of responding to it. Psychoanalytic approaches to psychosis have always attended first to this pain, seeing the dissolution of normal psychological functioning as the consequence of dynamic processes that accompany extreme and primitive affect. The dissociation between different psychological functions that Bleuler had described as pathognomonic of schizophrenic psychology is part of a violent mental fragmentation in which intensely hostile feelings threaten to overwhelm the patient and are split off from awareness. Whether or not they are also projected outwards, they remain in a largely unprocessed and unprocessable form. Although the different post-Freudian analytic schools have construed this situation in subtly different ways, the therapeutic task is essentially one of assisting extremely raw and often terrifying experiences to be recognized as internal events, but helping them to be re-integrated with the rest of the patient's affective experience. This is inevitably a gradual process, during which the analytical psychotherapist is exposed to extreme affects over long periods before any prospect of them being re-owned and emerges. The therapist's function is often spoken of as holding these affects on behalf of the patient, a situation encapsulated in the concept of 'containment'. It was introduced by Wilfred Bion, a protégé of Melanie Klein, who worked with many psychotic adult patients. (The behaviours and attitudes that later research has shown to characterize the expressed emotion that is counter-therapeutic when directed to these patients, represent the antithesis of those required for successful containment.) Much subsequent psychodynamic thinking about psychosis can be seen as attempts to enhance the containing function, not only within the traditional treatment situation, but within specifically convened therapeutic groups, and across staff teams and institutions.

Affective psychoses

There has been relatively little work on the psychological treatments of bipolar disorder. There are anecdotal and single-case reports, but few formal studies of adequate size. There are suggestions that group therapy and individual therapy might be useful, particularly in improving compliance, and most treatments studied have had a strong psycho-educational component. One theme has been to help the patient or family member to identify prodromal symptoms of relapse as early as possible (termed recognition of the 'illness signature'). Only small, preliminary studies have been reported as yet, but family interventions similar to those used with schizophrenia seem to be helpful.

Psychotherapy and the 'borderline' personality

The term 'borderline' denotes an unstable form of personality disorder. There have been many definitions, these rarely overlapping completely. A useful survey reported three features to be the most consistent, viz. continuing lability in mood, unstable personal relationships, and a tendency to acquire multiple psychiatric diagnoses (Higgit and Fonagy, 1992). Diagnoses of psychotic conditions are frequently among the latter, a reminder that originally, one of the 'borders' inhabited by borderline cases was that between neurosis and psychosis. Certainly, transient states of paranoia and even hallucinosis can be seen in these patients, although diagnostic revisions in manuals such as DSM-IV and ICD-10 have meant that some of them are now classified under 'schizotypal personality'.

As with any 'personality disorder', these patients are understood to have developmental problems evident from adolescence onwards. The earliest descriptions of borderline pathology were devised by North American psychoanalysts, and the condition has been seen as relatively amenable to psychotherapy. Although the degree of fragmentation between ego functions is not as severe as with psychotic illnesses, and any impairments of reality testing are correspondingly less profound, patients are likely at least to seek the kind of containment offered by analytic approaches. There is continuing debate about the most appropriate kind of strategy beyond initial engagement, expressed in the contrast between those emphasising early challenge and interpretation of processes actively maintaining these splits, and others in which the patient's efforts to sustain at least an illusion of wholeness are supported as part of an attempt to transcend the damaged functions through positive nurturing of the undeveloped capacity to relate. These therapies tend to be long (several years), intensive and uneven.

Borderline patients tend to be extremely demanding, often detracting from the care of other individuals if they live within institutions. Other therapeutic approaches are well recognized, especially the social and cognitive therapies. Social therapy, practised within a specialized hospital, employs techniques used historically with dyssocial or sociopathic people. By having them in a series of groups throughout a day's programme, learning of their effect on others and vice versa is encouraged; this is expected to promote social learning of the solidity of boundaries with others.

Cognitive therapy techniques were extended by Aaron Beck and his followers to address the needs of personality-disordered patients once clinical experience indicated that many patients presenting with depression and anxiety would not benefit from techniques targeting these symptoms unless attention was also paid to dysfunctional personality traits that accompanied them (Beck et al., 1990 and Chapter 9 of this volume). In the present-day management of borderline patients, two specific offshoots from the cognitive–behavioural tradition have attracted a good deal of attention and look likely to enjoy a significant place in future treatment. The first, dialectical behaviour therapy (DBT) was pioneered by Marcia Linehan and combines individual psychotherapy with group-based educational seminars that attribute patients' difficulties to innate abnormalities in emotional arousal as well as subsequent environmental failures (Linehan et al., 1991). Patients undergo both simultaneously, through a programme that may be two years or more in duration. Therapists aim to be unusually flexible both in the eclectic way they address situations in therapy (part of what is meant by 'dialectical' here) and in the way they hold themselves available for telephone contact by patients outside therapy sessions. The method has been heavily researched, showing itself effective in reducing self-harming behaviours.

The second development, Anthony Ryle's cognitive analytic therapy (CAT), is a structured short-term psychotherapy originally designed for use across a very broad range of clinical problems (Ryle, 1990 and Chapter 11). It has shown particular promise, in therapies of a year's duration or more, with borderline patients. In accordance with theories depicting the borderline person as having a number of poorly integrated 'self states', CAT presents patients with a diagram on which these different states and the shifts between them are represented as a basis for therapeutic work. Although CAT was devised primarily as an individual therapy, these diagrammatic formulations can also be shared with a staff team offering a more intensive programme on a day-patient or in-patient basis to facilitate the consistency and coherence in approach that is essential to success in these circumstances.

Psychotherapeutic Principles and the Care Programme Approach

The treatment of psychosis and, indeed, any severe and enduring mental illness needs to be co-ordinated between psychiatric and social agencies.

One of the main failings across many inquiries has been the need to communicate effectively between professionals. It is implied that patients also need to 'own' the proposed treatment programme. It is unusual, however, to take account of the communication difficulties experienced by patients in dealing with often terrifying experiences. It may be that the disordered communication is sometimes a product of brain dysfunction, but the content of the delusional beliefs and hallucinations of a psychosis are usually highly charged with meaning. One of the most important themes of the work of the last decade has been a return to attempts to understand the metaphorical meanings lying within the madness. In the past, this was often seen as an alternative to medication or social treatments. Now it is assumed that a good treatment approach needs not only to give expert advice on the best physical treatments, but also to provide a framework within which it is possible to communicate meaningfully.

Further reading

ARIETI, S. (1975). The psychotherapy of psychosis. In: S. Arieti (ed.) *American Handbook of Psychiatry* (4th edition). New York: Basic Books, 627–629.

BATESON, G., JACKSON, D. et al. (1956). Towards a theory of schizophrenia. *Behavioural Science* 1, 251–264.

BECK, A.T. (1952). Successful outpatient psychotherapy of a chronic schizophrenic with a delusion based on borrowed guilt. *Psychiatry* 15, 305–312.

BECK, A.T., FREEMAN, A et al (1990). Cognitive Therapy of Personality Disorders. New York: Guilford Press.

BROWN, G.W. and RUTTER, M. (1966). The measurement of family activities and relationships: a methodological study. *Human Relations* 19, 241–263.

COX, M. and THEILGAARD, A. (1997). *The Aeolian Mode*. London: Jessica Kingsley.

HADDOCK, G. and SLADE, P.D. (1996). *Cognitive–behavioural Interventions with Psychotic Disorders*. London: Routledge.

HIGGITT, A. and FONAGY, P. (1992). Psychotherapy in borderline and narcissistic personality disorders. *British Journal of Psychiatry* 161, 23–43.

JUNG, C.G. (1939). On the psychogenesis of schizophrenia. In: *Collected Works*, Vol. 3 (eds. H. Read, M. Fordham and G. Adler, 1960). London: Routledge and Kegan Paul, 233–249.

KINGDON, D. and TURKINGTON, D. (1997). Cognitive therapy of schizophrenia: collaborative and integrative approaches. In: C. Mace and F> Margison (eds). *Psychotherapy of Psychosis*. London: Gaskell, 114–29.

LAING, R.D. (1960). *The Divided Self*. London: Tavistock.

LINEHAN, M.M., ARMSTRON, H.E. et al. (1991) Cognitive-behavioural treatment of chronically parasuicidal borderline patients. *Archives of General Psychiatry* 48, 1060–1064.

MACE, C.J. and MARGISON, F.R. (1997). *Psychotherapy of Psychosis*. London: Gaskell Press.

RYLE, A. (1990). *Cognitive Analytic Therapy: Active Participation in Change*. Chichester: Wiley.

RYLE, A. (1997). The structure and development of borderline personality disorder: a proposed model. *British Journal of Psychiatry* 170, 82–87.

SULLIVAN, H.S. (1974). *Schizophenia as a Human Process*. New York: Norton.

Chapter 9
Cognitive Therapy

MARC SERFATY AND DAVID M CLARK

'Can you keep from crying by considering?', said Alice.
'That's the way it's done', the Queen said.

From *Alice Through the Looking Glass* by Lewis Carroll (1872)

Introduction

Cognitive therapy is a relatively recent form of psychotherapy which aims to alleviate emotional problems by helping individuals to identify and change faulty patterns of thinking. It is based on a cognitive model of emotional disorders (Beck, 1976). The central notion in this model is the idea that it is not events *per se* but rather people's *interpretations of events* which are responsible for the production of negative emotions such as anxiety, anger or depression. The interpretations considered important in *depression* relate to perceived loss of a relationship, status or efficacy. In *anxiety* the important interpretations, or cognitions, relate to perceived danger of such a loss, or of damage, sickness or death. Clearly, there are numerous occasions on which individuals experience genuine loss or are in objectively dangerous situations. Furthermore, many cases of anxiety and depression are triggered by adverse life events. However, cognitive theorists claim that, in pathological mood states, thinking is unrealistic in the sense that it involves an over-estimate of the loss or danger inherent in the person's situation, and that it is this *distorted* pattern of thinking which helps to maintain emotional disorders.

Cognitive therapy aims to modify individuals' interpretations of events, substituting unhelpful ways of thinking with more functional ones. Behavioural tasks are often used to help achieve this aim. However, the term 'cognitive' therapy is used because all the treatment procedures (whether 'cognitive' or 'behavioural') are explicitly aimed at modifying dysfunctional thinking. Cognitive therapy was originally developed as a treatment for depression, and then anxiety, but has now been adapted to treat a wider variety of disorders. In particular, new developments offer patients and therapists hope for the treatment of more difficult psychiatric disorders, such as treatment-resistant psychosis. In this chapter, a general description of the cognitive approach is provided, followed by specific treatment methods, including a description of procedures used in cognitive therapy psychosis.

Reciprocal Relationship between Thinking, Emotion and Behaviour

The cognitive model of emotional disorders assumes that there is a series of reciprocal relationships between thinking and behaviour, and between thinking and emotion. Examples of some of these reciprocal relationships, which play a key role in maintaining emotional states, are given below.

- Research into the effects of mood on memory (Teasdale, 1983) indicates that depressed mood facilitates the retrieval from memory of negative information and impairs retrieval of positive information. When taken in conjunction with the suggestion that certain types of negative thoughts produce depressed mood, this work indicates that a depressed person is trapped in a vicious circle in which negative thinking produces depressed mood and then depressed mood increases the probability of those negative thoughts which are likely to cause a further increase in depression, so perpetuating the disorder.
- A second vicious circle also exists in depression. Believing that they are ineffective and likely to fail, depressed people often withdraw from everyday activities. This means that they are unlikely to experience any positive interactions which might contradict their negative view of themselves and hence alleviate their depression.
- In *anxiety*, three further sets of vicious circles exist. First, once a person sees a situation as dangerous, he or she selectively attends to information which might strengthen the perception of danger. For example, a speaker who is anxious might look round the audience, notice that there are a few people at the back who seem to be going to sleep, and then think, 'They have already decided the talk is useless, and everyone else is going to start nodding off soon. I'm boring them'. Second, the symptoms of anxiety are often interpreted as further sources of danger producing a further vicious circle which tends to maintain or exacerbate an anxiety reaction. For example, blushing may be taken as an indication that one has made a fool of oneself leading to further embarrassment and blushing; a shaking hand may be taken as an indication of impending loss of control leading to more anxiety and shaking; or a racing heart may be taken as evidence of an impending heart attack, producing further anxiety and cardiac

symptoms. Third, anxious individuals engage in 'safety seeking behaviours' that are intended to prevent feared catastrophes from occurring. However, as their fears are unrealistic, the real function of the safety behaviours is to prevent disconfirmation of negative beliefs. For example, a socially anxious person who is concerned that other people will think he is boring, might make conscious efforts to remember what he has just said and compare it with what he is about to say while in a middle of a conversation. If the conversation seems to go well, his belief that he is fundamentally boring will not be changed because he will think 'I only got away with it because I engaged in the safety behaviour'. In addition, the safety behaviour may, paradoxically, lead other people to behave less warmly towards him because his mental preoccupation will make it appear that he is bored with them. In this way the safety behaviour confirms the negative belief.

• The reciprocal relationship between perceived danger and symptoms of anxiety plays a particularly important role in patients who suffer from panic attacks. The latter consist of a sudden onset, intense feeling of apprehension or impending doom associated with a range of physical sensations. Cognitive theories of panic propose that such attacks are caused by the misinterpretation of normal bodily sensations as indications of an impending physical or mental catastrophe (for example, perceiving palpitations as evidence of an impending heart attack, or perceiving unusual and racing thoughts as evidence that one is about to go mad). Such interpretations set up a vicious circle in which negative thoughts, anxiety and body sensations mutually *reinforce* each other. Figure 9.1 illustrates this process in a specific panic attack. Dotted lines indicate the way in which safety behaviours: (a) prevent disconfirmation of the patient's fears, and (b) exacerbate some of the physical sensations that accompany a panic attack.

Features of Cognitive Therapy

The suggestion that emotional disorders are maintained by unrealistic thinking leads naturally to the idea that emotional problems can be treated by teaching people to identify, evaluate and change their distorted thoughts and associated behaviours. A variety of cognitive and behavioural techniques are used to achieve this aim. Behavioural techniques play an important part in therapy because certain types of behaviour (such as avoidance and safety behaviours) help to maintain distorted beliefs. Also, one of the most effective ways of modifying beliefs is to test them out in real life.

Cognitive therapy is a relatively brief and time-limited treatment (between five and 25 weekly sessions) which aims to teach patients a series of skills that they can use not only to overcome their current difficul-

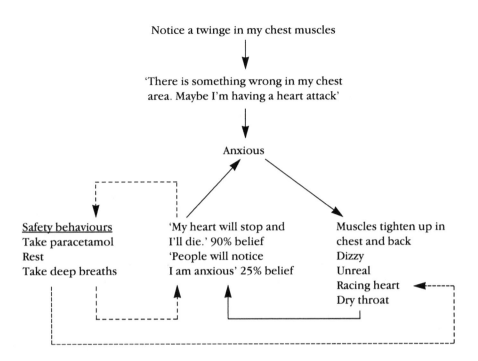

Figure 9.1 A specific panic attack. Reproduced with permission from Clark (1996).

ties, but also to deal with future emotional problems and setbacks. Therapy sessions are highly structured. They begin by setting an agenda, which lists items to be dealt with during the session. Patient and therapist agree the contents of the agenda. This usually includes a review of the previous week's homework and then covers one or two specific problems which will be the main focus of the session. Within the session, frequent feedback is used to guarantee mutual understanding and the session ends with a homework assignment which follows up the topic discussed during the session.

At the start of treatment, therapists aim to demonstrate the connection between thoughts and feelings (emotions). This can be done by reviewing examples from the patient's own experience and also by discussing hypothetical situations, for example imagining how you would feel if you are at home one night, heard a crash in another room, and then thought 'there is a burglar in the room', or instead, thought 'the window was left open and the wind has blown something over'. Similarly, a pounding heart experienced in anxiety states may be perceived as unpleasant, but when experienced as exciting; the same sensations are experienced, for example, when in love, or on a roller coaster ride they may be experienced as exciting. The cardinal difference will be the *appraisal* of the sensations. For some patients, it is also necessary to clarify the difference between thoughts and feelings to establish the existence of thought–feeling links.

Patients are trained to identify the cognitions that are associated with disturbed emotions. Sometimes these are images rather than thoughts, and initially can be difficult to identify, partly because they are very brief and come to mind without conscious effort. Negative automatic thoughts (NATs) are associated with thinking errors which will be described below. Once identified, attempts are made to modify the thoughts. Although therapists may be convinced of the irrationality of their patient's thoughts, they should not 'lecture' their patients. Instead, therapy is a collaborative exercise similar to that of a scientific team. Patients' thoughts are treated as hypotheses, with therapist and patient together collecting data to determine whether the hypotheses are accurate or helpful. The two main sources of data are discussion and behavioural experiments.

As previously mentioned, patients tend to make consistent errors in their thinking (see Beck, 1995, pp. 118–119). As the cognitive therapist needs to be aware of these *thinking errors*, a description is given below.

Although perception of an event may take place, the patient may selectively attend to negative aspects of a situation (**mental filter**) and disqualify positive events as 'not counting' (**disqualifying the positive**). Depressed individuals may jump to conclusions (**jumping to conclusions**) that others think negatively of them (**mind reading**) without evidence to support this belief and be convinced that they were personally responsible (**personalization**) for some negative event, even when this was not the case. The experience of negative emotions may reinforce a belief (**emotional reasoning**). Patients have a tendency to see things in absolute black and white terms (**all or nothing thinking**). If they perceive themselves as falling short of perfection, this thinking style encourages them to flip to the other side of the coin and see themselves as a total failure. Furthermore, there is a tendency to see a negative event as a never-ending pattern of defeat (**over-generalization**). Depressed individuals predict negative outcomes (**fortune telling**), make mountains out of molehills (**magnification and catastrophizing**) and belittle their own achievements (**minimization**). These thinking styles are further complicated by the individual's tendency to make demands of themselves and others (**should, must statements — making demands**) and feel angry or upset if these expectations are not realized, so that a belief arises that he or she is a failure and deserves to be punished. In addition, patients may form a negative image of themselves, which adds little to overcoming the problem (**labelling**). Fortunately, there are a number of techniques which are suitable to tackling these different thinking errors, which are described below.

Table 9.1 A daily record of dysfunctional thoughts

Situation Describe: 1. Actual event leading to unpleasant emotion, or 2. Stream of thoughts, daydream, or recollection, leading to unpleasant emotion	Emotions 1. Specify sad/anxious/angry 2. Rate degree of emotion, 1–100	Automatic thoughts 1. Write automatic thought(s) that preceded emotion(s) 2. Rate belief in automatic thought(s), 0–100%	Rational response 1. Write rational response to automatic thought(s) 2. Rate belief in rational response, 0–100%	Outcome 1. Re-rate belief in automatic thought(s) 0–100% 2. Specify and rate subsequent emotions, 0–100	Further action
Attending a social function at my husband's work. Don't know many people and most of them know each other. Not being included in the conversation.	1. Anxious 2. 70	1. I am boring tonight	There are lots of explanations for people having difficulty talking to a stranger other than finding them boring. Also I'm not evaluating other people so why should they be evaluating me	1. 10% 2. Anx. 0	Next time: 1. Give the other people some 'free information' about me to help them include me in their conversation 2. Ask them about themselves 3. Stop mind reading
		This means I'm a boring person	If I am boring tonight that doesn't mean I'm always boring. Anyway nobody is boring through and through		
		Everyone hates a boring person therefore nobody will like me	You don't have to be the life and soul of the party to be liked. Many 'quiet' people are liked and loved by others		
In supermarket, suddenly felt faint, hot and breathless	Panic 90	1. I'm going to collapse/faint 2. 80%	Just because I feel faint it doesn't mean to say I will faint. I've never fainted before when anxious. Furthermore one needs a blood pressure drop in order to faint and blood pressure is up in anxiety so I'm less likely to faint than if calm. I feel faint because of overbreathing and blood going to muscles. Both normal responses. 2. 95%	1. 10% 2. Panic 10	Next time as soon as I *feel* faint, rehearse answers to my thoughts, control breathing and check my pulse to see if my heart is beating which means it is strong

Verbal Challenging of Negative Thoughts

A daily record of dysfunctional thoughts is shown in Table 9.1. This sheet is used to record and evaluate negative thoughts. Several illustrations of such thoughts and patients' responses to them are given in the table.

Within treatment sessions, therapists ask a series of questions which are aimed at helping patients to identify rational answers to their negative thoughts. As elements of the therapy may be forgotten, sessions may be tape-recorded. This is a particularly helpful adjunct to treatment for patients who have concentration difficulties or do not like writing their thoughts down. The patient is encouraged to identify the cognitive distortions and replace the unhelpful (dysfunctional) thoughts with more functional ones. Between sessions, patients attempt to put into practice the self-evaluation skills they have learned in sessions by recording and challenging negative thoughts as they arise. Examples of some of the questions which are particularly useful in helping patients to identify answers to their negative thoughts are: 'What evidence do I have for this thought?', 'Is there an alternative way of looking at the situation?', 'How would someone else think in my situation?', 'Am I setting myself an unrealistic or unobtainable standard?' and 'Am I thinking in all-or-nothing terms?' In general, therapists prefer not to answer negative thoughts themselves, but instead ask questions that help patients to produce their own answers. This 'Socratic' style is used because research in social psychology suggests that people are more likely to believe information that contradicts their beliefs if they produce it themselves.

Emotional meanings can be represented in images as well as thoughts, and sometimes imagery exercises are required to fully transform meanings. For example, a mother who developed post-traumatic stress disorder (PTSD) following the death of her child in a house fire was greatly troubled by the idea that the child had died in agony. Discussion revealed that the fire had not reached the child, who was instead overcome by carbon monoxide fumes while asleep. This intervention had no impact until the mother vividly visualized the events, including all the corrective information.

Behavioural Experiments

In addition to discussing the evidence for and against negative beliefs, cognitive therapists also encourage patients to engage in behavioural experiments to test out their beliefs. An example of a behavioural experiment is provided by the case of a housewife who experienced frequent panic attacks which were frightening because she believed they meant she had a serious cardiac condition. Negative medical tests and reassurance from her physician failed to modify this belief. However, reproduction of her feared symptoms by voluntary hyperventilation allowed her to entertain the idea that her symptoms might be partly due to a stress-induced event. Her objection that she noticed her heartbeat most of the time, and that this must indicate that there was something wrong with her heart, was countered with the alternative suggestion that she noticed her heartbeat more because of her *fears*, which led her to focus on her body. To test this suggestion, she was asked to close her eyes and concentrate on her heartbeat. To her surprise she found that simply attending to her heartbeat enabled her to detect her pulse throughout her body and reproduce her most alarming symptoms.

Assumption Techniques

As well as dealing with specific thoughts that occur in particular situations, therapists also attempt to challenge general beliefs (dysfunctional assumptions), which may make an individual prone to becoming depressed or anxious in the first place. For example, a generally anxious patient who frequently has the thought, 'I will never get everything done', may be prone to this thought because of an extreme perfectionist belief such as 'I always have to do things perfectly'. One technique which could be used to challenge this belief would be discussion of its advantages and disadvantages. This discussion would reveal that the advantages of the belief (it can sometimes produce very good work) are vastly outweighed by its disadvantages (it produces considerable anxiety which prevents you from doing your best; it makes you unwilling to take risks, unnecessarily restricting your range and preventing you from making the mistakes which are necessary for learning; it does not allow you to let mistakes be noticed by others and therefore prevents you from obtaining valuable feedback).

Dealing with Thinking Errors

Some techniques suitable for the thinking errors described above are given below.

Methods for dealing with 'mental filtering' and 'disqualifying the positive'

A useful technique for patients who select negative aspects of a situation is to ask them to write down a **balance sheet** of evidence for and against the belief. This may be backed up by behavioural tasks which encourage them to check out others' beliefs. It is, nevertheless, important to ensure that patients select others with functional beliefs, otherwise the exercise may reinforce their own dysfunctional belief. For example, a patient suffering from a dirt phobia may have his or her belief about the possibility of contamination reinforced by another dirt-phobic patient. Patients may also be asked to increase their awareness of positive events.

Methods for dealing with 'fortune telling' (jumping to conclusions)

Patients may be asked to list their negative predictions and then undertake behavioural tasks to test whether their predictions are correct. As a number of outcomes may be dependent on their approach, it is important to consider how an individual's behaviour may influence the outcome. For example, depressed individuals may predict that whenever they go into a shop the shop assistant does not smile at them. They may be asked to go into the shop on several occasions, sometimes being bright and chatty and sometimes behaving in a depressed way. In this way individuals may test out their negative predictions.

Methods for dealing with 'mind reading'

Patients may be asked to verify the other person's belief. However, it is important to point out to patients that they may place themselves in a no-win situation, so just as they may disqualify a positive response as part of the respondent's innate niceness, so they need to collect other information which may disconfirm the belief.

Methods for dealing with 'personalization'

The therapist asks individuals what evidence there is that the other person is specifically reacting to them negatively. They are asked to observe the other person in a variety of other situations and collect information on the person's negative behaviour to others.

Methods for dealing with 'emotional reasoning'

The use of flash cards, index cards upon which the patient writes down helpful statements, for example, 'Even if I feel this strongly, it does not mean this is true' or 'I have felt this way before and have been wrong' can be useful.

Methods for dealing with 'all or nothing thinking'

All or nothing thinking (dichotomous reasoning) is one of the most prominent cognitive distortions and may be illustrated by use of visual analogue scales. For example, patients may hold the belief that 'people are either completely good or completely bad'. They should be asked to rate the degree of the belief. A visual analogue scale of the two extremes should then be drawn with the two extremes at either end. Patients should then be asked to indicate where they place themselves, as show in Figure 9.2.

Then the patient should be asked questions such as 'Where would you place Mother Theresa, Adolf Hitler, the man who lives next door (etc.)?' Patients should then be asked to re-rate the degree to which they hold the belief. Patients' view of themselves have become less polarized into two categories (dichotomous reasoning) (Figure 9.3).

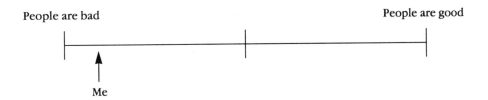

Figure 9.2 Visual analogue scale to represent patients' 'all or nothing' thinking.

Figure 9.3 Visual analogue scale to represent patients' restructured belief.

Methods of dealing with 'over-generalization'

Similar pictorial exercises may be performed using pie charts to illustrate over-generalization and magnification. Patients should be asked to draw a wedge in a pie chart to signify the proportion of the pie chart the belief takes up. For example, if a patient believes he or she has to be thin to be liked, he or she should be asked to represent that pictorially, as shown in Figure 9.4.

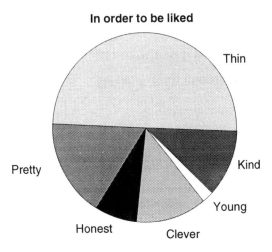

Figure 9.4 Pie chart to represent patients' over-generalization that thinness is a prerequisite of being liked.

Patients should be asked to list all factors which may make a person liked (or disliked). They are then asked to fit wedges on the pie chart which make up being liked. As can be seen from the pie chart, the degree to which patients believe that thinness is linked to size and shape is reduced (Figure 9.5).

In order to be liked

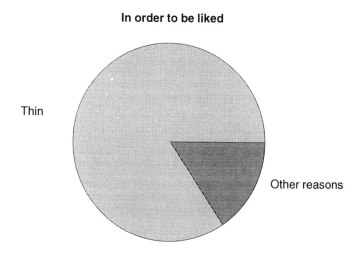

Figure 9.5 Pie chart to help patients' restructured beliefs.

Methods of dealing with 'magnification' and 'catastrophizing'

Judicious use of humour. By exaggerating the situation patients may see how unreasonable the thinking is. It is, however, important to do this in a way in which patients do not think they are being ridiculed. Visual analogue scales, described above, are also a useful technique in this instance.

Methods for dealing with 'labelling'

Patients may be encouraged to use imagery and role play to adopt a more positive image of themselves. For example, the submissive housewife who sees herself as a mouse could be asked to stand on a table and look down on her bombastic husband.

Methods of dealing with 'making demands'

A useful approach may be to adopt a philosophical or debating style by asking the patient to play devil's advocate. For example, by asking patients who are suffering from guilt, 'If it were someone you liked, would you think it is reasonable to punish them in the same way that you punish yourself?'

Cognitive Therapy in Psychosis (see also Chapter 9)

Cognitive therapy in schizophrenia was first described by Beck (1952). However, it is only recently that randomized controlled trials using cognitive behaviour therapy (CBT) as a treatment have been reported. Findings suggest that CBT substantially reduces the risk of relapse (Jones et al., 1998). A number of approaches have been described (e.g. Kingdon and Turkington, 1994). Cognitive treatments adopt the rationale that some of the symptoms (delusions and hallucinations) in schizophrenia may be viewed as points on a functional continuum. It is accepted that individuals who do not have schizophrenia may hold a number of beliefs without evidence, but in psychosis these beliefs are more firmly held and not understandable within the cultural context of the individual. It is also recognized that hallucinatory experiences may be part of normal experience, although in patients with schizophrenia, these experiences are more extreme and possibly less easily controlled. Emergence of symptoms and relapse of illness is also affected by raised anxiety levels. Dysfunctional assumptions discourage patients from reality-testing their beliefs. Labelling of patients and others as 'mad' is unlikely to help them to question their beliefs, but rather more likely to force them into a polarized position. These cognitive processes are further complicated by such patients' difficulties in reading non-verbal cues and communicating clearly with others. Furthermore, patients' behaviour may provoke hostile reactions in others, fuelling and reinforcing paranoid beliefs.

Using a collaborative process, the therapist targets the less firmly held beliefs first. Patients are helped to see their symptoms as part of a continuum ('normalizing rationale'). Cognitive techniques help patients to question the strength of the belief, the consequence of relinquishing the belief and also encourages the joint discovery of alternative explanations. Keeping a record of factors which exacerbate or alleviate hallucinatory experiences may be helpful in developing coping strategies. As symptoms may be associated with raised anxiety, reducing this may be helpful in disconfirming the belief that patients have no control over their illness. Patients are also encouraged to consider the effect their appearance and behaviour may have on others and consider alternative interpretations (other than paranoid) for other people's responses. For example, 'What would be your reaction if you were sitting in a café and the person near you was muttering and shouting?' Patients may then be asked to test various options by use of a variety of behavioural tasks and report back at the next therapy session. Improving insight and helping patients to restructure their beliefs about their illness should further facilitate engagement and compliance with medication (see Chapter 8).

In conclusion, although cognitive techniques may not always abolish psychotic symptoms, they may be useful in helping patients to gain insight into their illness; decatastrophizing the stigma associated with this; reducing the severity and frequency of symptoms; and helping them to adopt a more realistic understanding of how their behaviour may affect the reactions of others. Cognitive techniques are generally used in conjunction with medication.

Effectiveness of Cognitive Therapy

Cognitive therapy is a relatively recent development in psychotherapy. So far, controlled trials of the effectiveness of cognitive therapy have focused largely on its use as a treatment for depression, anxiety and eating disorders (see Clark and Fairburn, 1997; Hollon and Beck, 1994 for recent reviews). In *depression*, studies assessing immediate response to treatment indicate that cognitive therapy is at least as effective as tricyclic antidepressants and there is some evidence that cognitive therapy may be more effective at reducing relapse. In *anxiety*, cognitive therapy has been shown to be an effective treatment for social phobia, generalized anxiety disorder, panic disorder, hypochondriasis and post-traumatic stress disorder. In each of these conditions, cognitive therapy has been shown to be superior to alternative treatments that control for non-specific therapy factors, such as repeated assessment, expectation of improvement and therapist attention. In many anxiety disorders, cognitive therapy also compares favourably with well-conducted behavioural treatment. The successes of cognitive therapy in depression and anxiety, and more recently, in those with schizophrenia (Jones et al., 1998) has encouraged research workers to develop cognitive approaches to the treatment of other problems, such as personality disorders (Beck and Freeman, 1990) and substance abuse (Beck et al., 1993). The results of controlled trials evaluating the effectiveness of cognitive therapy in these areas are eagerly awaited.

References

BECK, A.T. (1952). Successful outpatient psychotherapy of a chronic schizophrenic with a delusion based on borrowed guilt. *Psychiatry* **15**, 305–312.

BECK, A.T. (1976). *Cognitive Therapy and the Emotional Disorders*. New York: International University Press.

BECK, A.T. (1995). *Cognitive Therapy: Basics and Beyond*. New York: Guilford Press.

BECK, A.T. and FREEMAN, A. (1990). *Cognitive Therapy of Personality Disorders*. New York: Guilford Press.

BECK, A.T., WRIGHT, F.D., NEWMAN, C.F. and LIESE, B.S. (1993). *Cognitive Therapy of Substance Abuse*. New York: Guilford Press.

CLARK, D.M. (1996). Panic disorder: from theory to therapy. In P.M. Salkovskis, ed, *Frontiers in Cognitive Therapy*. New York: Guilford Press; 318–344.

CLARK, D.M. and FAIRBURN, C.G. (1997). *Science and Practice of Cognitive Behaviour Therapy*. Oxford: Oxford University Press.

HOLLON, S.D. and BECK, A.T. (1994). Cognitive and cognitive–behavioural therapies. In A.E. Bergin and S.L. Garfield, eds, *Handbook of Psychotherapy and Behavioral Change*. New York: Wiley; 428–466.

JONES, C., CORMAC, L., MOTA, J., CAMPBELL, C. (1998). Cognitive behaviour therapy for schizophrenia (Colchrane Review). *The Colchrane Library*, Issue 1. Oxford: Update Software.

KINGDON, D.E. and TURKINGTON, D. (1994). *Cognitive Therapy of Schizophrenia*. Hove: Lawrence Erlbaum.

TEASDALE, J.D. (1983). Negative thinking in depression: cause, effect or reciprocal relationship? *Advances in Behaviour Research and Therapy* 5, 3–25.

Further Reading

The following books are recommended for readers interested in a more detailed description of how to do cognitive therapy.

BECK, A.T., RUSH, A.J., SHAW, B.F. and EMERY, G. (1979). *Cognitive Therapy of Depression*. New York: Guilford Press.

BECK, A.T., EMERY, G. and GREENBERG, R.L. (1985). *Anxiety Disorders and Phobias*. New York: Basic Books.

BURNS, D. (1980). *Feeling Good*. New York: New American Library.

HAWTON, K., SALKOVSKIS, P., KIRK, J. and CLARK, D.M. (1989). *Cognitive Behaviour Therapy for Psychiatric Problems: A Practical Guide*. Oxford: Oxford University Press.

PADESKY, C. and GREENBERGER, M. (1995). *Clinicians Guide to Mind over Mood*. New York: Guilford Press.

Chapter 10
Behaviour Therapy

ALAN KING

Although behaviour therapy is a relatively straightforward form of psychological treatment, an adequate definition of it is, necessarily, rather lengthy. Unlike most other forms of psychotherapy, it cannot be entirely defined on the basis of theory. Its effects, and various phenomena which have been observed during research into behaviour therapy, have been partially explained in terms of learning theory which derives from the work of Pavlov and of Skinner into classical and operant conditioning. Learning theory has not, however, proved to be a perfect model. In fact, the techniques which so characterize behaviour therapy are used not because their effect has been predicted according to theory, but because experience has demonstrated it. Furthermore, many of the techniques of modern behaviour therapy can be traced back to methods of treatment described in medical writings which long predate the evolution of learning theory. Behaviour therapy, therefore, is essentially *empirical* rather than theoretical and is best defined in descriptive terms.

Just as characteristic as its techniques, with their emphasis upon overt behaviour, is the particular approach which behaviour therapy takes towards clinical problems. In contrast to other forms of psychotherapy, which seek to examine the historical antecedents of a problem, behaviour therapy is *symptom-oriented*. As far as the behaviourist is concerned symptoms include not only the subjective experiences that tell us that we are unwell, but inappropriate behaviours, disturbing thoughts and abnormal emotional states. Behaviour therapy is directed towards the relief of these symptoms and this has made it relatively easy to establish specific therapeutic goals, a feature which gives behaviour therapy some of its structure. This is reinforced by the use of written or oral contracts and by the application of specified *time limits*, which are negotiated before treatment begins. Time limiting a treatment programme is possible because behavioural treatments tend to be *short term* so that the likely duration of therapy can be predicted. The precise duration of treatment is variable, depending upon the condition that is being treated, but six to ten sessions represent an average therapeutic investment. The therapist's style is outstandingly *directive* rather than reflective or interpretive and he or she, as well as the subject, takes an *active* role in treatment, with *collaboration* between them being an intrinsic feature of the process.

Behaviour therapy has been applied with varying degrees of success in a wide range of disorders, and new applications continue to be discovered. As far as its *clinical uses* are concerned, there is a spectrum of therapeutic styles which reflects differences in the various problems it is used to treat, and in the clientèle which presents them. On one hand, subjects who have a neurotic disorder tend to be well motivated for change through treatment. They are usually their own advocates and, as well as a behavioural component, their complaints include physical and emotional symptoms which are causing distress. By contrast, subjects in an institution for the chronically mentally disordered are generally poorly motivated for change. Usually, the complaint is made by a member of staff and is confined specifically to a subject's behaviour. These differences require rather distinct therapeutic approaches.

In the management of neurosis, negotiation and explanation are fundamental features. Therapy is client-directed, subjects are responsible for seeing through their own programmes and the observations by which progress is judged are based mainly upon their own subjective experience and personal records. However, although the results that can be achieved using operant methods in the management of the chronically mentally disordered do appear to improve if effective negotiation and explanation are possible, these features are rather less important here than they are in the treatment of neurosis. At the same time, subjects' conscious co-operation and collaboration tend to be equally less crucial. Finally, operant programmes are under the control of staff who also carry out the observations and data recording by which treatment progress is measured.

Behaviour Therapy in the Neuroses

Assessment

Identification of the problem is the first task. Depending upon whose opinion is asked, there may be several views about what constitutes the problem. Initially, at least, subjects' own views, defined as clearly and as free from jargon as possible, are the ones that are adopted. Alternatives are recorded and introduced later if necessary. A full psychiatric assessment will identify important aspects, such as current life stresses and any co-existing physical or psychiatric disorder that may influence a behavioural treatment.

Details of past and present treatment may suggest interventions that are likely to prove effective, and the assessment is not complete without some enquiry into the use of alcohol and tranquillizers, both of which can interfere with some forms of behavioural treatment.

The rest of the assessment, called a *functional* or *behavioural* analysis, is characteristic of the behavioural approach. This consists of a highly detailed account of the current determinants of the problem rather than of its historical antecedents. Predisposing factors, such as heredity or early formative experiences, indicate why a subject should develop this particular problem and not another. Precipitating factors, such as major life events, tell us why the problem should develop when it did. Behaviour therapy, however, is interested in a third group — the perpetuating factors. These are the 'here and now' reasons why the problem has continued long after the precipitating factors have ceased to exert their effect. If the perpetuating factors can be overcome then the problem ought to improve.

The analysis is made easier by examining the perpetuating factors under three headings (Figure 10.1): the 'As', 'Bs' and the 'Cs'.

Antecedents ('As')

The antecedents, or cues, may be external or internal. External cues include objects, situations, animals or people which immediately evoke subjects' symptoms. If these symptoms can be reproduced during the

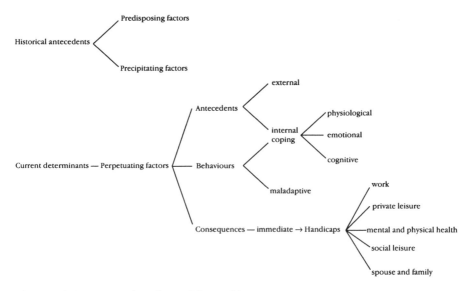

Figure 10.1 Functional analysis of the problem.

assessment session, either by introducing a relevant cue or by instructing the subject to carry out a simple manoeuvre such as overbreathing, immediate access is gained to the second group of cues. Internal cues are (1) *physical*, such as the bodily experiences that result from the physiological accompaniments of anxiety, (2) *emotional*, such as the fear experienced by phobic subjects and (3) *cognitive*, such as the disturbing thoughts and images that are so much a part of neurotic disorders.

Behaviours ('Bs')

These are the subject's overt responses. Those which maintain and strengthen the problem also restrict the subject's life in some way. They include avoidance, escape behaviours and ritualistic behaviours such as checking, cleaning and repeating. Sometimes the subject has discovered ways of coping with his problem such that the restrictions to his life are minimized. One of the tasks of treatment may be to improve upon these at the same time as overcoming the maladaptive behaviours by which subjects' lives are handicapped.

Consequences ('Cs')

Although the subject's response to his discomfort has the effect of relieving it, this occurs at the *price* of ever-increasing restrictions to his life. In addition, maladaptive behaviours are reinforced by the very fact that they relieve discomfort immediately. The problem may be made worse by the efforts of family and friends who, in their desire to be of help and to deal with the problem, inadvertently reinforce it.

Eventually, as the disorder develops, immediate restrictions become major handicaps which are commonly the reasons why professional help is sought. Important areas of life which are affected include work, personal leisure, domestic functioning and interpersonal relationships. As well as causing handicaps in just those areas that will later provide an arena for the subject to tackle his problem, neurotic disorders cause secondary handicaps in other areas of life which may not be directly related to the initial problem.

Preparing for treatment

By ensuring that the subject fully understands the principles and implications of behaviour therapy and that he knows what is likely to be expected of him in treatment, the therapist is able to maximize the chances that treatment will be accepted, and minimize the risk of subsequent drop-out. A Socratic method of explanation complements the commonsense approach of behaviour therapy. The rationale of treatment is explained and any odd ideas the subject may have about behaviour therapy are examined so that they do not discourage him from agreeing to a programme which is otherwise acceptable. Any distressing physical symptoms are discussed in full and their psychophysiological basis is explained. This indicates not only that therapists appreciate their subject's distress, but the more understanding the subject has of the nature of his symptoms, the less they will bother him and the less he will be troubled by fears of their possible consequences.

An explanation about treatment should cover several points:

- Treatment is *client-directed*: nothing is done without prior negotiation, no surprises are sprung upon the unsuspecting subject and his agreement is sought before any potentially distressing procedure is introduced. The therapist should always be prepared to take the same risks as those expected of a client.
- Most progress will be made *between* treatment sessions, during which time the subject is expected to complete, regularly and frequently, agreed 'homework' tasks. These may be time consuming, so the subject's application is essential and other activities may have to be relegated in importance, at least until treatment is completed.
- It is likely, although not essential for treatment to be effective, that programmes involving exposure to feared situations will evoke discomfort. However, this discomfort will decline, or habituate, if exposure is sufficiently prolonged. For the subject's benefit, habituation can be demonstrated either by devising an anxiety-provoking situation during the interview or by pointing out the way in which the subject's interview-related anxiety has declined since the start of the session.
- Tasks are tackled in a gradual fashion so that initial success with easier tasks restores confidence for more difficult ones. A formal hierarchy may be used but is not essential. Tasks should be repeatable and, as well as being components of treatment, it is ideal if they involve an additional pay-off for the subject.
- Treatment is usually time limited. Progress is reassessed after an agreed number of sessions to decide whether further contact is likely to be worthwhile.
- A friend or relative may be recruited and 'trained' to act as a co-therapist because it is unlikely that the therapist will be able to afford sufficient time to supervise all sessions.
- Before treatment begins, specific *therapeutic targets* are established for each problem. Targets should be:
    (a) precisely described in behavioural terms;
    (b) realistic;
    (c) relevant to the problem and representative of progress;

(d) morally and legally acceptable;
(e) desirable for the subject.

Recreating the subject's problems and symptoms during the assessment session is a great help towards deciding whether behavioural methods will be both suitable and acceptable. The height phobic, for example, may be asked to climb as far as he can up a fire-escape. This simple manoeuvre, called a *behavioural test*, not only leaves the subject in no doubt as to what may be expected of him in treatment, but it provides an unambiguous behavioural measure of the severity of the problem and indicates the level at which treatment must begin. It is also a convenient moment to test whether behavioural methods are likely to prove effective. The therapist uses prompting, praise and modelling to persuade the subject to improve upon his performance. The longer the subject tolerates the situation, the more likely his symptoms are to habituate and the more progress he will make. Performance here is a good indicator of how co-operative the subject will be in treatment and the therapist is given an opportunity to identify and discuss the subject's current coping strategies and any irrational ideas which might be maintaining his symptoms unnecessarily. It is, of course, a first step in treatment and, if it is carried out properly, *a test of behaviour therapy* leaves the subject with a sense of achievement from the first contact.

Measurement and record keeping

Behaviour therapists like their subjects to measure items such as symptom severity, problem severity and the degree of handicap in key areas of life. Measures applied before and after treatment and at follow-up indicate treatment progress, overall effectiveness and the durability of treatment. The ease of measurement has not only made efficacy studies possible, but it has important clinical implications, because the subject discovers that limits can now be applied to a symptom or problem which previously seemed to be boundless.

Standard questionnaires are available for some items but, for a symptom such as anxiety, a simple, visual analogue scale is quite sufficient. Its range is a matter of personal preference. Some therapists like to use a scale of 0 – 8 and others prefer 0 – 100. In either case, 0 represents the total absence of the symptom and the top of the scale represents the most severe the symptom has ever been. Somewhere between the two is a level at which the symptom becomes tolerable. It may be useful to incorporate this level into treatment targets. With a little instruction on the use of these scales, most subjects achieve a level of reliability from which treatment progress can be assessed.

Behaviour therapists also like their subjects to keep records in the form of a *daily diary*. This would contain information about task completion and associated symptom severity. A diary is also useful for getting at the cognitive components of a problem, because relevant details can be recorded as they occur. As well as providing information for the subject and therapist to process at their next meeting, the need to produce a diary encourages work on task assignments. The effort which has gone into producing a diary is also a good indicator of motivation in cases of doubt.

Factors influencing suitability for treatment

In the individual case, suitability for treatment depends upon certain features of the problem and upon factors in the client. The problem should be:

- Current.
- Predictable.
- Repetitive.
- Describable in behavioural terms.
- Sufficiently disabling to warrant the necessary therapeutic investment.

The client should:

- Understand and accept treatment.
- Not exhibit any psychiatric disorder which would contraindicate the use of behaviour therapy. No contraindications are absolute but four are important:
    - (a) severe depression;
    - (b) some forms of organic brain damage;
    - (c) active psychosis;
    - (d) a disorder of personality which results in subject's inability to stick to a structured treatment programme.

The diagnosis alone is a reliable guide as to whether a problem is likely to be suitable for behaviour therapy. For some conditions, behaviour therapy is the treatment of choice. These are:

- Simple phobias.
- Social anxiety and social skills dysfunction.
- Agoraphobia.
- Obsessive–compulsive rituals.
- Psychosexual dysfunction.
- Some childhood disorders such as school refusal.

There are many other conditions in which behaviour therapy has a role, though not necessarily as the treatment of choice. This list is not exhaustive.

- Depression.
- Alcoholism.
- Drug abuse.
- Smoking.
- Appetitive disorders.
- Habit disorders and tics.
- Hypochondriasis.
- Obsessional thoughts and ruminations.
- Grief reactions.
- Anxiety states.
- Marital dysfunction.
- Child abuse.
- Compulsive gambling.
- Some childhood disorders.

Working out a treatment package

The range of techniques which is available usually means that more than one approach can be offered to treat any given problem. In many cases, a package consisting of various techniques is used. Therapists may present the full range of techniques to the subject, cafeteria-style, with advice about the implications of each. The subject may be given the choice of those which he thinks will suit him best, though it must be said that therapists do guide the choice and would strongly advise a technique if it was particularly indicated for a specific problem.

As treatment progresses, the focus of therapy may switch from one problem to another. This is not unreasonable and behaviour therapy is flexible enough to accommodate such changes. However, the experienced therapist is always alert to the subject whose attention shifts from problem to problem so frequently that it is impossible to do much effective work upon any of them.

Efficacy, limitations and therapeutic failures

The disorders in which behaviour therapy may be usefully employed account for one in eight of psychiatric outpatient referrals. The effectiveness of behaviour therapy has been demonstrated in a number of controlled trials and single-case studies, but it has its critics. For example, because behaviour therapy is oriented towards the relief of symptoms, it has been suggested that its failure to deal with any underlying neurotic conflict might result in the emergence of fresh symptoms, a phenomenon known as *symptom substitution*. In fact, what evidence there is suggests that this occurs rarely, if at all. Furthermore, treatment gains appear not only to be maintained in the long run, but there is a progressive improvement in various areas of life following behaviour therapy.

Behavioural programmes are, however, not always successful. There are several reasons for this, some of which are avoidable. The most common, perhaps, is subjects' failure to comply with the agreed treatment programme. This may be because treatment tasks are too difficult or because co-existing life stresses are interfering with therapy. Some subjects are discouraged by counter-instructions from friends, neighbours, or family. Obsessional subjects may use mental 'tricks' or *internal avoidance* to 'make good' the omission of ritual. Where exposure methods are used, too short an exposure session is not only ineffective but may even make the problem worse, and there is a very small group of subjects whose anxiety fails to habituate even with prolonged exposure. Occasionally, the problem has been misidentified, with the result that treatment targets are wrong. Finally, there may be a co-existing psychiatric disorder, such as depression. Severe depression interferes with between-session improvements, even when there is good progress within treatment sessions. It must be treated before lasting therapeutic gains can be made.

Behaviour Therapy in Institutions

The skills which are required for independent living are frequently deficient in the behavioural repertoire of subjects who are cared for in the institutions for the chronically mentally disordered. In mental handicap these skills may never have been acquired and in chronic mental illness, particularly in chronic schizophrenia, skills may have been lost due to the ravages of the primary disorder or as a result of prolonged institutionalization. In some cases, aggressive, destructive and bizarre behaviours have taken their place. The aims of treatment are:

* To improve the quality of life of subjects.
* To establish the skills necessary for life in the community.
* To eliminate unwanted behaviours that constitute major management problems.

The methods used are based upon the principles of *operant conditioning*, which predict that behaviours are influenced by their consequences. Whenever possible, operant programmes emphasize the reinforcement of desirable behaviours. Aversive methods are used only when positive reinforcement and other methods of treatment have failed. Subjects, their relatives and the staff must be fully informed of the aims and methods of treatment, and the rights, privileges and standards of care of subjects should be rigorously maintained.

According to the principles of operant conditioning, the reinforcer principles should be delivered as soon as possible following the behaviour it is intended to reinforce. This is relatively simple where the therapist is working on a one-to-one basis with an individual. However, where few staff supervise many subjects, the practical problems of selecting and delivering the requisite reinforcer for each individual is overcome by the use of tokens (*secondary reinforcers*) which are contingent upon the required behaviour. Tokens may be exchanged later for goods and privileges (*primary reinforcers*).

Such programmes, known as *token economies*, have been criticized on academic and ethical grounds and the role of tokens as conditioned reinforcers has been questioned. Nevertheless, token economies do seem to be useful for producing desirable behavioural changes in subjects, and perhaps in the staff who supervise them.

Commonly used Behavioural Techniques

Methods of increasing desirable behaviours

An event which increases the likelihood that a behaviour will recur is a reinforcer. *Positive reinforcement* involves the addition of something that is equivalent to a reward, and *negative reinforcement* involves the removal of something that is aversive. Each increases the likelihood of recurrence of any behaviour upon which it is contingent. Sweets are useful as reinforcers for children, and tobacco, money and privileges for adults. The nature of the reinforcer depends upon the likes and dislikes of the individual and in all cases it is gradually replace by social reinforcement as targets are achieved.

In *shaping*, behaviours are achieved by reinforcing small steps or approximations towards the final response. *Chaining* involves the sequential linking of the component responses which constitute an organized behaviour, with reinforcement being contingent only upon the final response in the chain. Chaining is often most easily carried out in reverse, beginning with the terminal response and progressively building up prior behaviours. Responses can be initiated by verbal or physical *prompting*, or by *modelling* in which the therapist demonstrates the required behaviour to the subject. *Fading* involves gradually withdrawing prompts, as the behaviour is achieved.

These simple procedures have been applied with success to a range of human behaviours. Although operant methods are usually associated with the management of problems in institutions, it will be clear that the principles of reinforcement are equally fundamental to the treatment of neurotic disorders. Indeed, in some, such as certain forms of marital therapy, an operant approach may be the central feature of treatment.

Methods of reducing undesirable behaviours

Aversive techniques, which employ noxious stimuli to eliminate unwanted behaviours, were once used extensively in the management of sexual deviations, alcoholism, drug abuse and certain specific behaviours such as self-mutilation, which are seen in institutions. Electric shocks and chemically induce nausea were commonly used as aversive stimuli but the methods lost popularity partly because results were rather disappointing. In some instances, particularly with the mentally handicapped, aversive stimuli can paradoxically reinforce the undesirable behaviour.

Removing the subject from all reinforcers, called 'time out', is a form of *extinction* procedure in which unwanted behaviours gradually disappear because they are no longer reinforced. The use of aversive stimuli in imagination is called *covert sensitization* and has been used particularly in the management of deviant sexual behaviours and urges. It involves clients imagining themselves performing the deviant act and this is interrupted by an aversive scene, such as the approach of a policeman to arrest them for this behaviour.

The therapeutic component of the behavioural management of obsessive–compulsive rituals is called *response prevention*. It consists of preventing the subject from indulging in a ritual until the urge to do so has passed. Teaching subjects to interrupt intrusive, obsessional thoughts by shouting 'stop' is called *thought stopping*. Subjects then learn to internalize the order so that they can use the technique in any situation. Tics and habit disorders are managed by instructing subjects to follow the unwanted behaviour with one which is incompatible with it, a method known as *habit reversal*. Alternatively, subjects may be instructed to practise the unwanted behaviour until they tire of it. This is *satiation* or *massed practice*.

Self-observation, a feature of all *self-control* methods, can reduce the frequency of unwanted behaviours, such as cigarette smoking, by itself. It may be combined with *self-reinforcement*, where subjects reward themselves for periods of desirable behaviour, or *self-punishment* for failure to achieve an agreed target. A financial penalty is called a *response cost*. Reducing the opportunity for a behaviour by manipulating the conditions under which it occurs is known as *stimulus control* and has been used to treat appetitive disorders and alcohol abuse.

Methods of reducing anxiety and fear

Exposure to feared situations can be carried out slowly or rapidly. *Slow exposure, desensitization,* involves inducing a state of relaxation before a feared stimulus is introduced. Anxiety is minimized by choosing stimuli from a hierarchy of cues of increasing difficulty, hence the term '*systematic desensitization*', and by interrupting exposure as soon as subjects indicate arousal. The stimulus is reintroduced only when a state of relaxation has been re-established. It is supposed to work by weakening the fear-evoking property of the stimulus by presenting it only during relaxation — a state that is incompatible with fear. This principle is known as *reciprocal inhibition.* It is a slow, tedious method which has been largely superseded by *rapid exposure.* Here, anxiety is permitted but exposure is prolonged so that *habituation* occurs. When carried out *in vivo* it is sometimes called *flooding* and its use in imagination, at which time maximal anxiety levels are evoked, is called *implosion.* Exposure is useful whenever there is avoidance of feared situations. Its effect is impaired by depression and by excessive use of alcohol and tranquillizers.

Relaxation therapy can take several forms, though none seems to be more effective than another. Methods commonly involve progressive muscular relaxation or mental imagery. Taped instructions are useful and it is usual to link the relaxed state with a pleasant, imagined scene so that relaxation can be induced in any situation merely by recalling the scene.

Biofeedback consists of providing subjects with information about the state of their physiological functioning. One of the physiological accompaniments of anxiety, such as heart rate, galvanic skin response (GSR) or electromyogram (EMG), is converted electronically into a visual or auditory signal. Subjects learn to alter the signal and so their state of arousal. It has been used to treat generalized tension and anxiety. Migraine, tension headaches and other muscular dysfunctions may also respond.

Methods of altering social behaviours

Difficulties in forming and sustaining relationships with others are commonly associated with psychiatric disorders. *Social skill training* aims to modify subjects' social behaviour in order to help them to overcome these difficulties. There is some evidence that social skills training produces an improvement in overall psychological adjustment as well as in social competence.

Treatment usually involves a programmed course which is applied to a group of selected subjects. Behaviours are modelled by the therapist, and the group follows this with role-play and rehearsal under controlled conditions. The therapist's role is to guide, coach and encourage the group. Group members offer feedback with an initial emphasis upon successful aspects of performance. Shortcomings are examined later. Closed-circuit television and video play-back can be invaluable during feedback. Social interactions are examined in terms of separate components such as eye contact, posture, speaking skills, etc. This makes the role-play more manageable for the group and it helps to structure feedback. Exercises increase in complexity as skills develop.

Cognitive methods

For centuries it has been recognized that the influence of events upon our psychological equilibrium owes more to our attitudes towards those events than to their exact nature. Attitudes, thoughts, beliefs and perceptions are all cognitions. Those which are important in generating and maintaining mood disturbances tend to occur automatically, and so rapidly that they are usually beyond the subject's awareness. Hence a daily diary of negative thoughts is usually necessary to identify them. Once identified, their validity can be tested and alternatives considered.

A recognition of the influence of cognitions upon mood has led to the development of cognitive treatments for depressive illness. Depression, and the cognitions which are associated with it, are regarded as having a circular relationship with one another. As well as the patient keeping a diary of negative thoughts, the therapist and patient may agree behavioural tasks which are designed to demonstrate the irrational nature of cognitions and so reduce their depressive influence. At the same time, success in the behavioural task demonstrates the validity of alternative points of view.

In the last 20 years or so, cognitive and behavioural methods have been used increasingly side by side. Most therapists now practise this integrated form of treatment known as cognitive behaviour therapy (CBT).

There has been a progressive expansion of the range of neurotic disorders in which CBT has been shown to be effective and treatments have become increasingly efficient. Cognitive methods have been applied with considerable success in the treatment of psychotic symptoms and there is evidence that their use may reduce the frequency of hospital admissions in patients suffering from psychotic disorders.

Summary

Behaviour therapy is an empirically derived form of psychological treatment whose effectiveness has been demonstrated in a range of human disorders. It is distinguished by a characteristic symptom-oriented approach and by its emphasis upon the current determinants of the clinical problem rather than its historical antecedents. Treatment is often a matter of commonsense and follows logically from an accurate functional analysis.

The treatment of neurotic disorders is a collaborative process in which the subjects direct their own treatment with guidance from the therapist. Subjects are responsible for completing negotiated task assignments and for maintaining a daily record from which treatment progress can be assessed. In most cases a flexible, multi-technique approach is used.

For a basic introduction to behaviour therapy:

MARKS, I.M. (1978). *Living with Fear*. New York: McGraw-Hill.

For a more advanced account of cognitive behavioural therapy:

HAWTON, K., SALKOVSKIS, B.M., KIRK, J. and CLARKE, D.M. (1989). *Cognitive Behavior Therapy for Psychiatric Problems: A Practical Guide*. Oxford: Oxford University Press.

Chapter 11
Cognitive Analytic Therapy

ANTHONY RYLE

Introduction

People who seek psychotherapy have usually already tried commonsense solutions for their problems. They have also, in most cases, sought advice from friends. Friends, however, may have been chosen because they do not challenge what needs to be challenged. Psychotherapists offer something different; a safe, thoughtful relationship focusing on patients' needs and problems within which learning, which affects both knowledge and feeling, can take place. Therapists are essentially teachers but their teaching — especially in the psychodynamic tradition — pays particular attention to the therapy relationship, within which patients re-enact, and in time may learn to revise, their ways of relating to others and their sense of themselves.

Cognitive analytic therapy (CAT), as its name suggests, originated in the linking of ideas and methods from psychoanalytic and cognitive approaches. In the 20 years that have elapsed since the first argument for a common language for the psychotherapies (Ryle, 1978), the model has been elaborated and a number of therapeutic strategies developed. Today, CAT has its own theoretical base and its own methods of working with patients. It shares much with — but is clearly differentiated from, and is often critical of — the approaches from which it is derived.

Origins of CAT

The features of CAT can best be understood in terms of its development. Working in general practice during the early years of the National Health Service (NHS), to which I remain deeply committed, made me aware of the high prevalence of untreated emotional and psychological distress, and of the scarcity of appropriate resources. An investigation of families with young children on my practice list confirmed this high prevalence and suggested that individual and family interventions in primary care settings would be the most appropriate form of intervention (Ryle, 1967) — an idea given much prominence at present but still honoured more in the breach than the observance. The provision of treatment to those in need, rather than only to those who could pay, had been established as a basic principle in the NHS for most conditions, but not for psychotherapy. This reflected a general British prejudice against therapy and the assumption that it always need to be prolonged and therefore expensive, a prejudice that was also justified by its failure to demonstrate its efficacy. These factors, and the conservatism of the psychoanalytic institutions, meant that psychodynamic psychotherapy remained for a long time largely confined to private practice. The wish to develop an economically feasible and humanly effective model of therapy suitable for NHS needs was a main factor in the development of CAT, and linked to this was a desire to investigate the efficacy of dynamic therapies by use of measures which went beyond symptom relief and behavioural change.

The opportunity to pursue that research followed a move to the University Health Service at Sussex University. The research involved the use of repertory grid techniques (Kelly, 1955) which offer access to how individuals make sense of the important people in their lives or of their important relationships. Grids yield data in the form of correlations or graphs (which frighten most therapists!), but these can be restated in prose and considered alongside therapists' dynamic formulations. An example may illustrate this.

> In a map derived from his grid comparing significant people, a science student who was failing to attend any laboratory classes distinguished between people he saw as *likely to succeed, brutal and disliked* and those he saw as *creative and kind*. The former group were all male and included his father (a general); the latter were nearly all female, and included his mother and himself. Psychoanalytic explanations of his work failure might point to issues such as unconscious castration anxiety; by contrast, a description based on the grid pointed to the student's dichotomization of possible roles, and indicated the need to challenge the assumptions and escape the narrow options indicated by his 'map'.

Use of this technique with a large series of patients involved a continual comparison of grid and dynamic descriptions of the same individuals and contributed to the later integration of cognitive and psychoanalytic models. For the purposes of research into the outcome of psychotherapy, grids were also of value for descriptions of desirable change, made on the basis of the dynamic formulation of individuals' difficulties, these could be 'translated' into grid terms and this allowed specific predictions to be made as to how individually selected measures in pre-therapy grids should change on retesting with the grid if therapy has been successful (Ryle, 1975).

Defining the specific individual dynamic aims of each intervention through descriptions of the mental and behavioural processes responsible for the maintenance of these difficulties was an essential aspect of outcome research. Only on the basis of such descriptions, recorded at the start of therapy, could one specify which change would signify successful treatment, whether expressed in dynamic or in grid terms. Identifying and describing these features required active collaboration with patients and this work, which originated as part of the outcome research, turned out in practice to have a powerful therapeutic impact. This observation led to changes in practice and early *joint reformulation* became one of the main defining characteristic of what became CAT.

The Development of CAT in Practice

Early in the 1980s I became a consultant psychotherapist, required to provide a service for a population of 180 000 with the equivalent of a little over one full-time trained assistant. I depended upon trainees from various professions to carry out therapy. I decided to offer the minimum sufficient treatment to all patients referred, rather than to feel responsible only for those patients who found their way to the top of the waiting list. This situation — and the supervision of the volunteer therapists — was a spur to the refinement of the CAT model and over the next few years resulted in the establishment of a national organization offering formal training. The therapy was enriched through the incorporation of ideas and methods contributed by many of the trainees. The experience of treating a wide range of patients with non-psychotic illnesses, excluding only those with major current substance abuse, was encouraging: 16 CAT sessions turned out to be a safe intervention for the full range of referred patients, including those with personality disorders, and was a sufficient intervention for over two-thirds of subjects.

Basic CAT Theory

Cognitive analytic theory was derived from two main sources: from the re-instatement of object relations theory in cognitive terms (Ryle, 1985); and from the development of a sequential model linking cognitions, affects, beliefs, actions and consequences, influenced by cognitive–behavioural ideas. I sought also to take account of the increasingly detailed descriptions of early development derived from the observations of infants and infant–carer interactions which had been published in the last decade and which revised many of the previous ideas derived from psychoanalytic reconstructions. In its later developments the CAT model has further revised object relations theory through the introduction of ideas from Vygotsky (Ryle, 1991; Leiman, 1992, 1994). These ideas emphasize the role of language and other forms of *cultural transmission* in human development. Human babies are born into an environment where things and experiences are invested with meanings, and these meanings are mediated by *signs* acquired in interaction with others from the earliest months of life.

The basic unit of description of psychological processes used in the early phases of CAT was the *procedural sequence*. Procedures are described in terms of sequences of mental, behavioural and environmental processes involving, in turn, perception, appraisal, aims, action planning (including the anticipation of consequences), action and the appraisal of the consequences, on the basis of which the aim or the procedure may be revised. But, problematic procedures are *not* revised, despite their negative outcomes. Analysing these self-perpetuation procedural patterns, which maintain much psychological distress, demonstrated three overall patterns accounting for this non-revision:

- *Traps:* based on negative assumptions that generate behaviours which provoke consequences which (seem to) confirm the assumptions.
- *Dilemmas:* restriction of possible acts or roles due to falsely polarized options.
- *Snags:* appropriate aims are abandoned due to the (true or false) perception of the negative reactions of others, or to (conscious or unconscious) perceptions of danger or prohibition.

These patterns are described and examples of them are given in the *Psychotherapy File*. This is reproduced on page 168; it is usually given to patients during the first session. The psychotherapy file explains and illustrates these concepts and it may be helpful at this stage for readers to look at it and consider which parts might apply to themselves or their patients.

Later developments produced a more complex model, the *Procedural Sequence Object Relation Model*, which offers a fuller understanding, essential when working with more disordered patients. Therapy based on this model requires the identification of patients' *repertoire of reciprocal role procedures*. 'Role' here implies a pattern of experience, perception, knowledge and action; action including pursuing a relationship. The aim of enacting a role is to induce the response of the other, and hence the consequence of a *role procedure* will be success or failure in eliciting the expected or desired reciprocating role.

Early development

An individual's role procedures are acquired largely in early life through the patterns enacted and the meanings learned in relation to carers. These overall patterns are laid down in procedural memory and their origins are not directly accessible to conscious reflection or memory, although their manifestations in action *are*. This overall patterning of early role procedures is resistant to revision; moreover, stability is maintained because we all seek relationships which offer, or seem to offer, reciprocation to our procedures and which, therefore, serve to confirm our repertoire.

These early reciprocal role patterns, learned in relation to others, continue to shape our interpersonal relationships but they are also the basis of our relationship with ourselves; the 'voices' we internalize from those who are our first carers, companions and rivals become part of our conversation with ourselves.

In this view, whereas biology determines an infant's particular inborn traits, and while these will, in turn, influence the responses of parents and others, the particular parents' acts, their expressiveness, beliefs and fantasies (their role procedures) and their contribution to the child's developing system of understanding, play a crucial role in normal and abnormal development. Parents influence the child through the transmission and elaboration of non-verbal and verbal signs which bear both cultural and individual meanings and which determine the individual's assumptions about self and the world.

How will this basic reciprocal role repertoire, acquired in early life, shape and limit later patterns? An early reciprocal role pattern may be directly repeated in later relationships, with either pole (i.e. either the 'originally child' or 'originally parental' role) being enacted and the other elicited from others. For example, an individual with a *looking after to depending* reciprocal role pattern may seek either to offer care to dependent others or to be looked after by caring others. But some childhood roles may have been associated with unmanageable feelings (such as fear or anger) or unsayable thoughts and may have been forbidden or punished; such potential roles may therefore be avoided. One way of doing this is for the individual to play the reciprocal role and induce the feared or forbidden role in others. This process, described as *projective identification* in object relations theory, is seen in CAT as being a particular example of the general process of eliciting role reciprocation (Ryle, 1994; Sandler, 1976). If the pattern is stably maintained, the individual may remain unaware of that part of the self identified with the avoided role. For example, psychotherapists and other caring professionals may remain unaware of their own dependent needs. Therapists need to recognize the feelings elicited, often by non-verbal means, by their patients. Countertransference feelings are complex and may include:

- The felt response to invitations to reciprocate (reciprocating counter-transference).
- The empathetic echoing of feelings the patient may or may not be able to articulate (identifying countertransference).
- Reparative responses to patients' needs.
- Personal idiosyncrasies of the therapist.

These last (universally present) will make certain transference pressures more difficult to recognize or resist and require particularly well-trained self-reflection, something therapy and supervision will aim to enhance.

Roles and accompanying affects that were unmanageable during childhood are also commonly replaced by alternative enacted procedures. These are understood in classical psychoanalysis as *compromise formations* between the individual's conflicted desires (id) and internal prohibitions (superego) and the recognized reality of the situation (ego). In CAT *all* enacted procedures are seen to reflect such 'compromises'; those described as *ego defences* in psychoanalysis are those which involve a diminished awareness of the self and the world rather than specific inhibitions of feeling or memory. For example, *repressed anger* might be understood in CAT as involving the elaboration of complex alternative procedures to the direct expression of anger in which different (often less effective) forms of indirect assertion or resentful submission would operate, with accompanying negative assumptions about the self as weak or undeserving, and frequently accompanied by somatic symptoms. Therapy would aim to identify the replaced procedure, in this case expressed anger, examine the underlying assumptions about it and encourage realistic and adequately controlled forms of expression.

Practical Methods

CAT is normally given as a pre-determined 16-session intervention. Fewer sessions may be adequate for less disturbed patients, whereas personality-disordered patients may need 24 or more sessions; in all cases, the number is set in advance. Prior assessment for suitability and diagnosis is desirable and any gaps in the history should be filled in during the first few sessions.

Three phases of therapy are recognized, involving, in turn, reformulation, recognition and revision, and these will be considered in turn.

Reformulation

The aim of reformulation is to devise a clear, agreed description of patients' difficulties and of the continuing processes serving to perpetuate them. This involves therapists listening carefully to patients' stories, exploring and clarifying the feelings and meanings expressed in relation to the events described, and noting what patients convey through speech and non-verbal communications. At this stage it is often useful to focus on symptoms and behaviours and to ask patients to monitor their antecedent and accompanying thoughts and events, with the aim of identifying the affects and procedures which have been replaced. This method, derived from cognitive therapy, can be assigned as a 'homework' exercise. Patients' accounts of past and present relationships, whether accurate and objective or in some degree distorted, will reveal much about how they view and judge the self and about what response is expected or sought from the therapist, in this way giving evidence about the main reciprocal role patterns, including those of which patients are unaware. A well-tuned CAT ear will often pick up all the major problem procedures during the first session.

The experience of being listened to carefully is a powerful one, especially for emotionally deprived people; the risk of inducing magical dependency in the patient is reduced in CAT by the involvement of patients in active work from the beginning. At the end of the first session it is usual to give out the 'psychotherapy file' (see Appendix), which describes self-monitoring and lists traps, dilemmas and snags. Patients are asked to mark any descriptions which they feel apply to them. (The file may be read through with illiterate patients.) At the next session any marked descriptions are discussed. The file is not a questionnaire yielding scores, it is a basis for self-reflection (introducing new ways of thinking about the self) and for exploratory discussion. Over the first sessions other tasks may be proposed, such as the construction of life charts or family trees, or descriptions of the self such as a friendly observer might provide. In the therapy sessions, history-taking will be continued and whatever the patient offers, either spontaneously or through the homework tasks, will be considered. This material will be discussed, with possible links or patterns being considered; all such information, and the therapist's awareness of feelings evoked (countertransference) will be used as the basis for the formal reformulation. A draft of this is usually prepared by the therapist and considered at the fourth session; after revision, it is recorded in writing for both patient and therapist to provide a shared and agreed account of the agenda and aims of the therapy.

The *reformulation letter* represents therapists' understanding of the patients' present difficulty in terms of the past life. It offers an acknowledgement of what was experienced, clarifies what patients were and were not responsible for, and describes:

• Strategies or procedures learned from, often repeating that experience.

• Procedures or strategies which patients have developed in the attempt to deal with this experience.

The word *defence* can sound pejorative and is best avoided. The letter will usually end with a summary of the *problems* which trouble patients and of the *problem procedures* which maintain them. These problem procedures may be described as traps, dilemmas and snags, a process which offers a non-blaming explanation for their persistence. They may reflect the repetition of historically imposed role procedures. One example might read 'Faced in the past with your father's conditional, critical acceptance, you now either set yourself impossibly perfectionist goals, becoming guilty and depressed when you fail, or you avoid ever trying to achieve. Another example might be 'Having had to spare your handicapped sister's feelings as child, you learned either to avoid achievement or to dismantle it, as if you were guilty for being successful or happy.' In other cases, established avoidant, defensive or symptomatic procedures are described, for example, 'Seeking care but usually experiencing rejection and feeling unloved, you gave up hoping for emotional support and learned to use food as a comfort. Now, after binge eating, you feel overwhelmed with guilt so you make yourself sick, which makes you feel still more unlovable and empty.'

Such descriptions will be considered with patients, providing a summary of what they learned. Defensive procedures are described as *necessary strategies* rather then as *motivated defences*. They will be presented finally as part of the *reformulation letter*, as in the following example.

Elaine, a woman teacher, aged 26 years

Dear Elaine
Here is my letter trying to tell your story as I understand it .... [at this point the main historical issues and events were described]. ... I feel your recent severe recurrence of depression, and your past episodes, were brought about by three linked patterns. These patterns reflect the implicit 'instructions' you received early in you life. The main one was ambiguous: on the one hand, you had to achieve highly but were never judged to have done well enough and as a result were criticized; on the other, you mother seems to have been intolerant or envious of your successes. This *conditional, critical and undermining* attitude still operates inside you, as you constantly bully an irrationally guilty self, are always fearful of failure and always expect envy from others. For example, you could not enjoy your recent success in gaining a higher qualification. A second pattern contributing to your depression is your polarization in respect of your emotional needs; you act as if you must be either *totally competent and helpful*, never asking for help or support for yourself, or else you see yourself as *childish, vulnerable and undeserving*, which either leaves you feeling greedy

and demanding or not able to ask for anything. A third pattern has shaped your love affairs. If someone loves you, you feel safe and valuable in a way you never achieve on you own. But then you begin to anticipate rejection and feel the only way to keep the other's affection is to make no trouble of any sort so you become *placatory* and suppress your needs and feelings. As a predictable result, these unstated needs are ignored and not met, and in due course you become *resentful* and sink into a weepy, sexually withdrawn state which ultimately leads to the relationship ending.

This account does not describe all of you; it leaves out the ways in which you are a very competent teacher, and does not note how you have already begun to think about yourself in new ways. In the weeks to come we shall work at recognizing how the patterns described above are manifest in the day to day. We shall also watch out for how they may emerge in our relationship, for example you might see me as critical and demanding or, for fear of feeling childish, might only present your confident adult self who asks for nothing. As you learn to recognize these patterns, I believe that you will learn to challenge and control them and that the harshness and mistrust you feel towards yourself, and the criticism and rejection you expect from others, can be replaced by more trust and care.

In addition to describing problem procedures verbally in the letter, they may be mapped out in flow diagrams (*sequential diagrammatic reformulation*). These diagrams are best drawn around a central box listing the *repertoire of reciprocal roles* from which are generated interpersonal or self-management procedures. Elaine's sequential diagram is given in Figure 11.1. The reciprocal role pattern described in the central box represents the main legacy of her childhood. From the lower (child-derived pole) three procedures are generated:

- Striving (on the right) generates a dilemma: as if the choice was either perfection or failure; the former option produces success but is often undone by the undermining issuing from the upper (parental) pole; the latter returns her to guilt and depression.
- Seeking to be accepted (below) similarly generates a dilemma; Elaine feels she must either be a totally competent adult or, if she acknowledges her own needs, fears she will become an over-demanding baby.
- With lovers (on the left) she experiences the acceptance she so profoundly craves but the self-undermining assumptions generated from the parentally derived upper pole of the central reciprocal role pattern sabotage this and in due course she elicits rejection from the other.

The focus in the diagram on the basic reciprocal role repertoire from which the problem procedures are generated demonstrates clearly the common origin and form of the interpersonal and intrapersonal proced-

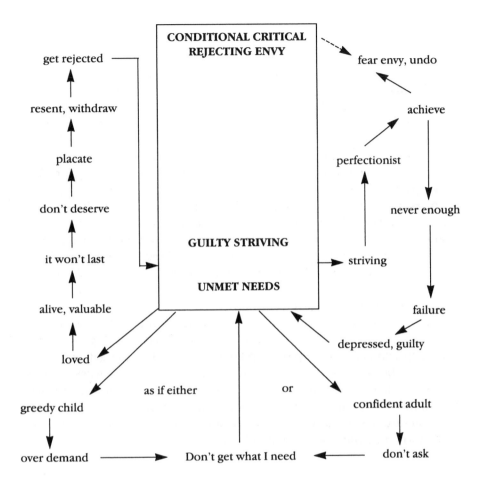

Figure 11.1 Elaine; sequential diagrammatic reformulation.

ures and shows how they reinforce the core assumptions. By providing a summary of the roles likely to be either played towards or elicited from others, it offers an invaluable guide to likely transference–countertransference interactions.

To summarize, the letter aims to offer a powerful retelling of the patient's experience, often serving to restore meaning and create a more coherent life narrative on which a less damaged sense of self may be built. It seeks to make clear what the patient was, and was not, responsible for. Its construction and final reading are usually experienced by patients as emotionally profound and the connection and containment provided by this serves, in most cases, to cement the therapeutic alliance. The diagram offers a shorthand map of currently operating procedures and plays a central role in the next phase of therapy.

Recognition

Almost all the stories told, memories and dreams recounted, and feelings and behaviours expressed in relation to the therapist during the early and middle phases of therapy, are examples of one or other of the patients' problem procedures. As this is recognized, the way in which revision has been so difficult in the past becomes clear, and this new awareness offers a new possibility of change. The diagram has two main functions here: it provides patients with a tool for self-reflection, enabling them to learn to recognize problem procedures — at first after, but in due course before, they operate — and it provides therapists with a basis for recognizing reported or enacted problem procedures and, crucially, enables collusive reciprocations to them to be avoided, or at least corrected. Therapeutic change is seen to derive largely from this enhanced self-reflective capacity on the part of patients and from acceptance and explicit, principled non-collusion on the part of therapists. In this way, reinforcement of historical problem procedures is avoided and new tools for self-reflection and a more benign parental figure are internalized.

During this phase, some specific techniques may be introduced. Thus, particular problems may be treated with behavioural programmes involving exposure or step-by-step change: underlying negative assumptions may be directly examined and challenged, and new ways of acting may be rehearsed through role play or empty chair techniques. All these techniques are applied within the context of a continuing awareness of the total picture. As therapy proceeds, patients increasingly use therapeutic tools and understandings independently.

Revision

Therapeutic change means procedural revision. Procedural revision may — indeed must — begin in the early stages, through patients' discovery that therapists offer trust and respect, and do not reinforce old patterns. But, the process of change is not a smooth one. As trust in the therapist is established, and as current procedures are better understood and controlled, patients feel safer and the unmanageable feelings associated with historically determined roles which have been kept at bay (repressed or dissociated) become more accessible. This process can be painful and frightening and therapists may be faced with the dilemma of either seeming too intrusive or standing back and seeming not to care; this is best discussed with patients and a manageable pace negotiated. In most cases patients will access feelings and memories only when they feel safe to do so. In CAT, direct challenge or interpretation of repression and other forms of defence and of most associated symptoms is seldom necessary; as safety is established, defensive avoidance fades and memories and feelings become more accessible.

Although the recognition and control of negative procedures is usually well advanced, the development of new procedures is seldom complete at the end of a 16-session therapy. Moreover, termination, although kept clearly on the agenda throughout therapy, is usually a difficult time, at which old procedures connected with abandonment or abuse are re-activated. At this stage therapists write a 'goodbye letter' which seeks to recapitulate what has been addressed in the therapy and to make an accurate evaluation of what has and has not been achieved. These letters should acknowledge and permit disappointment or anger as well as encouraging internalization of what was good. Patients are also invited to write their own evaluation. Many patients, after some distress at termination, discover that they are able to maintain the therapeutic process and act as their own therapist, using what was learned. Those who have ongoing significant relationships often find that these become less conflicted and more satisfying, although in some cases (an example of a snag) friends or partners may have been well-matched to the discarded procedures and may resent the change. It is important to leave time to see how far change is established and continues. Follow-up some three months later usually reveals how well the learning of therapy has been internalized, and any decisions about further needs will be taken at this stage.

How does CAT compare with other approaches?

All therapeutic activity involves joint work between therapist and patient. The CAT understanding of this work refers to Vygotsky who, writing of children's early learning, said that 'what the child does with an adult today she will do on her own tomorrow'. He described the role of the adult (or more experienced other) as being the joint elaboration with the child of new concepts and then the handing over of these to the child. In this sense the work of reformulation and the process of learning to apply this, as carried out in CAT, are a therapeutic application of Vygotsky's ideas. Vygotsky's concept of the 'zone of proximal development' (ZPD) is also relevant to therapy. The ZPD represents what the child does not know, but could acquire, given appropriate joint work and the sharing and transfer of concepts. We all have extensive ZPDs concerning forms of knowing which encompass feelings and meanings, and it is these that therapy needs to address. Therapy, as opposed to *cognitive instruction*, involves not only the internalization of specific concepts and tools but also the internalization of the therapist's person, whose 'voice' carries new meanings which can challenge or replace the neglecting or conditional or abusive voices from the past.

CAT and cognitive therapy

This Vygotskian understanding distinguishes CAT from cognitive and constructivist theories which describe individual development in terms suggesting too large a role for reason and evidence in human learning. Parents, teachers and therapists are influential figures, bearing individually and culturally shaped assumptions and meanings. The CAT therapist does not act as an authoritative teacher requiring good pupil behaviour; whatever the patient brings, whether co-operation, challenge or even (within limits) abuse, will be grist to the therapeutic mill. In this, in its collaborative style and in the integrative impact of reformulation I believe that CAT offers a more powerful intervention than does cognitive therapy, particularly for personality-disordered patients.

CAT and psychoanalytic psychotherapy

There are also many differences between CAT and other psychodynamic approaches, despite the common emphasis on transference and counter-transference. Within psychoanalysis, the self-psychology of Kohut and recent developments derived from attachment theory are closer to CAT than are classical or object relations approaches. But there are still many divergences. The reader will have noticed that the concept of 'the unconscious', central to psychoanalytic understandings, has played no part in the discussion so far. This is not because the role of unconscious thought processes is denied, but rather because our knowledge of them rests essentially on noticing what is done or said (or not done or not said) by the patient. The CAT therapist is good at describing these manifestations but does not *interpret* them, in the belief that to offer accounts of hidden processes within the patient implies a form of authority which diminishes the patient's agency. In any case, the various psychoanalytic theories underpinning such interpretations are imprecise, over-elaborated and contradictory. The CAT therapist aims to devise the most useful forms of *decription* of what is manifest and will do so in collaboration with the patient, which makes it unlikely that a totally useless or wrong idea will be imposed.

In contrast to both dynamic and cognitive therapies, attention is focused from the start on the most general, high-level descriptions; CAT is a 'top down' therapy, linking memories, thoughts and events wherever possible to the general patterns identified at the start. This, and the collaborative therapeutic relationship, may account for the speed with which change often occurs in CAT compared to other psychodynamic therapies.

Other Applications of CAT

The discussion so far has considered CAT as a general model applicable to the individual therapy of a wide range of patients. Detailed modifications specific to the treatment of different diagnostic groups have so far been described only in relation to eating disorders (Bell, 1996; Treasure and Ward, 1997), damaging patterns of self-care in insulin-dependent diabetic subjects (Fosbrook, 1996), work in forensic settings (Pollock and Kear-Colwell, 1994), substance abuse (Leighton, 1995) and borderline personality disorder (Ryle, 1997a). Work with borderline patients has involved increasing the number of sessions to 24 and has generated some theoretical developments. The proposed model (Ryle, 1997b) suggests that the harsh and abusive early experiences of these patients produce not only restrictions and distortions of the reciprocal role repertoire reflecting the internalization of destructive or restrictive parental figures, such as have been considered above, but also underdevelopment and disruption of the *metaprocedures* which link together and mobilize appropriately the repertoire. This *dissociation* is produced by external trauma and is responsible for the major instability and extremity which are core features of borderline patients. Instability is seen to reflect metaprocedural disruption and the alternating expression of a range of partially dissociated '*self states*'. Each of these has a specific reciprocal role repertoire, but self states are not sub-personalities with distinct biographies, memories and identities such as are described in cases of multiple personality disorder. Self states alternate in determining experience and behaviour, switches between them often being abrupt, confusing and not evidently provoked by external events. Some self states are characterized by very powerful feelings and loss of control and these provoke correspondingly powerful responses in others, including therapists. Diagrammatic mapping of borderline patients' range of self states and of shifts between them provides these distressed and distressing people with a basis for greater self-understanding and control and, ultimately, for integration and allows therapists to make sense of their confusion (Ryle, 1997a).

Other Applications of CAT Theory

Although developed primarily in relation to individual psychotherapy, the model of the individual developed in CAT emphasizes how a person's processes are maintained in interaction with others. The use of CAT ideas and methods in work with couples and with groups is an obvious extension; in particular, the model is essentially compatible with systems theory approaches. CAT is also being used increasingly as a basis for care planning and staff supervision and as a way of establishing a common understanding between staff and patients in residential and day hospital settings. An understanding of the collusions and splitting of staff groups, first described by Main (1957) is, in this way, made available to staff at all levels of training and to patients, and the patients' exposure to irrelevant or damaging interventions reflecting inadvertent collusions is much reduced.

Conclusion

At present, CAT represents one of the few attempts to integrate different models of psychotherapy both at the theoretical and practical level. The mutual competiveness and ignorance which has characterized schools of psychotherapy in the past may be receding, although it has to be said that the rather rapid spread of CAT owes nothing to either the support or criticism of the more established 'schools'. Over the next few decades it is to be hoped that the act of therapy will be based on a broad, shared understanding of human personality, a change to which CAT will have contributed.

References

BELL, L. (1996). Cognitive analytic therapy: its value in the treatment of people with eating disorders. *Clinical Psychology Forum* 92, 5–10.

FOSBROOK, J. (1996). Psychological treatment (CAT) with poorly controlled diabetic patients. *Practical Diabetes International* 13, 158–162.

KELLY, G.A. (1955). *Psychology of Personal Constructs*. New York: Norton.

LEIGHTON, T. (1995). A cognitive analytic understanding of 'twelve step' treatment. *New Directions in Study of Alcohol Group* 20, 31–41.

LEIMAN, M. (1992). The concept of sign in the work of Vygotsky, Winnicott and Bakhtin: further integration of object relations theory and activity theory. *British Journal of Medical Psychology* 65, 209–221.

LEIMAN, M. (1994). The development of cognitive analytic therapy. *International Journal of Short-term Psychotherapy* 9, 67–82.

MAIN, T.F. (1957). The ailment. *British Journal of Medical Psychology* 30, 129–145.

POLLOCK, P.H. and KEAR-COLWELL, J.J. (1994). Women who stab: a personal construct analysis of sexual victimisation and offending behaviour. *British Journal of Medical Psychology* 67, 13–22.

RYLE, A. (1967). *Neurosis in the Ordinary Family*. London: Tavistock.

RYLE, A. (1975). *Frames and Cages*. London: Chatto & Windus.

RYLE, A. (1978). A common language for the psychotherapies. *British Journal of Psychiatry* 132, 585–594.

RYLE, A. (1985). Cognitive theory, object relations and the self. *British Journal of Medical Psychology* 58, 1–7.

RYLE, A. (1991). Object relations theory and activity theory: a proposed link by way of the procedural sequence model. *British Journal of Medical Psychology* **64**, 307–316.

RYLE, A. (1994). Projective identification: a particular form of reciprocal role procedure. *British Journal of Medical Psychology* **67**, 107–114.

RYLE, A. (1997a). *Cognitive Analytic Therapy and Borderline Personality Disorder: The Model and the Method*. Chichester: Wiley.

RYLE, A. (1997b). The structure and development of borderline personality disorder: a proposed model. *British Journal of Psychiatry* **170**, 82–86.

SANDLER, J. (1976). Countertransference and role-responsiveness. *International Review of Psychoanalysis* **3**, 43–47.

TREASURE and WARD (1997). Cognitive Analytic Therapy in the treatment of anorexia nervosa. *Clinical Psychology and Psychotherapy* **4**(1), 62–71.

The psychotherapy file

An aid to understanding ourselves better.

In our life what has happened to us, and the sense we made of this, colours the way we see ourselves and others. How we see things is for us, how things are, and how we go about our lives seems 'obvious and right'. Sometimes, however, our familiar ways of understanding and acting can be the source of our problems. In order to solve our difficulties we may need to learn to recognise how what we do makes things worse. We can then work out new ways of thinking and acting.

These pages are intended to suggest ways of thinking about what you do; recognising your particular patterns is the first step in learning to gain more control and happiness in your life.

Keeping a diary of moods and behaviour

Symptoms, bad moods, unwanted thoughts or behaviours that come and go can be better understood and controlled if you learn to notice when they happen and what starts them off.

If you have a particular symptom or problem of this sort, start keeping a diary. The diary should be focussed on a particular mood, symptom or behaviour, and should be kept every day if possible. Try to record this sequence:

1. How you were feeling about yourself and others and the world before the problem came on.
2. Any external event, or any thought or image in your mind that was going on when the trouble started, or what seemed to start it off.
3. Once the trouble started, what were the thoughts, images or feelings you experienced?

By noticing and writing down in this way what you do and think at these times, you will learn to recognise and eventually have more control over how you act and think at the time. It is often the case that bad feelings like resentment, depression or physical symptoms are the result of ways of thinking and acting that are unhelpful. Diary keeping in this way gives you the chance to learn better ways of dealing with things.

It is helpful to keep a daily record for 1-2 weeks, than to discuss what you have recorded with your therapist or counsellor.

Patterns that do not work, but are hard to break

There are certain ways of thinking and acting that do not achieve what we want, but which are hard to change. Read through the lists on the following pages and mark how far you think they apply to you.

Applies strongly + +   Applies +   Does not apply 0

1. Traps

Traps are things we cannot escape from.. Certain kinds of thinking and acting result in a 'vicious circle' when, however hard we try, things seem to get worse instead of better. Trying to deal with feeling bad about ourselves, we think and act in ways that tend to confirm our badness.

Examples of Traps

1. Fear of hurting others trap

Feeling fearful of hurting others* we keep our feelings inside, or put our own needs aside. This tends to allow other people to ignore US or abuse us in various ways, which then leads to our feeling, or being, childishly angry. When we see ourselves behaving like this, it confirms our belief that we shouldn't be aggressive and reinforces our avoidance of standing up for our rights.

*People often get trapped in this way because they mix up aggression and assertion. Mostly, being assertive- asking for our rights- is perfectly acceptable. People who do not respect our rights as human beings must either be stood up to ot avoided.

2. Depressed thinking Trap

Feeling depressed, we are sure we wil manage a task or social situation badly. Being depressed, we are probably not as effective as we can be, and the depression leads us to exaggerate how badly we handled things. This makes us feel more depressed about ourselves.

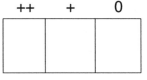

3. Trying to please Trap

Feeling uncertain about ourselves and anxious not to upset others, we try to please people by doing what they seem to want. As a result:
(1) we end up being taken advantage of by others which makes us angry, depressed or guilty, from which our uncertainty about ourselves is confirmed; or (2) sometimes we feel out of control because of the need to please, and start hiding away, putting things off, letting people down, which makes other people angry with us and increases our uncertainty.

4. Avoidance Trap

We feel ineffective and anxious about certain situations, such as crowded streets, open spaces, social gatherings. We try to go back into these situations, but feel even more anxiety. Avoiding them makes us feel better, so we stop trying. However, by constantly avoiding situations our lives are limited and we come to feel increasingly ineffective and anxious.

5. Social isolation Trap

Feeling under-confident about ourselves and anxious not to upset others, we worry that others will find us boring or stupid, so we don't look at people or respond to friendliness. People then see us as unfriendly, so we become more isolated from which we are convinced we are boring and stupid- and become more underconfident.

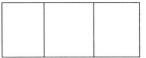

6. Low self-esteem Trap

Feeling worthless we feel that we cannot get what we want because 1) we will be punished, 2) that others will reject or abandon us, or 3) as if anything good we get is bound to go away or turn sour. 4) Sometimes it feels as if we must punish ourselves for being weak. From this we feel that everything is hopeless so we give up trying to do anything; this confirms and increases our sense of worthlessness.

2. Dilemmas (False choices and narrow options)

We often act as we do, even when we are not completely happy with it, because the only other ways we can imagine, seem as bad or even worse. Sometimes we assume connections that are not necessarily the case – as in

"If I do 'x' then 'y' will follow". These false choices can be described as either/or or if/then dilemmas. We often don't realise that we see things like this, but we act as if these were the only possible choices. Do you act as if any of the following false choices rule your life? Recognising them is the first step to changing them.

Choices about myself

I act AS IF:

	++	+	0
1. Either I keep feelings bottled up or I risk being rejected, hurting others, or making a mess.			
2. Either I feel I spoil myself and feel greedy or I deny myuself things and punish myself and feel miserable.			
3. If I try to be perfect, I feel depressed and angry; If I don't try to be perfect, I feel guilty, angry and dis-satisfied.			
4. If I must then I won't; it is as if when faced with a task I must either 1) gloomily submit or 2) passively resist. Other people's wishes, or even my own feel too demanding, so I put things off, avoid them.			
5. If I must not then I will; it is as if the only proof of my existence is my resistence. Other people's rules, or even my own feel too restricting, so I break rules and do things which are harmful to me.			

	++	+	0

6. If other people aren't expecting me to do things for them or look after them, then I feel anxious, lonely and out of control.
7. If I get what I want I feel childish and guilty; if I don't get what I want, I feel frustrated, angry and depressed.
8. Either I keep things (feelings, plans) in perfect order, or I fear a terrible mess.

Choices about how we relate to others:

I behave with others AS IF:

	++	+	0

1. Either I'm involved with someone and likely to get hurt or I don't get involved and stay in charge, but remain lonely.
2. Either I stick up for myself and nobody likes we, or I give in and get put on by others and feel cross and hurt.
3. Either I'm a brute or a martyr (secretly blaming the other).
4a. With others either I'm safely wrapped up in bliss or in combat;
4b. If in combat then I'm either a bully or a victim.
5. Either I look down on other people, or I feel they look down on me.
6a. Either I'm sustained by the admiration of others whom I admire or I feel exposed.
6b. If exposed then I feel either contemptuous of others or I feel contemptible.
7. Either I'm involved with others and feel engulfed, taken over or smothered, or I stay safe and uninvolved but feel lonely and isolated.
8. When I'm involved with someone whom I care about then either I have to give in or they have to give in.
9. When I'm involved with someone whom I depend on then either I have to give in or they have to give in.
10. As a woman either I have to do what others want or I stand up for my rights and get rejected.
10. As a man either I can't have any feelings or I am an emotional mess.

3. Snags

Snags are what is happening when we say "I want to have a better life, or I want to change my behaviour but...". Sometimes this comes from how we or our families thought about us when we were young; such as 'she was always the good child', or 'in our family we never...'. Sometimes the snags come from the important people in our lives not wanting us to change, or not able to cope with what our changing means to them. Often the resistance is more indirect, as when a parent, husband or wife becomes ill or depressed when we begin to get better.

In other cases, we seem to 'arrange' to avoid pleasure or success, or if they come, we have to pay in some way, by depression, or by spoiling things. Often this is because, as children, we came to feel guilty if things went well for us, or felt that we were envied for good luck or success. Sometimes we have come to feel responsible, unreasonably, for things that went wrong in the family, although we may not be aware that this is so. It is helpful to learn to recognise how this sort of pattern is stopping you getting on with your life, for only then can you learn to accept your right to a better life and begin to claim it.

You may get quite depressed when you begin to realise how often you stop your life being happier and more fulfilled. It is important to remember that t's not being stupid or bad, but rather that:

a) *We do these things because this is the way we learned to manage best when we were younger.*

b) *we don't have to keep on doing them now we are learning to recognise them.*

c) *by changing our behaviour, we can learn to control not only our own behaviour, but we also change the way other people behave to us.*

d) *although it may seem that others resist the changes we want for ourselves (for example, our parents, or our partners), we often under-estimate them; if we are firm about our right to change, those who care for us will usually accept the change.*

Do you recognise that you feel limited in your life:

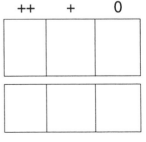

	++	+	0
1 For fear of the response of others: for example I must sabotage success 1) as if it deprives others, 2) as if others may envy me or 3) as if there are not enough good things to go around.			
2. By something inside tourself: for example I must sabotage good things as if I don't deserve them.			

4. Difficult and unstable states of mind

Some people find it difficult to keep control over their behaviour and experience because things feel very difficult and different at times. Indicate which, if any of the following apply to you:

	++	+	0
1. How I feel about myself and others can be unstable; I can switch from one state of mind to a completely different one.			
2. Some states may be accompanied by intense, extreme and uncontrollable emotions.			
3. Others by emotional blankness, feeling unreal, or feeling muddled.			
4. Some states are accompanied by feeling intensely guilty or angry with myself, wanting to hurt myself.			
5. or by feeling that others can't be trusted, are going to let me down, or hurt me.			
6. or by being unreasonably angry or hurtful to others.			
7. Sometimes the only way to cope with some confusing feelings is to blank them off and feel emotionally distant from others.			

The Psychotherapy File was developed by Dr Anthony Ryle, Emeritus Consultant Psychotherapist and Senior Research Fellow, Department of Psychiatry, United Medical & Dental Schools (UMDS) of Guys and St Thomas's Hospital, London SE1 9RT UK.

For further information about Cognitive Analytic Therapy - CAT please contact the CAT Co-ordinator, Munro Clinic, Guys Hospital, London SE1 9RT.

Different states

Everybody experiences changes in how they feel about themselves and the world. But for some people these changes are extreme, sometimes sudden and confusing. In such cases there are often a number of states which recur, and learning to recognise them and shifts between them can be very helpful. Below are a number of descriptions of such states. Identify those which you experience by ringing the number. You can delete or add words to the descriptions. and there is space to add any not listed.

1. Zombie. Cut off from feelings, cut off from others, disconnected.
2. Feeling bad but soldiering on, coping.
3. Out of control
4. Extra special. Looking down on others.
5. In control of self, of life, of other people.
6. Cheated by life, by others. Untrusting.
7. Provoking, teasing, seducing, winding-up others
8. Clinging, fearing abandonment.
9. Frenetically active. Too busy to think or feel.
10. Agitated, confused, anxious..
11. Feeling perfectly cared for, blissfully close to another.
12. Misunderstood, rejected, abandoned.
13. Contemptuously dismissive of myself.
14. Vulnerable, needy, passively helpless, waiting for rescue.
15. Envious, wanting to harm others, put them down, pull them down.
16. Protective, respecting of myself, of others.
17. Hurting myself, hurting others.
18. Resentfully submitting to demands.
19. Hurt, humiliated by others.
20. Secure in myself, able to be close to others.
21. Intensely critical of self, of others.
22. Frightened of others.

Chapter 12
Forensic Psychotherapy: The Dangerous Edge

GWEN ADSHEAD

'Our interest's on the dangerous edge of things'
Robert Browning, *Bishop Blougram's Apology*

Introduction

The term 'forensic' derives from the Latin word 'fora' or open space, which in Roman times was frequently the site of legal hearings and judgement. In psychiatric terms 'forensic' is a descriptor of those patients whose behaviour frightens people, is a cause of interpersonal harm, or leads to the patients being charged with some sort of illegality. Traditionally, such patients were excluded from psychotherapeutic work on the grounds that, by definition, these were people who acted, rather than thought, and so were not deemed to be psychologically minded. However, over the last 20 – 30 years, there has been more interest in looking at the psychological treatment of offenders generally; not least because of the apparent increase in violence and alienation in Western cultures.

'Forensic psychotherapy' is a term which covers a number of different types of psychotherapeutic practice. It includes:

- Psychoanalysis of patients with problems of anger or interpersonal violence.
- Psychoanalytic psychotherapy with offenders (either group or individual).
- The application of psychodynamic theory to understanding the genesis of offences, and the lives of offenders.
- The application of psychodynamic theory to the management of forensic institutions, such as secure units, special hospitals and prisons.

Clearly, not all these practices are the same, and the activities of forensic psychotherapists will be profoundly affected by the setting in which they find themselves. Different types of patient group will be found in different settings, and the therapeutic milieus are also likely to vary in nature and atmosphere.

Here, forensic psychotherapy is described first in terms of how psychodynamic theory may help to understand how people come to act illegally or violently towards others. Then something of forensic psychotherapeutic work in an institution is described. The chapter concludes with some thoughts about where forensic psychotherapy is going, and its connection with other systems that deal with offenders.

Deviance, Crime and Violence

Although the above terms tend to be used interchangeably, they are very different and mean different things. There are many ways to be *deviant* in Western societies, in ways which are not illegal. For example, there are many sexual practices which might be thought of as highly deviant in terms of local cultural norms but which are not illegal (for example, necrophilia (sexual interest in the dead) or erotic autostrangulation). If the deviant behaviour is causing harm, either to the practitioner or to someone else, then help may be sought. But it is likely that many people are deviant and never seek help because they do not perceive themselves as having a problem, and in fact, do not do so unless their behaviour results in dangerous consequences.

Crime is defined as behaviour which violates criminal statute laid down by law, that is, all criminals are law-breakers. However, the vast proportion of crime (94%) is property crime, i.e. variations on the theme of theft. Interpersonal *violence* is actually very uncommon (despite what one reads in the newspapers), and is by no means the norm. People who commit acts of criminal interpersonal violence are therefore rather unusual, in terms of crime, and worthy of further study and understanding; not least because, although violence is statistically unusual, it is still numerically frequent and carries a huge cost both for its victims and the perpetrators.

What deviant, criminal and violent offenders have in common is that they are the subject of censure and rejection by others after exposure. Such people (for understandable reasons) are often the subjects of prejudice, revenge and hate by other members of society. This is sometimes because of the hurt that they have caused; sometimes because they are feared and sometimes, the hate and fury expended on offenders reflects our fear or concern that they are not so different from us, as Shakespeare suggests in *King Lear*:

'Thou rascal beadle, hold thy bloody hand.
'Why does thou lash that whore? Strip thy own back.
Thou hotly lusts to use her in that kind
For which thou whip'st her.'

King Lear
IV.5. 152 – 154.

Thus, patients seen by forensic psychotherapists are individuals who are rejected and ashamed. As well as being angry people, they are also distressed, isolated and frightened. They differ from general psychiatric populations in many ways. First, the majority are male. Although there are many female offenders — and there is some evidence to suggest that female offenders are not detected or punished as much as men — there is no culture in the world where men do not make up the vast majority of offenders. This gender split remains unexplained by criminologists or forensic researchers, and is one of the most important questions facing society about crime and violence.

Forensic psychotherapeutic populations are usually young. This reflects in part the fact that crime is an activity of the young, and it is mainly those who are detected who are likely to be among those referred to forensic psychotherapists in the National Health Service (NHS). Of course, many deviant men and women who have not been detected by anyone may seek help from psychotherapists in the private sector, and the Portman Clinic in London is an NHS facility which offers help to patients who self-refer with deviant behaviour. Thus, forensic psychotherapists working at places like the Portman Clinic see a population of deviant people, both male and female, which may include the middle class, educated and affluent, whereas a forensic psychotherapist working in a prison will see a population largely consisting of deprived young men from broken homes, who have been raised in poverty, neglect and abandonment. These are people who were frequently abused and neglected by their parents, placed in care where they were further abused and neglected, who failed in every sort of education and who started offending at an early age.

Lastly, the men and women who are seen by forensic psychotherapists are often people who lack hope, and often need considerable assistance in seeking help. They rarely ask for psychological help voluntarily, but they are frequently detained involuntarily in settings where such help is on offer. Because psychotherapy is not a treatment which individuals can be made to take against their will, this is another reason why, for so long, psychotherapy was not thought of as a treatment for offenders. However, it is often the case that forensic patients may be interested in engaging in psychotherapy if the psychotherapist appears to be taking an interest in them. It is therefore perfectly possible for prisoners and detained patients to engage in psychotherapy, so long as there is proper attention to the professional boundaries between the patient and the therapist, and between the therapist and the rest of the institution.

Psychodynamic Theories of Deviance

The literature addressing the aetiology of deviance and crime is enormous, and we do not have space to review it here. Freud was not the first to look at the psychological roots of crime, but he was one of the first to consider *unconscious mechanisms* as being important (Freud, 1916). He argued that criminals act from an unconscious sense of guilt, that unconsciously they already see themselves as offenders, feel guilty and unconsciously act this out in order to get the punishment they feel they deserve. Although this formulation does not apply in every case, it is remarkable how many offenders describe a sense of relief at being imprisoned, and make comments such as, 'I feel I belong here'.

Many psychoanalysts, particularly those working with young offenders, have noted the overwhelming histories of deprivation and loss in the lives of such offenders. Winnicott (1984) suggested that antisocial behaviour was a way for the deprived delinquent to get the attention he/she needed, but had not previously received; Bowlby (1944) related persistent thieving to a sense of deprivation as a result of early maternal separation and loss. Bowlby's work with delinquents led him to develop further his theories about the importance of attachment to others for the formation of successful relationships with others in later life. He postulated that much family violence might be related to insecure attachment in the histories of family members (Bowlby, 1984).

Increased awareness of the prevalence of child abuse in all its forms has been important for psychodynamic understanding of offenders. It is now clear that histories of child abuse and neglect are very much more common in offenders than they are in non-offenders. Childhood abuse and neglect are risk factors for the later development of antisocial personality disorder, psychopathy and violence, especially in men (Luntz and Widom, 1994; Rivera and Widom, 1990; Weiler and Widom, 1996). Not everyone who is abused or neglected as a child will become potentially dangerous, because human beings have different levels of resilience to traumatic events, and because if enough good things happen, these may help to overcome the destructive effects of abuse. Therefore, in forensic psychotherapeutic practice, one is usually meeting not only people who have been severely traumatized as children, one is also meeting people who have had very few good experiences with caretakers.

Psychoanalytic theorists such as Fonagy (Fonagy and Target, 1996, 1997) have suggested that offenders are not able to think about themselves or others in the way non-offenders do. They do not have a sense of themselves as a person or self with a thinking mind; and they find it hard to conceive of others having minds or feelings, etc. This is more than just the lack of a sense of empathy with others (often the case with offenders); this relates to an absence of personal identity in their own internal world, and a failure to conceive of others as being real people with identities. This lack of sense of self comes about because of extreme experiences of fear, loss, grief or neglect in childhood. In particular, experiences of fear in early childhood may result in the child developing what is called a 'disorganized' sense of self in relation to others (Hesse, 1996). Given that physical and sexual abuse are both extremely frightening experiences for children, it is not hard to see how abuse might give rise to disorganized states of mind. There is now some evidence to suggest that offenders are more likely to have disorganized and insecure states of mind than non-offenders (Fonagy et al., 1997; van Ijzendoorn et al., 1997).

Psychodynamic theories of offending therefore focus on the damage to the sense of self, and the sense of others which has its origins in the child-hood of the offenders. One particular manifestation of psychological damage is a type of personality organization called *borderline*. The original formulation of the borderline personality implied that the patient's sense of self-identity lay on the 'border' between a psychotic state and a neurotic state. More recent formulations suggest that 'borderline' describes a state of disorganization of the personality. Diagnostic features include instability of mood, outburst of anger and heightened arousal, intense relationships which are abandoned as quickly as they are initiated, and brief psychotic episodes. It is not unusual for all individuals to exhibit mild variations of these aspects of interpersonal behaviour at different times; what is striking about the borderline patient is how all these diagnostic features combine to form an interactional mode which is self-defeating and self-destructive. Although borderline personality disorder (BPD) is commonly associated with women, it is also common (and often overlooked) in men. Patients with BPD are often unhappy people, who seek help, but find it hard to work with offered help. Such difficulty with carers probably reflects the association of BPD with childhood abuse; research suggests that more than half of those with a diagnosis of BPD diagnosis have been abused as children, leading to the suggestion that BPD may represent a type of chronic post-traumatic stress disorder (Herman et al., 1991; Herman, 1992).

Another manifestation of psychological damage is a type of thinking style called *perverse*. A perverse style can give rise to compulsive and stereotyped sets of behaviours called *perversions*. The term 'perverse' should not be

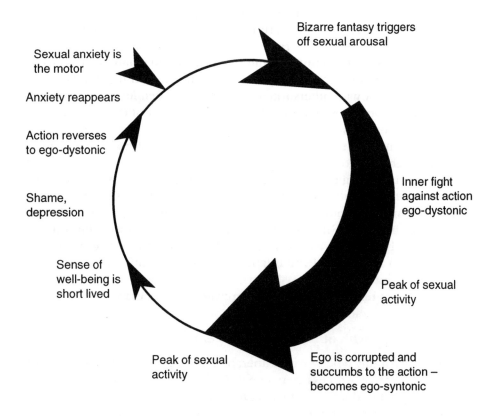

Figure 12.1 The circular motion of perversion. (Reproduced with permission from Welldon, 1996.)

confused with the pejorative way that the word 'pervert' is used; perverse thinking is a response to trauma (Milton, 1994) and anybody who has experienced trauma may come to use such thinking as a defence against rage, fear or psychosis. The key features of perverse behaviour are:

*   Acting rather than conscious thinking.
*   Unrealistic polarity of thought (e.g. she is either perfectly good, or the most evil person on the planet) (also applies to self concepts).
*   An urgent quality: action must take place now (a hint at the unconscious anxiety).
*   A confusion of the somatic and the psychic, so perverse behaviour requires the use of a body; a victim's body may be used, rather than the offender's.
*   A repetitive, compulsive quality, so that the behaviour goes in cycles (Welldon, 1990).

Given the description of BPD, and its association with early trauma, it is not surprising that patients with BPD exhibit both perverse thinking styles and, occasionally, perverse behaviour. Most sexual offending, including the sexual abuse of children, involves perverse mechanisms. Domestic violence between partners, other forms of child abuse and deliberate self-harming behaviour may also be understood as examples of perverse behaviour (they are also associated with a diagnosis of BPD). The common theme is that perverse behaviour tends to take place between people who are in relationship with each other; or the offender may imagine that there is a relationship.

It is worth noting at this point that most interpersonal violence takes place between people who know each other. Between 60% and 70% of rape and murder victims are known to the perpetrator and 80% of murdered children are killed by their parents or carers. Most child abuse is carried out by parents, step-parents or family relations. Therefore it is important to understand the relationship between offenders and their early carers and their relationship with their victims; this is obviously an area which can be explored through forensic psychotherapy.

Psychotherapy with offenders: assessment

Assessment for any type of psychotherapeutic work is complicated because it is a subjective process between two people. Psychotherapy is not something that is 'done to' patients; rather it is a process of self-discovery on their part whereby therapists act as companions, commentators and occasional guides. Not infrequently therapists also find out something about themselves too. Therefore it is no surprise that most efficacy/outcome studies show that psychotherapy is most effective when the patients, therapists and therapeutic style are well matched. This is important because, like any treatment, psychotherapy can be harmful if given inappropriately, or in the wrong 'dose'. Not everyone is suitable for all sorts of psychotherapy, and much of the professional skill of being a psychotherapist is in determining what — if any — psychotherapy would be useful for each patient.

Another important aspect of general psychotherapy which needs to be borne in mind at assessment is that, during therapy, patients will probably get in touch with parts of themselves that, they have tried very hard not to think about. Thus, in the initial stages they may find themselves feeling worse not better. Psychotherapy is not an instant cure, and both therapist and patient can find it frustrating and depressing. They may also become highly dependent on their therapists in ways that are surprising and anxiety-provoking.

This basic review about assessment for general psychotherapy has been provided in order to put the assessment of forensic patients for psychotherapy in context. Clearly, not all forensic patients will be suitable for psychodynamic psychotherapy. A lot depends on when they are referred and why. (This also applies to general patients.) Frequently, offenders are referred just after they have been apprehended and are facing court appearance and conviction. Sometimes, offenders (and their lawyers) may see referral for psychotherapy as a way of influencing the judge not to impose a custodial sentence. Alternatively, undergoing therapy may be a way for the battering man to persuade his wife to let him come home, or the paedophile father to persuade Social Services to let him have access to his children. In such cases, offenders are not curious about themselves or their offending, but want to use psychotherapy and the therapist as a means to an end. This is a nice example of how offending behaviour tends to be repeated in less obvious ways in the therapeutic process. The essence of interpersonal violence is to use another person as a *means*; as a *thing* rather than a *person*. In such circumstances, it is better not even to offer assessment until the court case is settled.

However, there are many cases where psychodynamic assessment of offenders, and a formulation of the reasons for their offending, may be helpful to both them and the judge who has to pass sentence on them. In particular, in cases of family violence, it may be important that offenders are not sent to prison, where they will just feel victimized and resentful. A Probation Order with conditions of residence or treatment can be a way of ensuring that offenders receive access to therapy, especially if they seem genuinely interested in participating. Most therapists advise against making the therapy itself a condition of the order, because offenders may then see the therapy as being 'done' to them, just as things were 'done' to them as children and as they 'did' things to their victims. However, this is not an absolute rule.

Assessment of offenders for forensic psychotherapy involves evaluation of the offender and his/her support system. Given that psychotherapy for offenders is likely to be more lengthy and often more disturbing than that for general patients, it is important to think about containment. Offenders who are distressed are likely to act dangerously, either with the therapist or others; thus if an offender is to remain in the community whilst having therapy, the therapy may need to take place more frequently than once a week, or could take the form of group therapy. In every case, therapists should have some link with the other agencies who are involved with offenders, either directly or indirectly. The more common situation is when offenders are already in-patients in a secure hospital, or inmates in prison. Such settings may provide more containment in terms of preventing dangerous acting out, but they are not necessarily supportive of offenders in distress.

Psychodynamic psychotherapy is not the only form of psychological therapy which is helpful for offenders, and the assessor should bear in mind the value of cognitive approaches (see Chapter 9), and the creative therapies. Many offenders who are referred for therapy have never had a chance to think about themselves before, and they may need an introduction, by way of other types of therapy.

Positive signs at interview include:

- Any history of an enduring attachment in their personal history.
- Any curiosity about why they are where they are.
- Any previous positive experience of carers.
- Expression of grief or distress (rare).

Negative signs at interview include:

- Complete denial of the offence.
- Complete responsibility for the offence attributed to the victim.
- Frank hostility to the assessor (i.e. a very paranoid stance that does not respond to empathy).
- Complete lack of curiosity, often expressed as intellectualization.

Negative signs indicate that offenders are not ready for therapy immediately; not that they will never be ready for psychotherapy. Offenders (like anyone else) do change with time, and the negative indicators described above may reflect the defences of someone who is terrified at finding himself in prison or a special hospital. Therefore, forensic psychotherapy assessment may often be a process which is repeated, and probably should not be attempted too soon after admission.

Assessors need to take a full history and obtain as much information as possible about both offences and offenders' personal histories before coming to any conclusions. This is particularly important in relation to deciding between group and individual therapy, and deciding whether the gender of the therapist is relevant. Offenders who have never had any sort of individual relationship with carers, who have been raised in very large families or in care, may benefit from lengthy individual work, at least initially. Offenders who have had some experience of positive care-taking may gain enormous benefit from group therapy. Offenders who have used the individual relationship to offend (such as child abusers, especially paedophiles and incest offenders), or who have experience of abuse by individuals, may also do much better in group. Any offenders whose offences suggest profound hostility to women will probably find a female therapist difficult to work with in the early stages (and the therapist will have a tough time too). Equally, offenders who say that they cannot work with one gender or another need to have that issue explored carefully at assessment. It is common for offenders to say that they will not work with a man (usually because of an early history of sexual abuse). Without being unduly authoritarian or confrontational, it may help to suggest to offenders that it is the man in themselves that they fear, and this needs to be worked with, not avoided.

Assessment begs the question of the purpose of psychotherapy for offenders. Is it to help them find out more about themselves, or is it to make them behave better? The view expressed that there is no point in offenders having therapy unless it is going to affect their behaviour i.e. stop them offending, is not uncommon. But forensic psychotherapists rarely hold this view. First, there is no intervention (apart from the death penalty) which guarantees an end to re-offending. The only thing which stops people offending is themselves; their view of themselves as people, and of others as people. Therefore, forensic psychotherapy aims to help offenders develop a sense of themselves, and a capacity to take their own needs seriously. Second, all therapists hope that their therapy will assist offenders not to re-offend. But if the main aim of therapy is to make patients behave better then patients are just a means to therapists' therapeutic ends. Offender patients have to learn to feel like real people; a state with which many offenders are quite unfamiliar.

The purpose of forensic psychotherapy then is to try to help offenders feel like real people; to become more real to themselves and their therapists. Therefore, when assessing offenders for forensic psychotherapy, therapists are assessing:

- Degree of resistance.
- Capacity to relate to someone else.
- Degree of damage to the sense of self.
- Extent to which this person has any sense of self or other curiosity about him- or herself.

Psychotherapy with offenders: treatment

Psychotherapy with offenders is not necessarily different from therapy with non-offenders. It is commonly assumed that the work is more dangerous, and certainly therapists would be foolish not to give some thought to the possible risks involved. Good 'rules of thumb' for the therapist include:

- Always letting someone else know where they are going.
- When they intend to return.
- Never let the patient block the exit.

Dangerous situations most commonly arise when patients are distressed or frightened, or feel humiliated. For many offenders, acting violently has been a way of coping with feelings of shame and/or humiliation. Most dangerous situations actually occur in the outpatient setting where there is no way of anticipating the state of the patient on arrival.

Clinical vignette
Henry arrived for his usual session (weekly for the last three years). As the session proceeded, it was clear that he was very angry; swearing, and making many menacing statements about how awful things were going to be in the future. Although the therapist was not personally threatened, it was clear that Henry was much more obviously unstable in his affect than usual. Gradually, it transpired that, at breakfast that same morning, Henry had asked a member of staff for a second glass of milk. The staff member said that seconds were against 'regulations', and deliberately (it seemed to Henry) poured a full jug of milk down the sink in front of him. Henry was overcome with murderous rage; he felt humiliated and spurned. He was able to link these feelings with his childhood experience of being abused by his father who had been a prison officer.

Offender patients often experience therapy (and the therapist) as the first consistent caring experience they have ever had. For some, this new experience will be highly anxiety-provoking, as patients believe either that the perfect carer has arrived but is about to vanish, or that the therapist is not really caring, and sooner or later will be revealed as untrustworthy or possibly abusive. In the early stages of therapy, (and intermittently thereafter) therapists are *always* in the position of either *victim* or *perpetrator*. This is the essence and work of forensic psychotherapy. Within the therapeutic space will be re-enacted not only interpersonal relationships from the patient's past but also the relationship with the victim.

Clinical vignette
The therapist was meeting Jim for the fourth or fifth time after agreeing to start individual work. In the middle of the session, having previously felt perfectly well, the therapist was overcome with a feeling of being stifled. The room suddenly seemed very hot, and after a few minutes the therapist got up and opened a window. Jim seemed unconcerned and continued to talk in a rather conversational and superficial way. Later, in supervision, the therapist was reminded that Jim's index offence had been to semi-strangle a young man, whom he had been holding hostage.

Therapists should expect the index offence to be symbolically re-enacted in the therapeutic space many times; although it is fortunately rare for the patient to physically re-enact the index offence. This is because it is the only way for offenders to think, by either enacting or projecting the feeling into someone else. As the therapeutic work progresses the patient should begin to use words and images instead of re-enactment and projection in order to tell their story. Being able to tell one's own story is the way that most people establish identity; so anything that assists the telling of the story is to be encouraged. Some forensic psychotherapists suggest that the use of metaphor and the creative arts is of especial benefit to forensic patients (Cox and Theilgaard, 1987; Cox, 1994).

Patients who have never felt cared for yearn for the perfect carer and become very attached to their therapists in an insecure way. They idealize them and identify with them; often in an unconscious attempt to prevent them going away. Since therapists are only human, they always fail to live up to their ideal, most obviously when they go on leave. Patients who have consciously idealized their therapist may be bitterly disappointed and furiously angry in the sessions; unconsciously, there may be considerable satisfaction or a strange relief that there is no ideal carer. Patients who have been abused may suggest that therapists have abused them again (i.e. the therapist is just like their abuser); this needs to be countered (gently) with the idea that being disappointed or let down is not the same as being abused. Otherwise the therapist is put in a position of either being an abuser or of being perfect and never-failing; note the polarity of thinking so characteristic of perverse mechanisms. It is important to note, too, that behind this idealization–denigration defence is the experience of grief for the real failures in care experienced by the patients during childhood.

Boundary maintenance and counter-transference

One of the most important aspects of forensic psychotherapy is the issue of security. By this is meant an internal sense of safety. It is the job of the therapist to make the therapeutic space as secure as possible. This is not a matter of external security (although it is sensible to pay attention to this), rather, it is a matter of maintaining the boundaries of the therapeutic space. In practice this means meeting at the same time, in the same place with everything being as consistent as possible. Generally speaking, there should be no contact between sessions, so that all material is contained within the therapeutic space. Therapists need to remain as therapists, i.e. people who make their skill available to patients in order to help them. If this ceases, the therapeutic space will be lost or damaged.

These are common enough boundaries in psychotherapy. All therapists know that boundaries are crossed occasionally; and it is the understanding of these instances that is important for both the therapist and the patient. However, in forensic work the stakes can be somewhat higher, so that if boundaries are crossed, there may be an abrupt reduction in the sense of security.

Clinical vignette

The therapist had been working with Mary for two years. One day, just before the therapist was due to go to the ward to see Mary, Mr Jenkins, the ward manager rang to say that the ward was being searched. 'However', said Mr Jenkins, 'we will do all we can to make sure that the session with Mary takes place.' The therapist arrived on the ward, which was in a rather chaotic state, with many strangers on the ward, and sniffer dogs outside. The session with Mary began on time, in the usual room, and apparently in the usual way. Mary looked glum. The therapist noted the external disturbance, and told Mary of Mr Jenkin's call. Mary seemed very angry, got up and walked out.

This vignette highlights how therapists must take note of external events in patients' lives. Mary's 'home' (the ward) was practically unsafe and frightening (readers may like to think how they would feel if strangers were searching their homes with dogs). Further, the therapist, by mentioning the call from Mr Jenkins, was talking about *her* experience, rather than allowing Mary to talk about *hers*. This type of boundary-crossing, although commonplace and apparently insignificant, meant a lot to Mary who later agreed with the therapist that therapy sometimes felt like 'being searched'.

Boundary crossings need to be thought about in supervision, which should be mandatory for all therapists working in forensic settings. They also need to be talked about with the patients, otherwise patients may be left feeling unsure about what has happened. This is a special problem for offenders who have been sexually abused by parents or carers. Perpetrators of child abuse rarely discuss what they are doing with children, and usually deny that anything happened at all. This leaves the victim uncertain as to what actually happened, and whether he or she can believe their own experience.

Boundary violations are another matter. These are the more serious boundary crossings which involve exploitation or abuse of patients by therapists. Sadly, this does occur in forensic settings, and is often a consequence of patients' vulnerability in their search for the perfect carer. Therapists feel under pressure not to disappoint patients. However, patients who have been sexually abused may behave in a sexual way towards therapists in the belief that this will prevent the therapist from abandoning them. Therapists who respond to sexual behaviour by the patient are, indeed, enacting the part of abuser, and exploiting the dependence and neediness of the patient. Other types of boundary violation include financial exploitation of patients (rare, but does occur), and physical or verbal abuse of patients. Such boundary violations are re-enactments of early abuse, which confirm patients' views of themselves and the world, and can badly set back the therapeutic process.

Boundary issues are linked with counter-transference, by which is meant all the feelings that therapists have about therapy and patients. Patients who lack voice and narrative may use therapists as a projection screen for their feelings and experience. Thus, careful attention to counter-transference may give therapists a great deal of information about patients' state of mind. It is particularly important to consider the counter-transference when one is feeling either very positive or very negative about a patient: it is especially important to ask oneself the (paradoxical) question, 'What am I *not* thinking about?'

Finally, it is important to be honest with patients, and to be as genuine as possible. It is especially important to be honest about feelings of fear, and to take them seriously. If a patient is frightening the therapist, this is clearly an important message that patient needs to convey, and it is vital that the patient is assured that the therapist has received the message. Otherwise patients may feel they have to amplify their message until the therapist *does* get it. Forensic psychotherapy is not about being a hero; brains, not brawn, are required. It is equally important not to abandon therapy just because a patient is aggressive or difficult. Most, if not all, forensic patients were abandoned when they became difficult as children; carefully thought-out perseverance within appropriate boundaries may be highly beneficial to such patients. Again, supervision is essential as a support to therapists with difficult patients. If therapy does have to end unexpectedly, it is particularly important not to terminate it abruptly, without the opportunity to say goodbye. Abrupt terminations resemble too closely a type of sudden death, with which offenders may be all too familiar.

Conclusion

Psychotherapy with offenders is hard but fascinating work. It raises some of the powerful and dramatic questions that human beings have to face: Why do people hurt each other? Is there such a thing as evil? Are there really people about whom we would say 'there is no hope'?

Forensic psychotherapy does not pretend to have the answers, but it offers a means of thinking about the unthinkable.

References

BOWLBY, J. (1944). Forty four juvenile thieves: their characters and home life. *International Journal of Psychoanalysis* 25, 19–52; 107–127.

BOWLBY, J. (1988). Violence in the family. In: Bowlby, J., *A Secure Base*. London: Routledge; 77–98.

COX, M. (1994). *Shakespeare as Prompter: The Amending Imagination and The Therapeutic Process*. London: Jessica Kingsley.

COX, M., and THEILGAARD, A. (1987). Mutative metaphors in psychotherapy. In: *The Aeolian Mode*. London: Tavistock/Routledge (Republished 1997. London, Jessica Kingsley Publishers.)

FONAGY, P. et al. (1997). Morality, disruptive behaviour, borderline, personality disorder, crime and their relationships to security of attachment. In: Atkinson, L. and Zucher, K. (eds), *Attachment and Psychotherapy*. New York: Guilford Press, 223–274.

FONAGY, P. and TARGET, M. (1996). Personality and sexual development, psychopathology and offending. In: Cox, M. and Cordess, C. eds, *Forensic Psychotherapy: Crime, Psychodynamics and the Offender Patient*. London: Jessica Kingsley, 117–152.

FREUD, A. (1916). Some character types met with in analytic work. In: Standard Edition. (Trans. J. Strachey). London: Hogarth; 309.

HERMAN, J., PERRY, C. and VAN DER KOLK, B. (1989). Childhood trauma and borderline personality disorder. *Americal Journal of Psychiatry* 146, 490–495.

HERMAN, J. (1992). Complex post-traumatic stress disorder. *Journal of Traumatic Stress* 5, 377–391.

HESSE, E. (1996) Discourse, memory and the adult attachment interview: a note with emphasis on the emerging Cannot Classify category. Infant Mental Health Journal 17, 4–11.

LUNTZ, B. and WIDOM, C. (1994). Antisocial personality disorder in abused and neglected children grown up. *American Journal of Psychiatry* 151, 670–674.

MILTON, J. (1994). Abuser and abused: perverse solutions following childhood abuse. *Psychoanalytic Psychotherapy* 8, 243–255.

RIVERA, B. and WIDOM, C. (1990). Childhood victimisation and violent offending. *Violence and Victims* 5, 19–35.

VAN IJZENDOORN, M. et al. (1997). Attachment representations of personality disordered criminal offenders. *American Journal of Orthopsychiatry* 67, 449–459.

WELLDON, E. (1996). Contrasts in male and female sexual perversions. In: Cordess, C. and Cox, M. (eds), *Forensic Psychotherapy: Crime, Psychodynamics and the Offender Patient*. London: Jessica Kingsley; 273–289.

WEILER, R.L. and WIDOM, C.S. (1996). Psychopathy and violent behaviour in abused and neglected young adults. *Criminal Behaviour and Mental Health* 6, 263–281.

WINNICOTT, D. (1984). In: Winnicott, C., Shepard, R. and Davis, M. eds, *Deprivation and Delinquency*. New York: Routledge.

Further reading

COX, M., CORDESS, C. (1996). *Forensic Psychotherapy: Theory and Practice* (Volumes 1 and 2). London: Jessica Kingsley.

MAIN, T. (1957). The ailment. *British Journal of Medical Psychology* 30, 129–145.

DE ZULUETA, F. (1993). *From Pain to Violence: The Traumatic Roots of Destructiveness*. London: Whurr Publishers.

Chapter 13
Postscript: Feelings and Counterfeelings in Doctors and Medical Students

HAROLD MAXWELL AND BARBARA SQUIRE

Choice of Profession

What makes someone become a doctor? Do the same factors also then help or hinder the experience of medical practice and dealing with patients? Is the high rate of breakdown among doctors (see below) a result of their working lives, or can it be explained in part by those psychological characteristics that made the individual choose a career in medicine in the first place?

Lief (1971) interviewed first-year medical students and reported that over one-third of those approached were motivated to study medicine as a partial response to unconscious neurotic drives and unresolved conflicts from childhood. Sklar (1991) states that it is quite common to find, in the history of the student/young doctor, illness in a sibling, parent or close relative that had a profound effect. In research comparing medical students with law students, Paris and Frank (1983) found that the medical students were more likely to have experienced serious health problems in their families. The child witnessing the stress of illness and disease in the family may attempt to take on responsibility for it, and an unconscious desire to 'make it better'.

Although this may be a valid reason for entering medicine, doctors should be aware of it in order to deal with some of the potential problems it may cause. Although some factors from childhood may enhance an individual's capabilities, others may predispose the doctor to experience some aspects of life in a negative way — negative affectivity. The desire to make it all better or to compensate for early experiences may result from, say, having a depressed parent or experiencing early abuse (Elliot and Guy, 1993), parental separation or illness. Johnson (1991) called this 'reparation for impotence'.

If such events do lead to the choice of medicine as a career, they may also lead to unrealistically high expectations of both the career and oneself. Uncertainty in the job, the perceived lack of support and increasing demands may compound this uncertainty and produce a sense of failure and self-blame (Firth-Cozens, 1997).

One response to carrying this burden would be to suppress childhood experiences so as to avoid confronting the pain that they may have engendered. To do so, however, would be to risk an inability to empathize with patients and to appear to be emotionally hard and uncaring (Sklar, 1991).

The importance of early *family relationships* has been shown in many studies of emotional problems in doctors. Relationships with cold and distant fathers were predictive of death from suicide and cancer (Thomas and Duszynski, 1974); absence of normal rebellion from parental ties and high levels of altruism leading to self-denial, can lead to aspects of psychopathology (Vaillant et al., 1972). Anxious, guilty relationships with *mothers* were strongly predictive of stress and self-criticism (Firth-Cozens, 1992); and early sibling rivalry seemed to result in high levels of stress and depression (Firth-Cozens, 1998).

High Rate of Breakdown

Although stress is common in most professions, the figures for doctors suggest that 28 – 30% of them suffer above the threshold level for stress as measured by the General Health Questionnaire (Wall et al., 1997) compared with a figure of 18% in workers outside the health professions. The figure of approximately 28% seems constant at all stages of medical careers. However, as Lief (1971) has claimed that over one-third of medical students are motivated to enter medicine in response to psychological conditions in childhood, it is perhaps not surprising that symptoms of stress are higher in doctors than in other professions.

Measurement of levels of *depression* is not so consistent, but the condition is thought to account for approximately 20 – 60% of psychiatric admissions among doctors (Rucinski and Cybulska, 1985). In a follow-up study, Reuben (1985) found a peak of depression of 38% among first-year medical students. By comparison, the rates of mental health problems in the general population are one in six for depression, one in ten for anxiety and one in 100 for bipolar disease (Bird, 1999).

There has, in fact, been an increasing incidence of mental illness among both general practitioners (Sutherland and Cooper, 1993) and hospital consultants. The former have especially high levels of anxiety and depression. About a quarter of doctors in one study scored as instances of anxiety and one tenth had clinical depression (Caplan, 1994). Chambers and Campbell (1996) found similar rates in their study of over 600 general practitioners, with many more displaying borderline symptoms.

Although some attribute doctors' widespread distress to the complex dynamics of doctor–patient relationships, an alternative explanation for the high rate of breakdown among doctors may be the denial of personal vulnerability. If the doctor relates self-image to the idealized parent figure from childhood then to admit to not being able to cope is to question that ideal. The culture of medical training, with its emphasis on self-sacrifice and looking after others, may merely enhance a lack of self-care and denial of vulnerability in those predisposed to it. This may lead to a reliance on drugs and alcohol, which may start in the student years and carry on throughout working life.

In his 1990 study, Garrud reported that 24% of house officers thought that they would be 'letting everyone down if ill'. Therefore possible drug abuse through self-prescription could continue, either to enable the doctor to carry on with work, or to mask the effects of physical and/or mental ill health 'because of the need to appear professional, efficient and able to cope with life's stresses'. It was also found that, of the general practitioners studied, a quarter had at sometime prescribed sleeping tablets for themselves (Richards, 1989).

Feelings of Doctors in Training

Undergraduate medical training includes emphasis on the importance of mental factors in illness and its treatment; but doctors who are not interested in the emotional life of both healthy and ill people may be less than skilful in their handling of the doctor–patient relationship and the process of healing. A poor capacity for introspection is often responsible for this trait.

Psychology courses in the preclinical curriculum that concentrate on academic and experimental factors and/or are preoccupied with measurement of detail, cannot meet the requirements of students wishing to develop depth of understanding for patients. Students will need to deal with the emotions that their patients might create in them — for example, anger, sympathy, empathy and antipathy.

Patients' emotional or psychic states may stir up complementary responses in doctors. If the student is aware of them, these responses are much less likely to interfere in communication with their patients and can be analysed for their meaning (Zinn, 1988). However, although the student has to maintain the ability to empathize, one underlying objective of medical education is to 'harden' the student. This is right and proper. Who would want to be treated by a surgeon who had qualms about sticking a knife into another person's body, or a doctor who fainted at the sight of blood? The student has to undergo an inevitable 'toughening up'. Such training often begins in the dissecting room – a major fault of the medical system, whereby the process of making a doctor begins with death rather than birth. It represents a lack of responsiveness to changing medical needs and an overemphasis of biomedical models while ignoring the psychosocial aspects of health and disease. Medical training concentrates on acute care in hospital, tending to neglect primary care, and produces graduates oriented towards disease rather than health; *cure* rather than *care*.

Some medical institutions have attempted to counteract this. In Israel, for example, an intensive programme called Hospitalization Week was developed with the goal of giving first-year medical students an opportunity to understand the complexity of the needs and problems of patients in hospital. Students accompanied patients from their arrival at Accident and Emergency departments throughout their stay in hospital (Carmel and Bernstein, 1986). Further curriculum reforms were developed to counteract the usual brief and unrepeated student–patient encounters, with early clinical exposure from the first week at medical school. It was found to motivate students in their care for *people*, as their first patient was not a cadaver on the dissecting table (Benor, 1987).

The process that students undergo in order to defend themselves against anxieties may become so exaggerated that they may build armour around themselves so that feelings are never acknowledged. The future doctor may then be left untouched by death and pain. Patients are frequently disheartened when confronted by such a practitioner. In such cases, emotional messages cannot be transmitted between the patient and doctor through the process of *infectivity* (Zinn, 1988), so that diagnostic information about the patient, which could have been gained by the doctor monitoring his or her own feelings, is lost. *Infective feelings* include fear, anxiety, hopelessness and sadness. Self-awareness is the key to using reactions to patients to improve the doctor–patient relationship.

Perhaps, given that there is evidence to suggest that at least some students enter medical training to compensate for factors in childhood, a more careful selection process for entry into medical school would be beneficial. In Australia a follow-up study over 20 years found that students chosen for their ability to empathy and problem-solving, had better quality of life and job satisfaction than those chosen traditionally (Powis and Rolfe, 1998). The introduction of such changes in the selection system for entry to medical school could reduce the high rate of psychological problems among medical students. The extension of such changes into the selection process for entry into the medical specialities would go some way towards maximizing the person–job fit.

High Subjectivity Specialities

In a recent study, Firth- Cozens (in press) found that psychiatrists were the most stressed and negative about their jobs, whereas surgeons were the least. Although the different emotional demands of the jobs could explain this, the differences in stress and negativity were apparent even when the subjects were medical students some ten years earlier, before they had made the choice of speciality. Is it possible then that some psychiatrists, for example, enter the speciality to deal with their own unresolved psycholog-ical problems, partly by dealing with similar problems in their patients? Certainly, suicide is more common among psychiatrists than among other senior doctors (Carpenter et al., 1997).

There is a lack of career counselling at all stages of undergraduate and postgraduate training (Firth-Cozens, in press). Given the reluctance of many doctors to seek counselling for problems such as depression and drug abuse, perhaps this is not surprising. Doctors seem to have funda-mental difficulties in seeking help and have apparently casual attitudes to self-prescribing (Baldwin et al., 1997). Part of this reluctance to ask for help may be connected to doctors splitting off the diseased, disabled and incompetent parts of themselves and seeing them as the exclusive preroga-tive of patients.

Treatment with drugs is, for obvious reasons, not uncommon among doctors as a way of dealing with their own stress. The availability of drugs and the high rate of self-prescription leads to many problems. Perhaps not surprisingly, there is a high rate of drug abuse among anaesthetists, although sadly death is often the first indication of such problems (O'Connor and Spickard, 1997). Lutsky et al. (1993) found that 16% of anaesthetists were substance dependent, alcoholism being the most common. However, another study (Hughes et al., 1992) found that substance abuse was more common among house officers in emergency medicine and psychiatry, with unsupervised benzodiazepine use the highest among psychiatrists. Vaillant (1992) stated that doctors were 'five times as likely to take sedatives and minor tranquillizers without medical supervision'. An American study found that a staggering 73% of doctors surveyed had used psychoactive drugs that were not prescribed (Lutsky et al., 1994).

Emotional Responses in Clinicians

The emotional responses of doctors to their patients may be used in two quite separate ways: to gain information about patients and to gain insight into doctors' own personalities. Encounters with patients, like all human interactions, have unavoidable emotional content (Zinn, 1988). Despite the maintenance of proper clinical distance, it is impossible not to have normal reactions to patients who, for example, are hard to like, or infuriate with lack of compliance with treatment. The sadness experienced when a patient dies does not represent a breakdown of scientific objectivity, nor do feelings of guilt, even when all procedures have been carried out correctly and everything that could have been done for the patient has been done. Doctors who trained with their own mental burdens may take on the additional stress of medical guilt. Care is required to recognize that what is being experienced is a *projection*, in other words, *differentiation* must be made from the patient (Sklar, 1991).

One method of investigating the anxieties and feelings of both medical students and qualified doctors is through training seminars. Difficulties in development of skills for the doctor–patient relationship arise because such skills they cannot really be taught, only experienced. Balint's studies with general practitioners led to the development of such seminars (see Chapter 7). The aim is to develop sensitivity to the patients' emotional problems, thereby enabling doctors to understand those problems more precisely and in greater depth and to acquire skills and understanding for a greater therapeutic effect. To quote Balint:

> A precondition for the acquisition of this increased sensitivity is a general loosening up of the doctor's personality, especially with regard to his professional work. He must be able to notice and to tolerate emotional factors in his patients that he rejected or ignored before and he must learn to accept them as worthy of his attention. (Balint, 1957)

In Israel workshops have been developed to increase *empathy* through the development of interviewing skills. Kramer et al. (1989), however, found that simply being taught these skills by experienced practitioners was not enough, students needed to take active roles to stimulate the practice of interview techniques. A further study also carried out in Israel examined the personality traits and socio-organizational factors that enhanced compassionate–empathetic behaviour in doctors — qualities that are much appreciated by patients. Carmel and Glick (1996) found that doctors who were more recently qualified and were satisfied with their work were more likely to be compassionate–empathetic but they were also much more likely to suffer emotional exhaustion.

Empathy in doctors, therefore, is not without personal cost. The BMA found it necessary to run a help line. First set up in 1996, it has since been relaunched under the name of 'BMA Counselling, a Service for Members and their Families'. In its first two years the service received over 6000 calls, with the largest number (well over 2000) related to emotional issues — anxiety, stress and depression (Beecham, 1998). In Australia, a suicide hotline has been set up. Doctors in New South Wales are 50% more likely to kill themselves than the rest of the population, with women, young doctors and resident medical officers at greatest risk (Zinn, 1997). However, the very fact that such services exist indicates a change in attitudes and self-awareness, and it is now more socially acceptable to admit to having too much stress in your own life (Weaver, 1999).

A Final Note

In the various types of psychotherapy described in this book, the amount of personal involvement by the clinicians concerned will vary from the *transference* of psychoanalytic or dynamic models to the more directive approaches of the cognitive–behavioural therapies. In the final instance, however, it is individual practitioners and their degree of empathetic kindness that will often prove the salient feature in the outcome of treatment therapy, irrespective of specialty. Perhaps, at the beginning of the twenty-first century, one may echo the regret noted by one correspondent, that the advent of 'walk-in health centres' may presage the end of a particular kind of general practice (O'Connell, 1999). This at one time may have involved family doctors working single-handed from their own homes and offering their own *psychotherapy*. Notwithstanding the advances in modern medicine in its technical aspects, many will regret the passing of this very personal relationship, which was experienced by so many as the very cornerstone of medical practice.

References

BALDWIN, P.J., DODD, M., WRATE, R.W. (1997). Young doctors' health — 1. How do working conditions affect attitudes, health and performance? *Social Science and Medicine* 45, 35–40.

BALINT, M. (1957) *The Doctor, His Patient and the Illness.* London: Pitman Medical.

BEECHAM, L. (1998). BMA's counselling service takes over 6000 calls. *British Medical Journal* 316, 1250.

BENOR, D.E. (1987). Early clinical program for novice medical students: 13 year's experience at Ben-Gurion University of the Negev. *Israel Journal of Medical Sciences* 23, 1013–1021.

BIRD, L. (1999). *The Fundamental Facts: All the Latest Facts and Fiction on Mental Illness.* London: Mental Health Foundation.

CAPLAN, R.P. (1994). Stress, anxiety and depression in hospital consultants, general practitioners and senior health managers. *British Medical Journal* 309, 1261–1263.

CARMEL, S., BERNSTEIN, J. (1986). Identifying with the patient: an intensive programme for medical students. *Medical Education* 20, 432–436.

CARMEL, S., GLICK, S.M. (1996). Compassionate–empathic physicians: personality traits and social-organizational factors that enhance or inhibit this behaviour pattern. *Social Science and Medicine* 43, 1253–1261.

CARPENTER, L.M., SWERDLOW, A.J., FEAR, N.T. (1997). Mortality of doctors in different specialities: findings from a cohort of 20 000 NHS consultants. *Occupational and Environmental Medicine* **54**, 388–395.

CHAMBERS, R., CAMPBELL, I. (1996). Anxiety and depression in general practitioners: associations with type of practice, fundholding and other personal characteristics. *Family Practice* **13**, 170–173.

ELLIOT, D.M., GUY, J.D. (1993). Mental health professionals versus non-mental health professionals: childhood trauma and adult functioning. *Professional Psychology: Research and Practice* **24**, 83–90.

FIRTH-COZENS, J. (1992). The role of early experiences in the perception of organizational stress: fusing clinical and organizational perspectives. *Journal of Occupational and Organizational Psychology* **65**, 61–75.

FIRTH-COZENS, J. (1997). Depression in doctors. In: C. Katona, M.M. Robertson, (eds), *Depression and Physical Illness*. Chichester: Wiley.

FIRTH-COZENS, J. (1998). Individual and organizational predictors of depression in general practitioners. *British Journal of General Practice* **48**, 1647–1651.

FIRTH-COZENS, J. (In press). The psychological problems of doctors. In: J. Firth-Cozens and R. Payne. *Stress in Health Professionals*. Chichester: Wiley.

GARRUD, P. (1990). Counselling needs and experience of junior hospital doctors. *British Medical Journal* **300**, 445–447.

HUGHES, P.H., BALDWIN, D.C., STEPHAN, D.V., CONARD, S., STORR, C.L. (1992). Resident physicians' substance abuse by specialty. *American Journal of Psychiatry* **143**, 1348–1354.

JOHNSON, W.D.K. (1991). Predisposition to emotional distress and psychiatric illness amongst doctors: the role of unconscious and experimental factors. *British Journal of Medical Psychology* **64**, 317–329.

KRAMER, D., BER, R., MOORE, M. (1989). Increasing empathy among medical students. *Medical Education* **23**, 168–173.

LIEF, H.I. (1971). Personality characteristics of medical students. In: R.H. Coombs and C.E. Vincent. *Psychological Aspects of Medical Training*. Springfield, IL: Thomas.

LUTSKY, I., HOPWOOD, N., ABRAM, S.E., et al. (1993). Psychoactive substance abuse among American anesthesiologists: a 30-year retrospective study. *Canadian Journal of Anesthesiology* **40**, 915–921.

LUTSKY, I., HOPWOOD, N., ABRAM, S.E., et al. (1994). The use of psychoactive substances in three medical specialities: anesthesia, medicine and surgery. *Canadian Journal of Anesthesiology* **41**, 561–567.

O'CONNELL, S. (1999). The introduction of walk in health centres — the end of general practice? *British Medical Journal* **318**, 1146.

O'CONNOR, P.G., SPICKARD, A. JR. (1997). Physician impairment by substance abuse. *Medical Clinics of North America* **81**, 1037–1052.

PARIS, J., FRANK, H. (1983). Psychological determinants of a medical career. *Canadian Journal of Psychiatry* **28**, 354–357.

POWIS, D.A., ROLFE, I. (1998). Selection and performance of medical students at Newcastle, New South Wales. *Education for Health* **11**, 15–23.

REUBEN, D.B. (1985). Depressive symptoms in medical house officers: effects of level of training and work rotation. *Archives of Internal Medicine* **145**, 286–288.

RICHARDS, C. (1989). *The Health of Doctors*. London: King Edward's Hospital Fund for London.

RUCINSKI, J., CYBULSKA, E. (1985). Mentally ill doctors. *British Journal of Hospital Medicine* **33**, 90–94.

SKLAR, J. (1991). The trainee's feelings and the clinical relationship. In: *Psychotherapy. An Outline for Trainee Psychiatrists, Medical Students and Practitioners*: second edition. London: Whurr Publishers; 48–54.

SUTHERLAND, V.J., COOPER, C. (1993). Identifying distress among general practitioners: predictors of psychological ill health and job dissatisfaction. *Social Science Medicine* **37**, 578–581.

THOMAS, C.B., DUSZYNSKI, K.R. (1974). Closeness to parents and the family constellation in a prospective study of five disease states. *Johns Hopkins Medical Journal* **134**, 251–157.

VAILLANT, G.E., SOBOWALE, N.C., McARTHUR, C. (1972). Some psychological vulnerabilities of physicians. *New England Journal of Medicine* **287**, 372–375.

VAILLANT, G.E. (1992). Physician, cherish thyself: the hazards of self prescription. *Journal of the American Medical Association* **287**, 2373–2374.

WALL, T.D., BOLDER, R.I., BORRIL, C.S. et al. (1997). Minor psychiatric disorder in NHS trust staff: occupational and gender differences. *British Journal of Psychiatry* **171**, 519–523.

WEAVER, J. (1999). Keeping stress under control. *BMA News Review* Feb 27, 32–33.

ZINN, C. (1997). Suicide hotline to be set to for Australian doctors. *British Medical Journal* **314**, 1711.

ZINN, W.M. (1988). Doctors have feelings too. *Journal of the American Medical Association* **259**, 3296–3298.

Further general reading

AVELINE, M. (1992). *From Medicine to Psychotherapy*. London: Whurr Publishers.

BROWN, D. and PEDDER, J. (1991). *Introduction to Psychotherapy*. London: Tavistock Publications.

HOLMES, J. (ed)., (1991). *A Textbook of Psychotherapy in Psychiatric Practice*. Edinburgh: Churchill Livingstone.

LOMAS, P. (1973). *True and False Experiences*. London: Allen Lane.

RIPPERE, V. and WILLIAMS, R. (1985). *The Wounded Healers*. Chichester: Wiley.

STORR, A. (1979). *The Art of Psychotherapy*. London: Secker & Warburg; Heinemann Medical.

Index